Writing & Freedom

WILLIAM F. MYERS

Writing & Freedom

FROM NOTHING TO PERSONS AND BACK

Franciscan University Press

Franciscan University Press
1235 University Boulevard
Steubenville, OH 43952
740-283-3771

Distributed by:
The Catholic University of America Press
c/o HFS
P.O. Box 50370
Baltimore, MD 21211
800-537-5487

Library of Congress Cataloging-in-Publication Data
Names: Myers, William F., author.
Title: Writing and freedom : from nothing to persons and back / William F. Myers.
Other titles: From nothing to persons and back
Description: Steubenville, OH : Franciscan University Press, [2018] | Includes bibliographical references and index.
Identifiers: LCCN 2018008244 | ISBN 0999513400 (978-0-9995134-0-8)
Subjects: LCSH: Religion and literature. | Atheism in literature. | Nothing (Philosophy) | Persons--Philosophy. | Liberty in literature. | God in literature.
Classification: LCC PN49 M94 2018 | DDC 820.9/38--dc23
LC record available at https://lccn.loc.gov/2018008244

Dust Jacket and Text Design: Kachergis Book Design
Dust Jacket Image: *The Angel Standing in the Sun*, by Joseph Mallord Wiliam Turner, 1846. The Archangel Michael with flaming sword on Judgment Day. From Tate Britain, London.
Printed in the United States of America.
ISBN: 978-0-9995134-0-8

To the past and present
students and teachers of
Leicester's oldest adult
education institution,
the once and future
VAUGHAN COLLEGE

Contents

One must have a mind of winter
To regard the frost and the boughs
Of the pine-trees crusted with snow;

And have been cold a long time
To behold the junipers shagged with ice,
The spruces rough in the distant glitter

Of the January sun; and not to think
Of any misery in the sound of the wind,
In the sound of a few leaves,

Which is the sound of the land
Full of the same wind
That is blowing in the same bare place

For the listener, who listens in the snow,
And, nothing himself, beholds
Nothing that is not there and the nothing that is.

—Wallace Stevens, "The Snow Man"

Epigraph. Wallace Stevens, "The Snow Man," *Poetry*, 19, no. 1 (Oct. 1921): 4–5.

Introduction

Writing is a stage or set on which the freedom of persons is articulated and enacted. Take the essay. An essay stands on its own. It is a ruminant form that ends but does not come to a conclusion. Though the essays in this book have been put in a definite order, lines of thought recur and move on, and the book has a goal, it respects the essay form and does not come to a conclusion, either. If there is repetition—that, after all, is an aspect of rumination in man and beast,—and if there is a moral—intellectual, ethical, or religious—it is a moral exemplified in the essay form. "Can philosophy systematically cultivate the equivocal?," asks Paul Ricoeur[1] (1913–2005). Can the essay, "the literary form with the least configuration,"[2] move beyond casual meditation into disciplined philosophical discourse, and what relation has the latter to literature?

The five writers considered in Part I—George Eliot (Marian Evans) (1819–80), Walter Pater (1839–94), Oscar Wilde (1854–1900), Thomas Hardy (1854–1900), and Rudyard Kipling (1865–1936)—were all philosophically literate and provide the foundation for my consideration of English philosophy in the nineteenth century and the larger philosophical tradition from René Descartes (1596–1650)

1. Ricoeur, *Freud and Philosophy*, 1970, 41.

2. Ricoeur, *Oneself as Another*, 149.

into the twentieth century. My treatment of that tradition is, I hope, serious but not comprehensive. The essay form deals with issues in patches. It is "economical" in the sense that term has in the writings of John Henry Newman (1801–90), Newman's thought being central to this book.

Newman's economical principle was a daring position for a nineteenth-century thinker to adopt, since, from the Greeks, philosophy had been based on the assumption that everything must (somehow) be connected, and that it is the task of philosophy to explore as much of this connectedness as possible. The ancient tradition of comprehensive skepticism, initiated by Pyrrho of Elis (c. 360–270 BCE), is the negative version of this project. Newman's "economical principle," of separated manifestations of certainty in a sea of unknowing, might seem, in his own words, "to cut off all ties which bind the mind to the universe" and "to end to a dreary and hopeless scepticism."[3] It was certainly condemned by his opponents as religious obscurantism, and by many Christians as potentially atheistic. But (as on a number of issues) Newman's position was prescient. Many recent philosophers, and scientists, have accepted that, in Thomas Nagel's words, "the methods needed to understand ourselves do not exist ... we must be resigned to achieving [truth] to a very limited extent and without certainty."[4] (I refer a lot to Nagel in this introduction, not least because he is the polar opposite in current American philosophy of Daniel C. Dennett, whose conclusions, as the reader of this book will discover, are not mine.)

Newman distinguishes between notional and real assent. He holds that publicly expressible theories can never amount to "knowledge." They are "economical" ways of ordering concepts, *always* partial and subject to refutation or improvement. They can be recognized as tenable, given what Newman calls notional assent. Their

3. Quoted in Myers, *Thoughtful Heart,* 59.

4. Nagel, *View from Nowhere,* 10.

implications can be analyzed. But Newman also believes in the possibility of "certitude" based on "imaginative or real assent,"[5] "Real assent" being the work of "implicit reason" or the "illative sense." It engages directly with "experiences and their images that strike and occupy the mind, as abstractions and their combinations do not."[6] Unlike notional assent, real assent is "proper to the individual, and as such, thwarts rather than promotes the intercourse of man with man."[7] Generals on the battlefield may give orders, or skilled craftsmen complete tasks, and even peasants express judgments they know to be true, without being able to lay out their reasons for acting or thinking as they do—but that does not make their actions or judgments irrational. Mathematicians such as Sir Isaac Newton (1643–1727) also "see the truth all of a heap, by one act." "Newton's great trouble was to *find* his proofs";[8] "the proof of [his] rule for ascertaining the imaginary roots of equations" was only discovered in Newman's lifetime. It took "near two hundred years *to prove* a truth which Newton *saw* by his genius."[9] Relevant here is the assertion of Albert Einstein (1879–1955) "that the fundamental insights from which our scientific understanding of the world derive cannot be reached by logical thinking or by observation, but only by feeling *into* things (*Einfühlung*), intuition, acts of creation."[10] Einstein's *Einfühlung* and Newman's Illative Sense are barely distinguishable, and both are implicitly rational.

There are numerous illustrations of *Einfühlung* and/or the Illative Sense in the literary works discussed in these essays. The Illative Sense is integral to Newman's presentation of his protagonist in *Callista,* but it is also strongly suggested in Kipling's Peroo in the short

5. Newman, *Grammar of Assent,* 62.
6. Newman, *Grammar of Assent,* 50.
7. Newman, *Grammar of Assent,* 82.
8. Newman, in Myers, *Thoughtful Heart,* 62.
9. Newman, in Myers, *Thoughtful Heart,* 119–120.
10. Magee, *Ultimate Questions,* 96.

story "The Bridge Builders," and in Hardy's Arabella in *Jude the Obscure,* both expert in their engagement with the world but incapable of, or at any rate not interested in, rational explanation. Then there is the complex of unstated understandings between Milton and Lawrence, in the sonnet discussed in chapter 5, "Writing and Freedom." Transference in psychoanalytical theory and practice examined in chapter 1, "George Eliot: Is Submission a Virtue?," and chapter 7, "Five Suppositions," depends on preverbal insights. This is also true of criticism in literature and art, examined in chapter 9, "Good, Happy, and Free." Even when a critical judgment only takes shape in the writing, the written word always falls short of what is *grasped*. In criticism, as in all other forms of theorizing, the Notional is forever "not all" (and essays are always incomplete).

Free will is the central concern of this book. There are two components in free-will theory—autonomy and freedom—and two notions of freedom—the freedom of "spontaneity" and the freedom of "indifference." Hardline materialists and determinists deny autonomy to the human subject and represent choice as just a happening in the world, the experience of agency being an illusion or rationalization: as Nagel puts it, there is "no room for agency in a world of neural impulses, chemical reactions, and bone and muscle movements."[11] Yet, as he also points out, it seems impossible "to dissolve our unanalyzed sense of autonomy and responsibility."[12] Newman agrees. "I put out my hand," he writes, "and stop the pendulum of a clock. The clock stops . . . Here is a force, Volition, which impedes, or strengthens, or quickens . . . the operations of physical laws."[13] Newman treats agency simply as (in Nagel's words) "a basic . . . psychophysical category—reducible to neither physical nor to other mental terms." Thinking solely in terms of sensation, feeling, belief, inten-

11. Nagel, *View from Nowhere,* 111.

12. Nagel, *View from Nowhere,* 113.

13. Newman, in Myers, *Thoughtful Heart,* 107.

tion, and desire, as well as physical events, would remove "agency," Nagel thinks, "from our picture of the world."

The claim that people are not just agents but free agents adds to the problem. For a determinist and atheist, like William Godwin (1756–1836), free will is a fantasy, but others find an apparently satisfactory understanding of freedom in the freedom of "spontaneity." This requires actions to be governed by reason, or preference, or perceived need, and not to be subject to *external* compulsion. It has an established place in the tradition. Godfried Leibniz (1646–1716) holds that an action is free provided it is (1) not logically necessary and (2) motivated (i.e., *determined*) by reason; in the view of John Locke (1632–1704), the unconstrained agent as a whole and not the will is free. Wiping your nose is a free act, sneezing is not, and coughing sometimes is and sometimes isn't. David Hume (1711–76) expresses this argument with greater clarity. Dennett thinks that decision-making depends on "heuristic procedures" that rely "on some 'random' generation of considerations"[14] in brains functioning as computer-like systems. It is enough for the alternative courses of action to be more or less rational or desirable, and the agent not subject to strong pressures from without. This is the sort of free will that he finds "worth wanting."

To many, however, a stronger version of freedom is required, choosing in which there is no randomness and that is fully conscious. Just as the moral dimension is subsumed into something else if it is described in terms of (say) the greatest happiness, or social conditioning, or convenience, so freedom would seem to become something else when it is limited to the absence of external coercion, and especially when it is undetectably heuristic. The problem, however, is that the freedom of indifference apparently takes the human subject out of our picture of the world, making us, as Nagel puts it, "the absolute source of what we do ... creating ourselves out of

14. Dennett, *Consciousness Explained*, 119.

nothing, so to speak."[15] The very notion of *self-creation* suggests that human beings are either divine or mad.

Nevertheless, Newman cannot get himself "with patience to consider the argument against the freedom of the will." Though he cannot reconcile free will "with the reign of Law," he finds it "absurd to say that a thing does not exist because we cannot reconcile it with another thing that exists."[16] Many people, however, including Nagel, would regard this as nonsense. For them, "nothing believable"[17] has been proposed on the subject of free will, even though, as Nagel points out, "it is not clear how someone can be morally responsible for doing wrong, if freedom is a condition of responsibility."[18] One of the hoped-for outcomes of this book is to suggest a point of view from which full, "godlike" freedom of the will can be included in a picture of world.

The other major fissure in philosophy is the problem of combining, as Nagel puts it, "the perspective of a particular person inside the world with an objective view of that same world, the person and his viewpoint included."[19] This is the contemporary version of Descartes's difficulty with accounting for the relation of soul and body. In pre-Cartesian thinking, the world simply is as it is perceived, and people act in it in the light of reason, emotion, and sense-experience. Descartes's starting point is doubt: *nothing* should be asserted as true if it is *possible* for it to be false. Experience of the external world, of the body, and the self might all be illusions generated by a malicious demon. From the existence of the doubt itself, however, a doubter—that is, "a thinking thing" (*res cogitans*)[20]—can be *inferred*.[21] Descartes

15. Nagel, *View from Nowhere*, 117–18.

16. Newman, in Myers, *Thoughtful Heart*, 111.

17. Nagel, *View from Nowhere*, 112.

18. Nagel, *View from Nowhere*, 137.

19. Nagel, *View from Nowhere*, 3.

20. Descartes, *Key Philosophical Writings*, 143.

21. My claim that Descartes's ego is only inferred is controversial. See chap. 9 in this volume and Myers, *Thoughtful Heart*, 247–49.

also claims that the existence of God can be known "clearly and distinctly," simply by entertaining "the idea ... of a supremely perfect Being."[22] Because he is unable to "conceive [conceptualize] God without existence," it follows "that existence is inseparable from Him, and hence that He really exists." In other words, only "the necessity of the existence of God"[23] would make the *thought* of God possible. (This is a difficult argument to grasp, never mind accept, but it is one that at least for a time the young Bertrand Russell [1872–1970], in a state of some excitement, thought was "sound,"[24] and I shall return to it, not directly in relation to the existence of God, but to that of right and wrong.) Convinced of God's existence and that God cannot be a deceiver, Descartes accepts the reality of the world as he finds it. But this leaves unresolved the problem of the interaction of body ("corporeal substance" or *res extensa*) and soul (a thinking thing or *res cogitans*). "The main objection to dualism," Nagel writes, "is that it postulates an additional, non-physical substance, without explaining how *it* can support objective mental states whereas the brain can't."[25]

Descartes speculates about the pineal gland as a point of contact between the immaterial "I" and the material world. His disciples Arnold Geulincx (1624–69) and Nicholas Malebranche (1638–1715) argue that the thinking domain and the extended domain are coordinated by divine *fiat*. Baruch Spinoza (1632–77) eliminates the division between thinking and the object of thought by uniting the whole of reality in a single entity, God or Nature. Leibniz envisages a universe, presided over by God and consisting of an infinite number of "monads," with each monad containing of a complete register of *all* its relations, past, present, and future, including its choices, with every other monad. But none of these carefully constructed solutions is susceptible to proof.

22. Descartes, *Key Philosophical Writings*, 171.

23. Descartes, *Key Philosophical Writings*, 172.

24. Russell, *Autobiography*, 65.

25. Nagel, *View from Nowhere*, 29.

A more influential tradition privileges experience over the world experienced. Locke argues that personal identity consists in continuity of consciousness, rather than in the continuity of the substance in which the consciousness happens to be, body or soul. George Berkeley (1685–1753) argues that the world has no existence outside perceiving minds. Hume holds that there are just sequences of experience-data, "ideas," to be described and empirically assessed according to the ways they "associate" together in regular formations. In experience, there is no personal "I"; therefore no personal "I" exists.

One of the projects of philosophers from Descartes to Hume, then, was to resolve the problem raised by the *cogito* either by relying on God or bypassing one side of the problem—reality as it exists independently of human perception. But science made this privileging of the experiencing subject increasingly unconvincing. Descartes had argued that animals might be "machines." Thomas Huxley (1825–95) suggested that consciousness in animals might be "a collateral product" of the bodily machine.[26] He called this "epiphenomenalism" and tried to work out a more nuanced view of brain and mind in human beings. Yet the notion of human consciousness as a stream of epiphenomena is currently very much alive.[27] Huxley was a disciple of Charles Darwin (1809–82), and Dennett is a committed neo-Darwinist. The "real" world with which scientifically minded philosophers, from Herbert Spencer (1820–1903) to Dennett, wish to engage is thus a world in which the philosophers themselves are products of the evolutionary processes that they describe.

As early as the 1820s, speculation about evolution became widespread. In France Auguste Comte (1798–1857) and in England Spencer produced theories of biological, mental, and social evolution, which relied on the claims of Jean-Baptiste Lamarck (1744–1829)

26. Quoted in Baggini, *Freedom Regained*, 15.

27. Baggini, *Freedom Regained*, cites the philosopher John Searle to this effect. See also Hofstadter and Dennett, *The Mind's I*, and Dennett, *Consciousness Explained*.

that bodily and mental skills, moral qualities, and even memories were inheritable. Though the detailed scientific work of Darwin and Gregor Mendel (1822–84) was inconsistent with it, Lamarckianism had considerable influence on literature in writers such as George Eliot and Hardy. They and present-day neo-Darwinists face a difficulty, however. In evolutionary theory, the relation between the environment and the senses of animals determines their reproductive potential. A moth attracted to candlelight dies. Human thinking is different. The mistakes human beings make are not like the fatal confusion of the moth seeking to mate by the light of the moon. Radical disagreement and therefore error are so widespread that they must have evolutionary *value,* say, by ensuring the cohesion of human groups and therefore enhancing the life chances of individuals: loyalty, for a time, trumps truth. But this must apply to scientific thought also. Neo-Darwinist thinking must not only be provisional but also incapable of fully articulating its own limitations. "An evolutionary explanation of our theorizing faculty," Nagel argues, does not "provide ... confirmation of its capacity to get at the truth."[28] Any attempt to exclude subjectivity is bound to be self-defeating. He holds on the one hand that "the objective standpoint, even at its limit, is too essential a part of us to be suppressed without dishonesty," and on the other that "the objective self, noticing that it is personally identical with the object of its detachment, comes to feel trapped."[29] And so "the basis of most real knowledge must be a priori and drawn from within ourselves."[30] If, instead, we "survey the world from a standpoint completely detached from all interests, we discover that there is *nothing*—no values left ... The result," Nagel concludes, "is objective nihilism."[31]

Friedrich Nietzsche (1844–1900) embraced objective nihilism:

28. Nagel, *View from Nowhere,* 79.

29. Nagel, *View from Nowhere,* 210.

30. Nagel, *View from Nowhere,* 83.

31. Nagel, *View from Nowhere,* 166.

it was not just God whose "death" he proclaimed but, in the words of Roland Barthes (1915–80), that of God's "hypostases—reason, science, law;"[32] language, according to Nietzsche, being nothing but a set of unstable metaphors and the notion of "truth" in language a consoling, cowardly illusion. For the radical philosopher Slavoj Žižek, "the Real" is precisely *not* what is grasped as the true but what "makes every articulated truth forever 'not-all.'"[33] "The Real" is atheistic darkness. And, according to psychoanalyst Jacques Lacan (1901–81), it is by this darkness—this "nothing that is"—that human life is collusively *driven*. It gives rise to what he calls *Jouissance*, a never quite acknowledged dance around "Nothing," on which the social bond is based. It haunts the writing of Wilde, and more surprisingly Newman's novel, *Callista*. George Eliot, Pater, Wilde, Hardy, and Kipling in their different ways also approached the Nothing disclosed by the "death of God" with carefully judged intellectual and moral responsibility. In the five late Victorian fictions discussed in Part I, the past is not viewed, selectively, nostalgically, as perhaps was commonly the case in earlier Victorian fictions, to secure the present as a base from which the future can be approached with confidence, converting "memory into action, remembrance into prediction, the past into promise."[34] Rather, it is emptied of meaning, the future being devoid of it. *Nevertheless*, these novelists attach themselves to notions of justice and right.

Immanuel Kant (1724–1804), whom many regard as a more significant philosopher than either of Descartes or Hume, has particular relevance to the essays in Part II. Kant identifies two modes of reason: pure and practical. Pure reason establishes the limits and identifies the contents of understanding, which *constructs* world, including time and space, by imposing on experience its own a priori intuitions and concepts, such as quantity, cause, absolute begin-

32. Barthes, *Image Music Text*, 147.
33. Žižek, *Plague of Fantasies*, 217.
34. Dames, *Amnesiac Selves*, 166.

nings, infinity, substance without accidents, arithmetic, and (Euclidean) geometry. Mind is not passively subject to the laws of nature, or the "laws of association," by which Humean "ideas" are organized. Rather it "gives laws to nature and even ... [renders] nature possible." Yet it is unable affirm or deny whether space—either as the mind engages with it or as it obtains in reality—is infinite. Nor can it affirm the bare possibility of "*God, freedom,* and *immortality.*" A "*necessary* being [God] ... would have to be known as given *outside ourselves,*"[35] and what is outside ourselves is unknowable. This applies also to immortality. As for freedom, even the "*possibility* of freedom" is "beyond the power of the mind to cognize."[36] (One of the principal themes of the essays in Parts II and III is to show that, on the contrary, freedom is both possible and cognizable.)

In the name of practical reason, however, Kant then insists on restraining "the officious pretensions of understanding,"[37] on abolishing "*knowledge,* to make room for *belief.*"[38] Free will cannot be treated by pure reason as even possible. *Nevertheless,* its logic must be explored because it is morally necessary. Similarly, though "the character of permanence" cannot be attributed to the "thinking subject"[39] because "permanence" is associated with the concept of substance and is therefore subject to the limitations of pure reason, *nevertheless,* the personal "I" is granted "pure apperception"[40] in practical reason and asserted not just as an idea, but—which makes this a daring assertion indeed—as "a thing-in-itself." This, Kant writes defiantly, "no doubt" it *is.*[41] According to Kant, then, the *only* "thing-in-itself" that the thinking subject can engage with is the thinking subject itself.

35. Kant, *Critique of Pure Reason,* 200.
36. Kant, *Critique of Pure Reason,* 329.
37. Kant, *Critique of Judgement,* preface, 4.
38. Kant, *Critique of Pure Reason,* 18.
39. Kant, *Critique of Pure Reason,* 230.
40. Kant, *Critique of Pure Reason,* 94.
41. Kant, *Critique of Judgement,* introduction, 13.

Kant held that the mind cannot know whether space is infinite. But it *can* think infinity and thereby discover its *own* "appropriate sublimity . . . even above nature,"[42] above, that is, the confined territory of the Understanding: it is *not* confined to pure reason. It can also legislate for itself at the level of "delight," making what, internally, it sees as possible harmonize with "the external possibility of nature"; "the theoretical faculty gets bound up into unity with the practical in an intimate and obscure manner."[43] Morality, however, does not come easy: "duplicity . . . lies hidden in the depth of the heart, because man manages to falsify his innermost sentiments before his own conscience."[44]

This side of Kant is especially relevant to the essays in Part II. Descartes claimed to find rational evidence for the personal "I" in (I argue) the *ergo* of *Cogito ergo sum*. All that this can signify about that personal "I," however, is that it can validly infer. Descartes's personal "I" would be Kant's pure reasoner if pure reason admitted the personal "I." But Kant's often overlooked penetration "into the unfathomable depths and abyss of [the] heart"[45] places practical reason and judgment (i.e., moral insight, aesthetic delight, "freedom," and therefore the manner in which the personal "I" might, may, must be perceived) alongside pure reason. The one thing in itself, to which the mind has undoubted if necessarily indirect access, is not just Descartes's "thinking thing" but a delighting, self-deceiving, morally responsible, potentially wicked thing as well. The range and character of its "therefores" intellectual and practical—"*This* is what I will do!"—are rich and constantly enlarging. In Ricoeur's words, "we have to recover the . . . positing of the self, in all the density of its works."[46]

42. Kant, *Critique of Judgement*, Part I, 112.

43. Kant, *Critique of Judgement*, Part I, 224*ff*.

44. Immanuel Kant, "On the Failure of All Attempted Theodicies," in Despland, *Kant on History and Religion*, 296.

45. Kant, *Doctrine of Virtue*, 107.

46. Ricoeur, *Freud and Philosophy*, 45.

The writers discussed in the essays in Part II—the pre-Cartesian John Milton (1608–74) and the Romantic and post-Romantic William Blake (1757–1827), William Wordsworth (1770–1850), Christina Rossetti (1830–94), Emily Dickinson (1830–86), and Gerard Manley Hopkins (1844–89)—elucidate and celebrate this wealth of inferred personal being, passionately if indirectly known. Their disclosures are layered. At the level of language, there is free play within precise signification. At the level of willing, there is choice, delight, and darkness—Milton inviting a friend to dinner, Satan staring in hatred at the naked glory of Adam and Eve, Wordsworth's Johnny gazing at the moon (what an *ergo* is there!), Blake's hate-driven baby. Next there is the correlative choosing by the poets themselves—*this* is what I will show and how I will show it. And finally there is what reading these texts, and these essays, reveals about the reader. "Five Suppositions" (chap. 7), for example, circulates without coming to rest, yet even if the reader is puzzled or angry in consequence, that puzzlement or anger is an indicator—indirect, partial, but precise—of what the reader *is*.

Parts II and III also address religious issues, religion being, of course, philosophically contentious. Here I rely heavily on both Kant and Newman. Newman had only sketchy knowledge of Kant, yet their thinking converges. Like Kant, Newman holds that space is just "our mode of conceiving of matter," and he does not "believe in time."[47] Kant, however, maintains that the properties of a thing "as it is in itself" cannot "migrate into [the] faculty of representation,"[48] but Newman rejects "absolute scepticism about everything external to consciousness."[49] He holds that *formal relations* are transferable from one medium to another. There is correspondence between spatial data expressed as fluxions and their mathematical equivalents in

47. Newman, in Myers, *Thoughtful Heart*, 54.

48. Kant, *Prolegomena to Any Future Metaphysics*, 34.

49. Newman, in Myers, *Thoughtful Heart*, 87.

differentials in which "space and time, and sense does [sic] not enter into consideration."[50] As in an equation such as $M = (a - b - x + y)^3$, a *single* change in M could produce a *series* of changes on the right, so a *single* datum in the world might generate a *series* of temporal and/or spatial reconfigurations in experience. Pater also holds this insight or intuition, and in *Tractatus Logico- Philosophicus,* Ludwig Wittgenstein (1889–1951) writes, "A gramophone, the musical idea, the written notes, and the sound-waves all stand to one another in the same internal relation of depicting that holds between language and the world," and "are all constructed according to a common logical pattern."[51]

There is no basis in Kant's pure reason for the being of God. Even so, on this issue there is common ground between him and Newman. Contemptuous of the so-called argument from design, Newman points to "the difficulty of assuming design because there is order."[52] Also, if order in the world is taken as evidence of the *mind* of a designer, phenomena "quite as forcibly" prove that *matter* really exists. But this, Newman points out, "leads to a Dualism—for when do we learn from the visible world that Mind can create Matter?"[53] So Nagel was not the first to see this difficulty.

How, then, does Newman justify belief in God? The mind, he argues, makes moral judgments that cannot be explained in terms of causes. Nothing in what Kant calls pure reason, or in what others think of as scientific, empirical truth, really explains the moral sense. Nevertheless, Newman feels justified in asserting its validity. The sense of moral obligation, like reason and a sense of the beautiful, is "bound up with the very idea or fact of [his own] existence," that is, with his capacity to see connections and reach conclusions. It carries an inchoate sense of accountability *to* as well as account-

50. Newman, in Myers, *Thoughtful Heart,* 98.

51. Wittgenstein, *Tractatus Logico-Philosophicus,* 20.

52. Newman, in Myers, *Thoughtful Heart,* 64.

53. Newman, in Myers, *Thoughtful Heart,* 65.

ability *for*. Initially, this "feeling … of right and wrong *under a special sanction*"[54] is just a way of being aware of oneself, but when the "idea of God [is] suggested," "the suggestions of conscience"[55] come to be adequately understood. The inference of God is thus grounded in self-experiencing, as are the inferences of the personal "I" and the world. From conscience, Newman can conclude rationally *that* God exists without knowing *God*. This is different from Descartes's ontological argument, and it brings Newman into an interesting relation to Kant. Like Newman, Kant accepts the principle of "accountability *to*", and that "accountability *to*" in turn entails a *notion* of "God"; "there is in our moral habits of thought," he writes, "a pure moral need for the real existence of a Being … a moral Legislator existing apart from the world, and to do so without regard to theoretical proof … but on a purely moral ground."[56] "God" cannot be endorsed by the Understanding, but if human beings want to *act* as moral agents—and Kant thinks they should—they must act *as if* they were accountable to "God."

In these essays, I pay more attention to good conscience than to bad, as presented (in my account) by Milton, Jane Austen (1775–1817), George Eliot, Newman, Wilde, and Hardy. Newman writes of "a grateful cheerfulness when we go right, which is just what we feel in pleasing … a father or revered superior."[57] His argument has an additional interest for me, since it almost amounts to an "ontological argument" for the existence of a moral order. When I grasp laws of optics, I realize that there is no such entity as a rainbow, that interactions between sunlight, droplets of water, and the eye generate the rainbow mirage. But intuitions of rightness and wrongness cannot be similarly accounted for as (say) outcomes of group opinion or social self-interest, or inherited programming, or tricks of

54. Newman, in Myers, *Thoughtful Heart*, 55.

55. Newman, in Myers, *Thoughtful Heart*, 45–46.

56. Kant, *Doctrine of Virtue* 107.

57. Kant, *Doctrine of Virtue*, 58.

language, or "dread of castration,"[58] because if that is *all* they are, they are like the rainbow. The intuition of rightness and wrongness as such is thus a truth independent of minds thinking about it, even though its being thought about is the only evidence of its existence; "if values are objective," Nagel argues, "they must be so in their own right."[59]

In his "Lecture on Ethics"—a beautifully formed "essay" as I understand the term, because you have to read it to the end to know where it is going—Wittgenstein turns this argument on its head, or appears to do so. If "a man could write a book on Ethics which really was a book about Ethics," he declares, "this book would, with an explosion, destroy all the other books in the world."[60] Statements about values are either relative or absolute. Relative statements such as "This man is a good runner" can be analyzed in terms of facts. Being a good runner means (say) "he runs a certain number of miles in a certain number of minutes." But calling a person "good" or an action "right" in an absolute sense is without meaning because it is without factual content. "There are no propositions, which, in any absolute sense, are sublime, important, or trivial."[61] So "a certain characteristic misuse of our language runs through all ethical or religious expressions."[62] They depend on analogy or simile or allegory. "But," Wittgenstein insists, "a simile must be the simile for something . . . I must also be able to drop the simile and simply to state the facts without it."[63] He would soon abandon this view of language, but his later account of "language games" would leave no room for "absolute" statements either.

Within his argument, however, there is what may be called a

58. Ricoeur, *Rule of Metaphor*, 382.

59. Nagel, *View from Nowhere*, 139.

60. Wittgenstein, "Lecture on Ethics," 2–3.

61. Wittgenstein, "Lecture on Ethics," 2.

62. Wittgenstein, "Lecture on Ethics," 4.

63. Wittgenstein, "Lecture on Ethics," 5.

counter-thrust—not an argument but a stance. Ethical claims, Wittgenstein suggests, have the same status as statements about miracles, a view not dissimilar to an argument of Newman's, as outlined in "Good, Happy, and Free" (chap. 9), except that, according to Wittgenstein, such statements are not just nonsense, "nonsensicality [is] of their very essence." If one of his listeners suddenly grew a lion's head and started roaring, Wittgenstein "would fetch a doctor and have the case scientifically investigated and *if it were not for hurting him* ... would have him vivisected" (my emphasis). Later he compares making absolute religious or ethical statements to "running against the walls of our cage"—that is, the cage of language—and describes the practice as "absolutely hopeless." (Was the lion image still in his head?) He concludes:

> Ethics so far as it springs from the desire to say something about ... the absolute good ... can be no science. What it says does not add to our knowledge in any sense. But it is a document of a tendency in the human mind which I personally cannot help respecting deeply and I would not for my life ridicule it.[64]

And so, ironically or solemnly, Wittgenstein concludes his deconstruction of ethics in full ethical mode. The alert reader or listener might recall some earlier throwaway or facetious remarks in the lecture—"all of us who, like myself, are still tempted to use such expressions as 'absolute good,' 'absolute value' etc.,"[65] "the experiences I have mentioned ... seem to those who have experienced them, for instance to me."[66] In effect, Wittgenstein cannot rid himself of a kind of inner nonsensicality. The touch paper has been lit, the cage door swings open—perhaps on Kant's practical reason.

By *fiat*, Kant is a dualist. For justification, pure reason is Wittgensteinian: it requires "theoretical proof" ("*knowledge*"). Practical

64. Wittgenstein, "Lecture on Ethics," 6.
65. Wittgenstein, "Lecture on Ethics," 3.
66. Wittgenstein, "Lecture on Ethics," 5.

reason, however, requires "a purely moral ground" ("*belief*"). Those commentators on Kant who prefer *Critique of Pure Reason* over his other writings would do well to acknowledge that their preference cannot be itself the work of pure reason. Objectivity, Nagel claims, may have "to rest on an unexamined subjective base"[67] or upon what the Nobel Laureate Jacques Monod (1910–76) calls "*an ethical postulate.*"[68] Commitment to pure reason is necessarily an act of practical reason, so that pure reason is (logically? practically? morally?) dependent on what it is at pains to eliminate.

For Newman, an ongoing personal "I" is indirectly inferred from his logical, emotional, aesthetic, and moral "therefores." If it were immediate and given, the I, in Nagel's words, could only be thought of as "a pure, featureless mental receptacle" and consequently "inadequate to bear the weight of personal identity."[69] An inference, from a series of intellectual, aesthetic, emotional, and moral "therefores," however, "does not," as Nagel puts it, "tell us fully what kind of thing we are . . . the principle of our identity . . . [being] partly hidden from us."[70] Nevertheless, it can be understood as an unfolding process of self-disclosure and self-discovery, which entails a complementary unfolding of awareness of others, where (I hold) the roots of morality and freedom are to be found, freedom (the full freedom of indifference) being a relationship of reciprocity and equality between persons. Freedom so understood is, I argue, especially in Part III, "Freedom and God," intrinsic to the mystery ("the nothing that is") of all meaningful relations between people, between them and God, and—here I speak as one less wise—in the very life of the Godhead.

67. Nagel, *View from Nowhere*, 68.

68. Monod, *Chance and Necessity*, 161. Cf. "In our account of how science might be acquired we do not try to justify science by some prior or firmer philosophy" (Quine, *Roots of Reference*, 34). The philosopher rejects what the scientist, a Nobel Laureate, sees as necessary.

69. Nagel, *View from Nowhere*, 33.

70. Nagel, *View from Nowhere*, 39.

"Philosophy is ethical to the extent that it leads from alienation to freedom and beatitude."[71]

Because this book moves between literary criticism, philosophy, theology, science, and scriptural studies, I try to clarify my line of thought for readers not familiar with the texts I am writing about. I describe plot and character in works of fiction and theoretical notions in science, philosophy, and literary theory in ways that specialists may find superficial. I ask for their forbearance. I am far from being a specialist in the fields I trespass upon, but then the essay is not a form for specialists, and if there are howlers, there are howlers (a.k.a. *Jouissance*).

I have nothing to say about ethics—for example, about judging between competing grants of freedom involving more than one other person—or the claims on conscience of differing values, such as justice, charity, obedience to law (divine or human), violence (divine or human),[72] and freedom itself. I leave it to others to explore the implications for ethics of freedom as I understand it, from Plato (428/27–348/47 BCE), Aristotle (384–322 BCE), St. Augustine, St. Thomas Aquinas (1225–74), Hume, Kant, and John Stuart Mill (1803–73) to the work of contemporaries such as Derek Parfitt (1942–2017), Martha Nussbaum, and Alasdair MacIntyre. Apart from Ricoeur, I have nothing to say either about analytical philosophy, the "grammar" of the grant of freedom. Hence the absence of references to important philosophers such as Elizabeth Anscombe (1919–2001), Willard Van Orman Quine (1908–2000), and Donald Davidson (1917–2003).

71. Ricoeur, *Rule of Metaphor*, 45.

72. This book went to press before I became acquainted with *Divine Violence and the Christus Victor Atonement Model*, by Martyn John Smith (2016), which argues powerfully for the view that "violence" is a divine predicate and consequently in some sense a human good. If sustainable, Smith's work would considerably complicate ethics in general, my ontological argument for the existence of right and wrong, and divine freedom as I understand it.

Most of these essays are published here for the first time. But substantial parts of the essay on George Eliot (chap. 1) are taken from my book *The Teaching of George Eliot* (1984); some material in "Writing and Freedom" (chap. 5) and "Transcendental Relativism; or, The Death of God and the Jesus Thought Experiment" (chap. 10) are taken from my book *Milton and Free Will* (1987). "'What Do You Want?' Newman's 'Interminable Scepticism'" (chap. 8) is based on a paper given at an academic conference but not published. "What It's Like to Be a Person" (chap. 6) was originally an Aquinas Lecture given at Holy Cross Priory Leicester, and then became the basis for a module on a part-time humanities degree for mature students. "Good, Happy, and Free" (chap. 9) is based on my Newman Lecture given to the Leicester Theological Society in 2015. In arranging these essays, I have had to modify them in places, to avoid repetition on the one hand and to point up connections on the other. Each is an essay in its own right, though I hope that they also fall into place in a larger whole, in the manner (say) of a song cycle or a carefully arranged sequence of poems.

Part I

Virtue and Necessity

1

George Eliot

IS SUBMISSION A VIRTUE?

> Den Himmel überlasen wir
> Den Engeln und den Spatzen
>
> We leave Heaven to the angels and the sparrows
>
> —*Heinrich Heine*

From early adulthood, George Eliot immersed herself in German and French atheism, and dutifully *submitted* to its logic. But she knew also that the peremptory and absolute concept of Duty,[1] the high calling to Altruism and faithfulness to truth, was difficult, perhaps impossible, to defend in the context of the atheism she had morally to affirm. This contradiction, unrecognized by contemporaries such as John Stuart Mill and Herbert Spencer, is at the heart of her last novel, *Daniel Deronda,* in which three conventions of the genre are replaced by the depiction of catastrophic spiritual failure that perhaps only a skilled psychoanalyst could have resolved. In

1. I capitalize "Duty," "Altruism," and "Submission" when they refer to the concepts in Comte's system, as reflected in the writings of George Eliot. I also capitalize "Meliorism" when referring to George Eliot's special use of the word, and *Jouissance,* perhaps just for the hell of it.

consequence, an untellable tale is *not* told. Yet the novel also presents ordinary people exemplifying life-sustaining virtue.

Atheism was central to nineteenth-century European philosophy. Auguste Comte, the founder of "Positivism," believed that human thought evolved through three stages, based on religion (the Theological Stage advancing from animism, through polytheism, to monotheism), abstract theorizing (the Metaphysical Stage), and finally scientific empiricism and altruism in morality (the Positive Stage) in which Submission to authority—intellectual, political, familial, and moral—would sustain personal and social well-being, with Altruism governing personal and social relations. The cult of the divine would be replaced by the cult of the human. Ludwig Feuerbach (1804–72) interpreted religious ideas as modes of human self-understanding, the qualities attributed to God—knowledge, power, mercy, justice—being a form of unconscious self-assessment by humanity; "theology" had now to give way to "anthropology," in effect what is now known as "humanism." Thus both Comte and Feuerbach envisaged religion, to which they attached considerable importance, being redirected from the illusory worship of the divine to a liberating celebration of the human.

Karl Marx (1818–83), in his "Theses on Feuerbach," disagreed. Feuerbach apparently thought that changing the way human beings perceived themselves would change the world. Marx argued that material circumstances determined the way human beings perceived themselves and currently divided humanity into mutually antagonistic classes, resulting in false consciousness or "alienation" (i.e., madness), of which religious belief was a flagrant, if understandable, instance. You didn't change the world by having better ideas about it; you transformed thinking and values by changing the world, by revolution. Arthur Schopenhauer (1788–1860) was a more pessimistic atheist. For him, underlying matter and its laws was an inchoate will to exist in nature itself, a barely self-comprehending cosmic "drive" that had no regard for the paltry willing of individual consciousnesses even though it gave rise to them. Nietzsche embraced this prioritizing of the will. For him, however, will manifested itself in the individual's encounter with a universe in which God was dead, the ancient notions of good and evil were no longer relevant, and all values were "transvalued." Altruism and Submission were not on Marx's agenda. Nor on Schopenhauer's or Nietzsche's.

Atheism was less central and adventurous in British philosophy. Herbert Spencer was an avowed atheist. For him, modern religious experience consisted of wonder at the vastness and complexity of reality, and a fear that "of all that is thus incomprehensible to us, there exists no comprehension anywhere"[2]—worshipping "the question mark as a god"[3] was Nietzsche's description of atheism like this. Spencer's *The Principles of Psychology* (1855) proposed a theory of evolution, one and continuous, from molecules to the industrial state and modern culture: "the ascending developments of Life in general," he wrote, "has continued throughout human civilization … The gradual evolution of Science and Art … abundantly exemplifies this."[4] His theory depended on Lamarck's belief that physical and psychological developments in the lives of individuals (the acquired skills of a carpenter, the battle skills of a soldier) could be transmitted to their descendants. People's reactions to landscapes, for example, were a mixture of personal and inherited experience. Particular memories of "trees … flowers … fields … streams … precipices" and "incidental feelings" associated with them, intermingled with "deeper, but now vague, combinations of states which were organized in the race during barbarous times, when its pleasurable activities were chiefly among the woods and waters."[5]

Charles Darwin recognized almost from the beginning that his

2. Spencer, *Autobiography*, 2:469.

3. Nietzsche, *Genealogy of Morals*, 292.

4. Spencer, *Principles of Psychology*, 464.

5. Spencer, *Principles of Psychology*, 599.

research had atheistic implications. *On the Origin of Species by Means of Natural Selection* (1859), published four years after Spencer's *Principles of Psychology*, focuses on the cumulative outcomes of small changes in biological structures over the generations. Darwin only partially sanctioned the transmission of acquired bodily characteristics,[6] but more readily envisaged the transmission of psychological experience—in his final work, *The Formation of Vegetable Mould through the Actions of Worms* (1881), he suggests that earthworms and worker-ants might inherit specific "habits" and "knowledge" from their immediate ancestors.[7] Lamarckian ideas about the mind and race flourished well into the twentieth century. As late as 1950, Paul Ricoeur wrote of the unconscious as "vital, sexual, infantile, perhaps even ancestral,"[8] and even now neo-Darwinists speculate that thoughts and feelings developed among humanity's hunter-gatherer ancestors have been transmitted to their present descendants through the genetic code.

In Mill's last major work, *An Examination of Sir William Hamilton's Philosophy* (1865), evolution is not mentioned. It would have been difficult to reconcile it with the book's premise that every mind begins as a blank upon which experiences accumulate according to "Laws of Association." For Mill, "individuality is the same thing with development,"[9] but if inherited ancestral experiences or the unconscious operation of sociological or physical processes affected thought and/or behavior, the experiential stream would be unable to explain itself to itself. Strict logic, therefore, led Mill to assert that the "initiation of all wise or noble things, comes from individuals; generally at first from some one individual,"[10] by which he meant individual consciousnesses, starting from scratch each time. The

6. See Darwin, *On the Origin of Species*, 108–9.

7. See Darwin, *Formation of Vegetable Mould*, 32, 35.

8. Ricoeur, *Freedom and Nature*, 401.

9. *On Liberty*, in Mill, *Essays on Politics and Society*, 10.

10. Mill, *Essays on Politics and Society*, 13.

past influenced the present through remembered experiences, imitation of others, and socially preserved traditions. There was only one set of data, a stream of sensations or ideas, which "associated" in each mind with strict but complex regularity, so that demonstrably high-quality streams generated demonstrably high-quality thinking and feeling.

Spencer and Mill and others like Thomas Huxley argued for the *moral* superiority of atheism over belief. This Nietzsche condemned as being pitiably "English."[11] Such thinkers, he brutally declared, were at heart "wan atheists, Antichrists, immoralists, nihilists, sceptics," imprisoned in an intellectual culture, the "restless activity" of which "thinly [veiled] a lack of ideal, the want of a great love."[12] Out of a still essentially Christian reverence for "truth," "English psychologists"—Spencer and Mill presumably among them—pushed

> into the foreground the nasty part of the psyche, looking for the effective motor forces of human development in the very last place we would have wished to have found them, e.g., in the inertia of habit, in forgetfulness, in the blind and fortuitous association of ideas: always in something that is purely passive, automatic, reflexive, molecular, and, moreover, profoundly stupid.[13]

Real freedom could only exist for those who asserted that "Nothing is true; everything is permitted."[14]

Nietzsche regarded George Eliot as typically "English"—"little" and "moralistic."[15] On one celebrated occasion, "taking as her text the three words which have been used so often as the inspiring trumpet-calls of men—the words, *God, Immortality, Duty*—[she] pronounced, with terrible earnestness, how inconceivable was the *first,* how unbelievable the *second,* yet how peremptory or absolute

11. *Twilight of the Idols,* in Nietzsche, *Portable Nietzsche,* 515.
12. Nietzsche, *Birth of Tragedy,* 285–86.
13. Nietzsche, *Birth of Tragedy,* 285–86.
14. Nietzsche, *Birth of Tragedy,* 287.
15. Nietzsche, *Portable Nietzsche,* 515.

the *third*."[16] She believed in "progress" on Comtean lines, in the doctrines of Altruism and Submission, moral, intellectual, and social development being governed by evolutionary processes. Her "Meliorism" (as she called it) was also influenced by Feuerbach—she translated *The Essence of Christianity* (1841) into English in 1854. She was also indebted to Spencer. She believed in heredity, the unconscious and physiological processes (particularly on issues relating to race and gender), and economic and cultural structures operating according to their own laws—railways and telegraphs facilitated the exchange of "sympathy" rather than (say) xenophobia or lust.[17] (What would she have made of the Internet?) Values were transmitted down the generations by passing between and slowly transforming human bodies, their nervous systems, even their appearance. There are *morally* different forms of inherited beauty in all George Eliot's novels. These "purely passive, automatic, reflexive, molecular" elements in her thinking explain Nietzsche's contempt. Her Meliorism is undoubtedly strained, her presentation of goodness often overwrought. Nevertheless, Nietzsche underestimated her. She was determined to "do without opium,"[18] and she engaged with the problems of the unconscious and of evil in a way that was outside the range of Spencer and Mill and in its fashion as challenging as Nietzsche's.

Without knowing that he is by birth a Jew, the eponymous hero of her last novel, *Daniel Deronda* (1876), feels powerfully drawn to Judaism and to Ezra Mordecai Cohen, a consumptive messianic Zionist, who is convinced that the apparently gentile Daniel will lead a Jewish return to Palestine. Both are programmed by inherited drives and sympathies into an affinity with each other and with the Zionist dream. "Have we not touched each other with invisible fibres," says

16. Myers, "George Eliot," 62.
17. Eliot, *Essays*, 402.
18. Eliot, *Letters*, 3:366.

Mordecai (the name he is usually known by), "have we not quivered together like the leaves from a common stem with stirrings from a common root?"[19]—*invisible* fibers are what Mill set his face against. For a Lamarckian, however, Mordecai's prophetic instincts with respect to Daniel—they have a quasi-visual character—make sense. Inherited cultural experience could make a person's mind-set and *future* personal development accessible to someone who shared that inheritance, in an intuitively symbolic or prophetic mode, an "effect of brooding passionate thought of many ancestors," as the modern-minded Daniel speculates; "the stolen offspring of some mountain tribe brought up in a city of the plain" would experience "the ancestral life . . . as a dim longing for unknown objects and sensations."[20] Mental "enlargement" for George Eliot uses mysterious, preconscious resources of ancestral experience, a notion completely unacceptable to Mill.

But such a preconscious core functioning over the generations as a benign, "always already" drive toward Altruism and rationality makes wickedness a problem. If wicked impulses and experiences were as inheritable as benign ones, how could the race advance? George Eliot meets this problem by allowing some innate functions—love of power and fear, for example—to result in bad behavior, but they can be transformed by enlargement of the sympathies. In *The Mill on the Floss* (1860), love of power in the confident, self-centered boy, Tom Tulliver, matures into a sense of seriousness and responsibility, and when, during a flood that drowns him and his sister he at last discovers "the depths in life, that had lain beyond his vision,"[21] his fear becomes quasi-religious awe. In general, however, Meliorism requires that wickedness be understood as a negative effect, inherited narrowness of vision and lack of emotional resources, as exemplified, for ex-

19. Eliot, *Daniel Deronda*, 572.
20. Eliot, *Daniel Deronda*, 750.
21. Eliot, *Daniel Deronda*, 654.

ample, by Tito Milema, the gifted but shallow, self-absorbed central male character in George Eliot's historical novel *Romola*.

This approach to moral deficiency seems also to be operative in *Daniel Deronda*. The corrupt Henleigh Mallinger Grandcourt is ostentatiously negative: "it was perhaps not possible for a breathing man wide awake to look less animated."[22] His passions are "intermittent, flickering ... never flaming out strongly."[23] He spends hours "sitting meditatively on a sofa and abstaining from literature ... [in] a state ... something like premature age."[24] He is fond of yachting, with "its dreamy do-nothing absolutism, unmolested by social demands."[25] Daniel, by contrast, has a "calm intensity of life,"[26] even in idleness. After an afternoon rowing, he lies back and looks "all around him ... forgetting everything else in a half-speculative, half-involuntary identification of himself with the objects he is looking at."[27] He also has depths. Still unaware of his Jewish ancestry, he reacts strongly to a synagogue service, in a way that seems "beyond the occasion—what one might imagine to be a divine influx in the darkness, before there was any vision to interpret."[28] But in this novel, influxes that arise in darkness are not all "divine." In a series of disturbing images, Grandcourt is described as resembling "a handsome lizard of a hitherto unknown species, not of the lively, darting kind,"[29] looking "as neutral as an alligator."[30] The negating qualifications do not counter positive intimations of menace. There are *depths* to Grandcourt's negations. With cold, unemphatic determination, he pursues the novel's most important woman character, Gwendolen Harleth.

22. Eliot, *Daniel Deronda*, 111.
23. Eliot, *Daniel Deronda*, 156.
24. Eliot, *Daniel Deronda*, 319.
25. Eliot, *Daniel Deronda*, 668.
26. Eliot, *Daniel Deronda*, 162.
27. Eliot, *Daniel Deronda*, 189.
28. Eliot, *Daniel Deronda*, 368.
29. Eliot, *Daniel Deronda*, 137.
30. Eliot, *Daniel Deronda*, 157.

Gwendolen is immature, self-centered, beautiful, witty, and frightened of adult intimacy, especially the attentions of her innocently virile young cousin, Rex Gascoigne. She shies away, too, from Grandcourt's measured advances—"I did not encourage them," she tells her uncle, the Rev. Mr. Gascoigne. "I turned the conversation."[31] But she adds, "I am not stupid. I know that I must be married some time. And I don't see how I could do better than marry Mr Grandcourt. I mean to accept him, if possible."[32] The next day, "looking lovely and vigorous as a tall, newly opened lily," with "yesterday's self-distrust [seeming] no more than the transient shiver on the surface of a full stream,"[33] she is on the point of accepting him when she is dramatically confronted by his mistress, Mrs. Glasher, and two of the four children she has had by him. Appalled, Gwendolen promises proudly not to act in any way that would harm Mrs. Glasher's son, and flees aboard. But she has to return home on learning that the family's money has been lost in a fraud. Her aspirations to go on the stage are humiliatingly dismissed by the great musician Herr Klesmer, and she faces the degrading prospect of becoming a governess, while her mother, on whom she is childishly dependent, is reduced to poverty. With perfectly timed determination, Grandcourt renews his suit. Knowing that she knows about his secret family only makes him wish more strongly to master "this piquant combination of maidenliness and mischief . . . to triumph over [her] repugnance."[34] When she pulls away from his kisses, he is "contented to pay a large price for this new kind of love-making, which introduced marriage by the finest contrast"[35]—it won't *quite* be rape, just a cold-hearted exercise of sexual power.

Their wedding is observed by some countrywomen: "A quarrel

31. Eliot, *Daniel Deronda*, 141.
32. Eliot, *Daniel Deronda*, 143.
33. Eliot, *Daniel Deronda*, 145.
34. Eliot, *Daniel Deronda*, 301.
35. Eliot, *Daniel Deronda*, 328.

may end wi' the whip," says one, "but it begins wi' the tongue, and it's the women have got the most o' that."[36] The woman who hits out verbally on Gwendolen's wedding day, however, is Mrs. Glasher, and the pleasures awaiting Grandcourt are not the crudity of the whip, but the knowledge that Gwendolen has been brought "to accept him in spite of everything."[37] Later, when he talks to her about her relations with Daniel, who becomes her mentor and spiritual guide, Grandcourt is conscious of using "pincers on that white creature";[38] and when, against her wishes, he sends his man of affairs, Mr. Lush, to discuss the provisions for her and his illegitimate family in his will, the man's speech is "like a sharp knife-edge drawn across her skin."[39] On their extended yachting holiday, she feels "moral repulsion and cowed resistance . . . like an eating pain intensifying into torture"; "throned on her cushions at evening," she hopes "that Grandcourt in his march up and down [is] not going to pause near her." This "repulsion" may be "moral," but its implications are also sexual, as the imagery makes clear. Gwendolen, we are told, could no more quarrel with Grandcourt than she could with "a dangerous serpent ornamentally coiled in her cabin without invitation,"[40] a cabin "hung with silk, expanded with mirrors."[41] This pseudo-enlargement of an intimate space must have been especially unpleasant to the young wife who couldn't "bear any one to be very near to [her]" except her mother[42] and so, presumably, especially piquant to Grandcourt.

Gwendolen's acceptance of Grandcourt is partly explained in ways that Mill could countenance: the family's poverty, the subservience exacted from governesses. But the decision to marry Grand-

36. Eliot, *Daniel Deronda*, 354.
37. Eliot, *Daniel Deronda*, 320.
38. Eliot, *Daniel Deronda*, 588.
39. Eliot, *Daniel Deronda*, 600.
40. Eliot, *Daniel Deronda*, 672.
41. Eliot, *Daniel Deronda*, 670.
42. Eliot, *Daniel Deronda*, 82.

court goes deeper than "motives." It too is an influx in the darkness. In the opening scene, Gwendolen is described as having "got herself up as a sort of serpent."[43] Later we learn that she has an "undefinable stinging quality . . . a trace of demon ancestry."[44] These images suggest an instinctual *affinity* between Grandcourt's violent heart and her own. Referring to the chemistry of dynamite, George Eliot writes in reference to Grandcourt: "We mortals have a strange spiritual chemistry going on within us, so that a lazy stagnation or even a cottony milkiness may be preparing one knows not what biting or explosive material."[45] Gwendolen has her own line in violence. As a child, she strangled her sister's canary. Before meeting Grandcourt, she remarks, "I feel sure that with a little murdering he might get a title."[46] Lush thinks her "as dangerous as gunpowder."[47] Within months of their marriage, Gwendolen is fantasizing about Grandcourt's murder, secreting a knife in her dressing case, and Sir Hugo Mallinger, Daniel's Guardian, detects "gunpowder" in the whole "establishment."[48]

Gwendolen, however, is driven to seek pain as well as to inflict it, notably in her elaborately intertwined relations with Daniel and Grandcourt. In one chapter, she notes that her husband "delights in making the dogs and horses quail," and finds she can say nothing to him "that would not hurt her worse than submission,"[49] in the next she "submissively" asks Daniel to arrange for her to have singing lessons, and later looks up at him "with pain in her long eyes, like a wounded animal asking help."[50] When he subsequently speaks to her, her face manifests "that subtle change in nerve and

43. Eliot, *Daniel Deronda*, 12.
44. Eliot, *Daniel Deronda*, 68.
45. Eliot, *Daniel Deronda*, 319.
46. Eliot, *Daniel Deronda*, 96.
47. Eliot, *Daniel Deronda*, 162.
48. Eliot, *Daniel Deronda*, 454.
49. Eliot, *Daniel Deronda*, 427.
50. Eliot, *Daniel Deronda*, 439.

muscle which . . . is the subsidence of self assertion,"[51] while in her next scene with Grandcourt, she finds that resisting him would be "to defy the texture of her nerves and the palpitation of her heart."[52] Daniel impresses her "with the feeling of submission,"[53] and Grandcourt applies "the spiritual pressure that [makes] submission inevitable."[54] Spiritual director and sadistic sexual partner have, as it were, intuitive access to her secret self.

This would not have surprised Sigmund Freud (1856–1939), holding as he did that "ever-increasing reinforcement in our sense of guilt 'is a necessary condition of civilization,'"[55] which depends on the redirection of violent impulses from external objects toward the self. Guilt attaches to feelings rather than actions. Once the superego becomes omniscient judge, "the distinction . . . between doing something bad and wishing to do it disappears."[56] This happens to Gwendolen. On the yachting holiday, Grandcourt falls into the sea, and as he struggles in the water, she wills his death, and hesitates briefly before throwing him a rope. Grandcourt would have drowned anyway, but George Eliot endorses Daniel's uncompromising judgment that "the outward effectiveness of a criminal desire dominant enough to impel even a momentary act, cannot alter our judgment of the desire."[57] Gwendolen *ought* to feel conscience stricken. Her destiny is to "scourge" herself, always to feel afraid of herself. The "need for punishment," Freud writes, "is an instinctual manifestation on the part of the ego, which has become masochistic under the influence of a sadistic super-ego."[58] Gwendolen's "death-wish," her murderous impulses, and her collusion with Grandcourt's sadistic dominance

51. Eliot, *Daniel Deronda*, 446.
52. Eliot, *Daniel Deronda*, 447.
53. Eliot, *Daniel Deronda*, 547.
54. Eliot, *Daniel Deronda*, 555.
55. Freud, *Civilization and Its Discontents*, 80.
56. Freud, *Civilization and Its Discontents*, 69.
57. Eliot, *Daniel Deronda*, 696.
58. Freud, *Civilization and Its Discontents*, 84.

are indistinguishable from the impulses that drive her, under Daniel's direction, to submit to the uncompromising counsel of her sadistic superego, to inflict mental pain on herself for the purposes of moral regeneration.

The novel gives scrupulous attention to these contradictory responses. Consider the expression "a criminal desire dominant enough to impel even a momentary act." The mind is a field of hidden, complicated interacting forces, but George Eliot also sees "Gwendolen" somehow in their midst. In 1875, she wrote in a letter: "every fresh morning is an opportunity that one can look forward to for exerting one's will. I shall not be satisfied with your philosophy till you have conciliated necessitarianism—I hate the ugly word—with the practice of willing strongly, of willing to will strongly, and so on, that being what you certainly can do."[59] Mill wrote *An Examination of Sir William Hamilton's Philosophy* to refute the claim that moral responsibility requires "a free agent," determined neither by external or internal factors and thus *absolutely* free, and that "the legitimacy of retribution or punishment" depends on this version of free will. On determinist principles, Mill replies, punishment is justifiable if it benefits the offender or protects others; children and "adult communities which are still in the infantine stage of development"[60] may be punished for their own good. On Mill's principles, however, both the punished and the punisher act of necessity, the difference between them being in their capacity to "see" the effects of the original actions and "the utility" of the punishment. That the "seeing" of each is necessitated, that there is a vicious circle here is ignored. George Eliot's notion, on the other hand, "of willing strongly, of willing to will strongly, *and so on*," acknowledges that it is itself "willed" and thereby acknowledges the logical dilemma that Mill smooths over. The principle of willing and willing to will suggests a

59. Eliot, *Letters*, 6:166.

60. Mill, *Examination of Sir William Hamilton's Philosophy*, 459n.

vortex rather than a regress, drive without content, indistinguishable from "nothing," from that which lies outside all systems of difference, male and female, slave and free, gentile and Jew.

In *Daniel Deronda*, George Eliot looks into the abyss. Nevertheless, the novel struggles against its own nihilistic logic and ends uncertainly, in spite of itself. Daniel marries Ezra Mordecai's sister Mirah. All three plan to travel to Palestine, but Ezra dies before they can do so. The novel concludes with his last words to Daniel: "'Death is coming to me as the divine kiss which is both parting and reunion—which takes me from your bodily eyes and gives me full presence in your soul. Where thou goest, Daniel, I shall go. Is it not begun? Have I not breathed my soul into you? We shall live together.'" He then utters "in Hebrew the confession of the divine Unity" and dies some hours later.[61] The "biblical" rhetoric in which the Zionist dream is dressed is portentous and complacent, particularly in assuming the propriety, never mind the likelihood, of Orthodox Judaism allowing itself to be assimilated into a post-theistic humanism with religious trimmings, the divine Unity being *replaced* by unified humanity.

Gwendolen's future is even more troubling. The scene in which Daniel tells her that he is about to marry Mirah and leave England for Palestine is acutely embarrassing. She is shocked. "Her withered look of grief" reminds Daniel of someone suffering a bereavement that renders life forever joyless. He is unable to speak. Gwendolen tries to reassure him, speaking of her own worthlessness, the harm she has done him, and her determination to "try to live." But after his departure, she breaks down: "Through the day and half the night she [falls] continually into fits of shrieking, but [cries] in the midst of them to her mother, 'Don't be afraid. I shall live. I mean to live.'" She sleeps at last, and on waking says tenderly to her mother, "Ah, poor mamma! You have been sitting up with me. Don't be unhappy. I shall

61. Eliot, *Daniel Deronda*, 811.

live. I shall be better."[62] She is sufficiently recovered by the time of Daniel's wedding to send him a letter in which she writes: "*I have remembered your words—that I may live to be one of the best of women, who make others glad that they were born. I do not yet see how that can be, but you know better than I.*"[63] But does he?

Awkwardly as its final chapter reads, *Daniel Deronda* is nevertheless *calculated* to disturb convention. Daniel is the only one of George Eliot's protagonists to embark on a Great Action,[64] but his specific intentions and their outcome are absolutely unknowable. At the conclusion of all George Eliot's other novels, the surviving characters have imagined futures. As its readers in (say) 1890 finished *Daniel Deronda,* they could have had no idea what Daniel was supposed to have been doing in the East since the mid-1860s. (Historically, Zionism would not begin until 1898.) He would have disappeared into nothing. The conclusion of Gwendolen's narrative would have been as troubling. Following precedent (as set in George Eliot's own novels and in those of her contemporaries and predecessors), the first-time reader would have been almost incited to envisage a humble and wiser Gwendolen as the central figure of a Romance (marrΔ26

ying, if not Daniel, then, say, a matured and responsible Rex), or of a violent melodrama (in which she is suspected or actually guilty of murder), or of a tragedy (as the flawed or misunderstood young woman destined to die, repentant or unrepentant). Instead, she faces a future even more unknowable than Daniel's. She may *either* live to be one of the best of women *or* her life may be forever joyless.

There are two possible ways of accounting for this. First, though it is not set in the historical past, *Daniel Deronda* is a historical novel in the sense that it is about the historical potential of the present. Gwendolen is as important as Daniel in this respect. After her first

62. Eliot, *Daniel Deronda,* 806–7.

63. Eliot, *Daniel Deronda,* 810.

64. See Markovits, *Crisis of Action.*

meeting with Grandcourt, George Eliot speculates about the historical significance of a consciousness like Gwendolen's,

> busy with her small inferences of the way in which she could make her life pleasant … in a time, too, when … ideas were with fresh vigour making armies of themselves … when women on the other side of the world would not mourn for the husbands and sons who died bravely in a common cause, and men stinted of bread on our side of the world heard of that willing loss and were patient: a time when the soul of man was waking to impulses which for centuries had been beating in him unheard, until their full sum made new life of terror or of joy.
>
> What in the midst of that mighty drama are girls and their blind visions? They are the Yea and Nay of that good for which men are fighting. In these delicate vessels is borne onward through the ages the treasure of human affections.[65]

The reference is to the American Civil War, ending at the time in which the novel is set. Liberal and Lamarckian optimism is strongly in evidence—"ideas … with fresh vigour making armies of themselves … the soul of man … waking to impulses which for centuries had been beating in him unheard." But there are allusions also in the novel to another, more recent conflict, the Franco-Prussian War, which horrified the initially pro-Prussian George Eliot, making her feel dismay at the "moral condition" of Germany.[66] In *Daniel Deronda,* she seems to suggest that the forces of good and evil that contend on battlefields are in contention also in souls like Gwendolen's, and that it is in the latter rather than the former that the outcome of that contention ultimately depends. What happens to "girls and their blind visions" is *historically* as significant as what happened at Gettysburg and Sedan. The struggle between terror *or* joy, between the Yea *or* Nay of the good for which a war may be waged, the contention between Deronda and Grandcourt in Gwendolen's mind, a mind "as dangerous as gunpowder," *must* therefore remain

65. Eliot, *Daniel Deronda,* 124.
66. Eliot, *Letters,* 5:118.

unresolved. Anything more decisive, anything more conventional at the personal level, would empty Gwendolen of her historical significance as a delicate vessel through which the experience of the past is transmitted into an unknowable future.

The second explanation for the impasse with which the Gwendolen/Daniel relationship concludes involves different considerations. The relationship is structurally the most prominent in the novel, which opens with a question about Gwendolen even before she is named.

> Was she beautiful or not beautiful? And what was the secret of form or expression which gave the dynamic quality to her glance? Was the good or the evil genius dominant in those beams? Probably the evil; else why was the effect that of unrest rather than of undisturbed charm?[67]

These, we quickly learn, are *Daniel's* thoughts. He is watching Gwendolen gambling in the casino in Leubronn. She grows tense under his gaze. Leaving the casino, having lost heavily, she receives the letter from her mother telling her of the financial disaster. Determined not to disclose the reason for her return home, she sells a necklace. Daniel sees her do this, buys the necklace, and returns it to her. But Daniel (though this is only disclosed much later) is already in love with Mirah. Nevertheless, his seriously indecorous action initiates a relationship that is at least as pivotal as his love story. It is also unprecedented in literature, and possibly in life. But since it is not in any ordinary sense a love relationship, what is it?

From a Freudian perspective, it involves what looks like "transference," and it is worth exploring what, if this were so, it might entail. The narration allows the reader to connect with Gwendolen's fears and fantasies, if not her dreams, and the images associated with them. The most overt of these fantasies is suggested by the strangled canary and the secreted knife. There is also her insistence that a "picture of an upturned dead face, from which an obscure figure seemed

67. Eliot, *Daniel Deronda*, 7.

to be fleeing with outstretched arms,"[68] should be locked away, and the key in her sole possession. Similarly, the serpent images noted above terrify and fascinate her. In the opening scene of the novel, she has got herself up as a kind of serpent, yet a serpent also symbolizes Grandcourt's sadistic presence in her cabin. A series of horse images are similarly contradictory. As a young woman, she is like "a young race-horse . . . among untrimmed ponies and patient hacks,"[69] but she is also a rider of horses. When she and Rex go to the hunt, she tells him that she dreads the loss of freedom in marriage: she wants to "go to the North Pole, or ride steeplechases, or go to be a queen in the East." She has a "fierceness of maidenhood"[70] but is physically excited by the meet, and "in feeling something like a combination of dog and horse, with the superadded thrill of social vanities and consciousness of centaur-power." She says later that if she were to "do anything so horrible as to marry,"[71] she would expect her husband to keep horses. After accepting Grandcourt, she looks at the pair of horses "in their fine grooming" he has brought with him for them to ride together with "a thrill of exultation."[72] Later, however, Grandcourt, who delights "in making the dogs and horses quail," figuratively makes her "kneel down like a horse under training for the arena"[73] Yet it is also "with pain in her long eyes, like a wounded animal asking help,"[74] that she looks up at Daniel, when she asks him to help her get singing lessons. Gwendolen compulsively returns and fantasizes about whatever it is "serpents" and "horses" express and conceal in her psychic life.

This almost demands a psychoanalytical reading. "Metaphor,"

68. Eliot, *Daniel Deronda*, 27.
69. Eliot, *Daniel Deronda*, 25.
70. Eliot, *Daniel Deronda*, 70.
71. Eliot, *Daniel Deronda*, 77.
72. Eliot, *Daniel Deronda*, 304.
73. Eliot, *Daniel Deronda*, 439.
74. Eliot, *Daniel Deronda*, 439.

Ricoeur writes, "is nothing other than repression, and vice versa."[75] Something certainly seems repressed in the metaphors and fantasies within which Gwendolen encloses herself. Reality, in psychoanalytic theory (as interpreted by Ricoeur), is what the patient has "to reach through the obscure maze of fantasies,"[76] in and through a developing relation with an analyst. The meaning of the patient's fantasies "is *separated* from becoming conscious by a barrier ... the unconscious is inaccessible unless an appropriate technique is used."[77] A past drama that resists exposure is "untangled" by being "transposed into the dual relationship of analysis through the process of transference."[78] This technique, developed and modified by Freud over many years, involves engaging with the patient's "erotic" involvement with the analyst—the equivalent of Gwendolen's "submission" to Daniel—in order "to curb ... [the] compulsion to repeat" in and through "substitute satisfactions,"[79] and "to lead [her] back along the paths of remembering."[80] The "height of technique lies in the art of exploiting the transference-love *without satisfying it*."[81] The "analytic dialogue ... brings to light the demand in which desire ultimately consists; but only the technique of transference ... could reveal the fact that desire is at bottom an unanswered demand."[82] Initially and necessarily, the dynamics of the transference, unique to each psychoanalytical relationship, are hidden from the patient. Hence the need for the analyst's "psychoanalytic purification," for "the rule of remaining opaque to one's patients, of foregoing all educative ambition, as well as all therapeutic ambition, etc." and for linking the analysis required of analysts in training to "recognizing and overcoming the "counter-

75. Ricoeur, *Rule of Metaphor*, 402.
76. Ricoeur, *Rule of Metaphor*, 387.
77. Ricoeur, *Rule of Metaphor*, 392.
78. Ricoeur, *Rule of Metaphor*, 372.
79. Ricoeur, *Rule of Metaphor*, 417.
80. Ricoeur, *Rule of Metaphor*, 415.
81. Ricoeur, *Rule of Metaphor*, 416. Ricoeur's emphasis.
82. Ricoeur, *Rule of Metaphor*, 417.

transference."[83] In Freud's words, "the analyst ... must take care not to steer away from the transference-love, or to repulse it or to make it distasteful to the patient; but ... must resolutely withhold any response to it."[84] Daniel clearly does not satisfy Gwendolen's "transference-love" (if that is what it is), nor does he "repulse it or make it distasteful" to Gwendolen, but he remains (as historically he necessarily would have been) an "empirical" psychologist capable only of seeking to change Gwendolen's behavior. If per impossibile he had been an analyst, he would have understood her behavior to be "a segment of meaning."[85]

Even those who reject psychoanalysis might be impressed by the ways in which Daniel and Gwendolen's relationship strikingly anticipates and necessarily falls short of Freudian theory and technique. As with Zionism (both arose in late 1890s Vienna), George Eliot gets things both right and wrong. As Gwendolen's spiritual guide, Daniel does *not* make her feelings for him repulsive or distasteful to her. But because he has not had analysis and training himself, he inevitably *fails* to remain opaque to her and he *does* attempt to educate her. However (to adopt the words used of Dorothea Brooke in *Middlemarch*), it is not possible to state, "exactly what else that was in [his] power [he] ought rather to have done."[86] He is not a qualified psychoanalyst—how could he be? For that reason, the barrier between Gwendolen's unconscious and her fantasies and behavior as an adult remains in place, even for George Eliot as narrator, and certainly for any critic of the novel. Speculation about Gwendolen's history—that she was abused, say, by her stepfather—would be futile and impertinent. *Only* in the intersubjectivity of one-to-one *work* by Gwendolen and a qualified analyst could a unique healing story about her past be constructed and accepted. It would not necessar-

83. Ricoeur, *Rule of Metaphor*, 409nn81, 82.

84. Quoted in Ricoeur, *Rule of Metaphor*, 418n97.

85. Ricoeur, *Rule of Metaphor*, 369.

86. Eliot, *Middlemarch*, 894.

ily reconstruct exactly what took place (no story can), but it would heal; "strictly speaking, there are no 'facts' in psychoanalysis, for the analyst does not observe, he interprets."[87] It is thus part of George Eliot's intuitive wisdom as a novelist that that story, like the story of Daniel's Great Action, remains untold. In her final novel, George Eliot moves out of the narrative assumptions and clarifications that served her so well in *Middlemarch* into the emptiness and the darkness both of human history and the human mind.

In other respects, however, *Daniel Deronda* is embedded in the realistic tradition. Both the Jewish and English worlds are substantial and human. Daniel's passionately orthodox grandfather, his gifted, but self-absorbed mother, the "complacently lively and unrefined"[88] Orthodox family with whom Ezra Mordecai lodges, his and Mirah's seedy father, living on the edges of show business and ready to sell his daughter to a wealthy client, build up a picture of Jewish life almost as circumstantial as the brilliantly observed milieu of the Gascoignes and Mallingers—Freud remarked on George Eliot's knowledge of aspects of Jewish life that "we speak of only among ourselves."[89]

The "supererogatory" hospitality shown to Ezra Mordecai by the cheerfully coarse, "typically Jewish" pawnbroker and his family has not, I think, received sufficient recognition. It does not offset, but it does modify, the dangerous darkness I have detected in the novel. This hospitality has its limits. At the Sabbath meal, Ezra Mordecai is given "the thin tails of the fried fish … and in general the sort of share assigned to a poor relation."[90] "You may think us a little weak ourselves," Cohen says to Daniel later. "But my wife and mother wouldn't part with him if he was a still worse encumbrance. It isn't that we don't know the long and the short of matters, but it's our

87. Ricoeur, *Rule of Metaphor*, 365.
88. Eliot, *Daniel Deronda*, 389.
89. Jones, *Life and Work of Sigmund Freud*, 166.
90. Eliot, *Daniel Deronda*, 397.

principle. There's fools that do business at a loss and don't know it. I'm not one of 'em."[91] The fish tails, Cohen's fear of seeming "weak" and less than "business-like," and his endearing, slightly absurd demonstration of acumen in assessing the "profit" he has incurred by looking after Mordecai embed his virtue in the anxieties, tensions, and achievements of a specific immigrant community in a specific time and place. His family thereby points to a thoroughly human way of practicing works of "supererogation"—good works that are over and above what strict justice obliges us to do. The Cohens have learned, apparently, what Alasdair MacIntyre calls "the virtue of just generosity," based on "communal relationships that engage our affections ... extend beyond ... long-term relationships ... to relationships of hospitality to passing strangers, and, through the exercise of the virtue of *misericordia* [uncondescending pity] ... include those whose urgent need confronts the members of ... [the] community."[92]

MacIntyre holds that everyone everywhere needs to exercise "the capacities of an independent practical reasoner" in order to flourish "in a specifically human way."[93] We also need relationships with others if we are to learn how "to evaluate, modify, or reject our own practical judgments ... to imagine ... alternative possible futures ... [and] to enquire rationally what the pursuit of our good here and now requires and how our desires must be directed and, if necessary, redirected."[94] Indispensable for such is "honesty, primarily truthfulness about ourselves, both to ourselves and to others."[95] It "is only through the acquisition and exercise of the virtues that individuals and communities can flourish."[96] The substance of these claims is that the "common good cannot ... be ... constructed" out of the sum

91. Eliot, *Daniel Deronda*, 519.
92. MacIntyre, *Dependent Rational Animals*, 126.
93. MacIntyre, *Dependent Rational Animals*, 77.
94. MacIntyre, *Dependent Rational Animals*, 83.
95. MacIntyre, *Dependent Rational Animals*, 95.
96. MacIntyre, *Dependent Rational Animals*, 112.

"of individual goods."[97] The individual participates in community, and separating the individual from collective good or benefits from virtues is mistaken. George Eliot would have found MacIntyre's moral reasoning easier going than Mill's. MacIntyre's discussion of "why human beings need the virtues" questions the stability of any utilitarian scheme that attempts to admit works of supererogation—it is *not* "purely passive, automatic, reflexive, molecular, and . . . profoundly stupid"; he also questions the humanity of any that does not. And if I am right, George Eliot's depiction of it in the Cohen family does the same.

In her construction of evil and her construction of the good, in her vision of the vortex of human willing in a necessitated universe, in her resistance in the construction of her final novel to the demands of convention for closure, and in her depiction of familial "virtue" encompassing *misericordia,* George Eliot's "open necessitarianism" is both logically and affectively incompatible with the "closed necessitarianism" of Mill because it articulates questions for which there seems to be no coherent answer. Nietzsche would have done well to read her more attentively than he apparently did.

97. MacIntyre, *Dependent Rational Animals,* 109.

2

Walter Pater and Oscar Wilde

SEEING AND SUFFERING

Walter Pater was an atheist who disapproved of Mill. He initiated the British "Decadent" movement in 1867 with an essay on Samuel Taylor Coleridge (1772–1834) that draws on Hamilton's thinking, which Mill strongly opposed. Pater's thought is proto-Nietzschean, proto-postmodernist and still surprisingly relevant. Intellectually, he was a major influence on Oscar Wilde. But because Wilde committed his life and not just his intellect to Pater's ideas, he achieved a seriousness in his writing, that his timid mentor could not match. Pater was the Seer, Wilde the Protagonist. Pater opened the door of Decadence, and Wilde passed through it into the Nothing on which the common life of humanity is (or seems to be) based.

In his essay "On Style" (1873), Pater praises the "fascinating precision" with which Hamilton's editor and defender, Henry Longueville Mansel (1820–71), argues that logic as such, rather than some "principle" or "soul," secures "the unity, the strict identity with itself of the apprehending mind."[1] He certainly knew the extensive quotations

1. Pater, *Essays on Literature and Art*, 21. My reading of Pater differs from Kate Hext's *Walter Pater*. Hext holds that "a unified and at least semi-stable self" (41) formed "the faltering centre" (1) of Pater's aestheticism. Insofar as Pater's thinking is influenced by that of Hamilton and his supporters, it offers, in my view, more than an "awkwardly woolly" suggestion "that there

from Hamilton in Mill's *An Examination of Sir William Hamilton's Philosophy*, which was reviewed in the *Westminster Review* alongside his essay on Coleridge. Modern thought, Pater contends, in opposition to Mill, is "distinguished from ancient by its cultivation of the 'relative' spirit in place of the 'absolute.'" Mill was an anti-relativist, committed to the visible operations of law. Ancient philosophy, too, Pater claims, tried "to arrest every object in an eternal outline, to fix thought in a necessary formula," but the best modern thinkers have recognized that "nothing is or can be rightly known except under relative conditions."[2] Characteristically, however, Pater then praises Coleridge for *resisting* relativism, for belonging to a generation of thinkers—Newman is another—whose "ideas, moralities, modes of inward life" are repressed by the new, but who stick to them nonetheless.

Pater advances this paradox because for him "Nothing is true." Thinkers like Mill believe that the modern is more truthful than the ancient, but for Pater, the "modern" is only "different." "Nature . . . evolves ideas, moralities, modes of inward life, and represses them in turn." The modern is just a "current of new life," which "weaker minds" fail to notice and to which "clearer minds abandon themselves." Thinkers like Coleridge and Newman, however, "feel the change" but *choose* not to abandon themselves to it. By willfully defending lost causes, they enrich "the passing stage of culture [with] the charm of what is chastened, high-strung, athletic." "How often," Pater asks, "in the higher class of theological writings . . . does the modern aspirant to perfect culture find the expression of the inmost delicacies of his life, the same yet different!"[3] Philosophy is an intel-

---

is *something* beyond our comprehension" (60) that resists explanation. Beneath the (delightfully) unstable aesthetic surface on which Pater dwells, lingeringly and sometimes playfully, but usually with tough-minded intelligence, is a philosophically sophisticated *explanation* of mental formation that accounts both for the personal formation of characters as different as Marius and Lord Henry, and for its tragic incompleteness in each of them. Nor in my mind is Pater's prose "stuttering" (71). Within the limits I identify later, I find it deft and hard-headed.

2. Pater, *Essays on Literature and Art*, 1.

3. Pater, *Essays on Literature and Art*, 21.

lectual Olympiad in which stylish losers attract as much esteem as forceful winners. Mill, for Pater, is a winner without style.

At another level, however, truth does matter. Relativism, Pater provocatively insists, is a consequence of the *success* of thinkers like Comte, Mill, and Darwin, all of whom were anti-relativists. Far from discovering unvarying laws of nature, the sciences "reveal types of life evanescing into each other by inexpressible refinements of change." The "relative spirit" invades "moral philosophy from ... the inductive sciences," introducing new ideas about "the relations of body and mind, good and evil, freedom and necessity." Human beings are "the most complex of the products of nature. Character merges into temperament; the nervous system refines itself into intellect. [The] physical organism is played upon not only by the physical conditions about it, but by remote laws of inheritance." We are swayed "through the medium of language and ideas" by "the mind of the [human] race," and "the character of the age."

Contradictory statements about us are equally valid: we are "so receptive" to "the influences of the world and of society," that every hour of life is "unique, changed altogether by a stray word, or glance or touch." The "truth of eternal outlines effected once for all" is replaced by "a world of fine gradations and subtly linked conditions, shifting intricately as we ourselves change," and we progress by "clearing of the organs of observation and perfecting of analysis to make what we can of these."[4]

Pater understands what this implies. If mental states are just outcomes of physical states, one cannot judge their truth, since those judgments must be the outcome of other physical states. In 1867, in an essay on the German art historian Johann Joachim Wincklemann (1717–68), Pater explores the physical determinism that seems to follow from this. In "the face of modern life," he declares, of "the universality of ... law ... penetrating us with a network, subtler than

4. Pater, *Essays on Literature and Art*, 2.

our subtlest nerves, yet bearing in it the central forces of the world," the spirit needs a *new* "sense of freedom" to replace free will. This art can provide. By representing "men and women in these bewildering toils ... [art can] give the spirit at least an equivalent for the sense of freedom." It can show "this entanglement, this network of law" as a "tragic situation, in which certain groups of noble men and women work out for themselves a supreme dénouement." Who, he asks, "would fret against the chain of circumstance which endows one at the end with those great experiences?"[5] Who would worry about losing free will if the payoff were an experience of an exquisite yearning for freedom fascinatingly intertwined with knowledge of iron necessity? The tragic paradox of the necessitarian willing to will is the ultimate sublime, or at any rate an experience to be relished. This approaches but ultimately falls short of what later thinkers would call *Jouissance*. Pater's modern men and women are "free," even if they are not the authors of their own actions. Specifically in reading novels, they can escape from an enslaving "penetration" of mind by scientific law, but only by finding an "equivalent" to freedom, and relishing it just because it is not really freedom at all. They are dominated by empiricist ideas, but they can still develop the *fiction* of personal autonomy and ensure their own blitheness and repose.

Pater's relativism, however, is not merely negative. He condemns Coleridge's account of art as too passive: it makes "the associative act [look] like some organic process of assimilation,"[6] a Nietzschean criticism of the essential passivity of mental life as viewed by the theorists of Associationism. For Pater, the artist has an *active* intellect, attaining "clearness of idea" by analysis, "then ... clearness of expression." The artist "moves over his work, calculating the tenderest tone, and restraining the subtlest curve." Great art displays a "power of understanding," a "logical process of construction," and "supreme intellec-

5. Pater, *Essays on Literature and Art*, 218.
6. Pater, *Essays on Literature and Art*, 16.

tual dexterity."[7] And it is not just the differences between sensations that art cultivates. It "begets an intellectual finesse, of which the ethical result is a delicate and tender justness in the criticism of human life."[8] Consequently, "the mind of the artist … is what is infinitely precious, and the work of art only as the index of it." Art presupposes an intimate connection between "moments of strange excitement" and "an external, concrete form, a statue, or play, or picture," between "the power of the understanding" and a "logical process of construction."[9] Formal relations in one system can be "represented" in another—a "tone" or a "curve" translated into thought and feeling or an algebraic formula. Pater uses Hamilton's claim that certain measurable relations are knowable because they are translatable between different media to explain the relations between minds and works of art. Just as a piece of music can be represented in a score, beautiful forms can be written into the emotions and the will.

These ideas dominate Pater's novel *Marius the Epicurean* (1885). Marius is a young Roman of the second century with the attitudes and feelings of a nineteenth-century bachelor-don. A fatherless only child and titular head of his family, he presides over the rituals of his family estate, adhering to a "religion of usages and sentiment rather than of facts and belief,"[10] a pagan version of undogmatic, slightly snobbish Anglicanism, "staid, ideal and comely," sanctioning "high scrupulosity" in domestic life, and valued as a hereditary distinction that gives his household "that aristocratic atmosphere which separated [his family] from newly-made people."[11]

Many late nineteenth-century relativists were syncretists. When Marius visits the shrine of "that mild and philanthropic son of Apollo," Aesculapius, the god of "bodily health," Pater carefully notes that

7. Pater, *Essays on Literature and Art*, 17.
8. Pater, *Essays on Literature and Art*, 26.
9. Pater, *Essays on Literature and Art*, 17.
10. Pater, *Marius the Epicurean*, 2.
11. Pater, *Marius the Epicurean*, 5–6.

the terms *salus* and *salvator* ("salvation" and "savior") related at this period to "bodily sanity"; the epigraph of the chapter, *Dilexi decorum domus tuæ* ("I have loved the beauty of thy house"), is from the Vulgate (Catholic) version of Psalm 26 (27),[12] and Pater translates "Huc profectus filius Dei, maxime amavit hunc locum" as "Being come unto this place the son of God loved it exceedingly," thus conflating "the god's son," Aesculapius, with "the Son of God," Christ.[13] The shrine encourages Marius to "keep the eye clear ... to discriminate ... to meditate much on beautiful visible objects," for their own sake and in expectation of their "conforming the seer to themselves"—making Marius *like* what he observes—so that, in a provocative allusion to the Book of Revelation, he may at last enjoy "some vision, as of a new city coming down 'like a bride out of heaven.'"[14] He approaches this ideal when his priest-instructor silently lifts "a cunningly contrived panel" to reveal "like the vision of a new world ... a green meadow at the foot of the steep olive-clad rocks below, [where] the novices were taking their exercise."[15] The bodies of naked young men at play are secretly available for their superiors' gaze.

In adolescence, Marius attends the Roman equivalent of an English "public school," where he becomes attached to the brilliant, beautiful Flavian, "who loved dress, and dainty food, and flowers, and seemed to have a natural alliance with, and claim upon everything else which was physically select and bright."[16] In "a world where manhood comes early," Flavian, unlike Marius, is familiar with "the seductions of [a] luxurious town," and the key to their friendship is their joint reading of a lubricious, exotically religious fantasy, *The Golden Book* of Apuleius (125–180 CE). But this phase of Marius's life ends with Flavian's death, which they both accept entails his final extinction.

12. Pater, *Marius the Epicurean*, 22.
13. Pater, *Marius the Epicurean*, 29.
14. Pater, *Marius the Epicurean*, 26.
15. Pater, *Marius the Epicurean*, 32–33.
16. Pater, *Marius the Epicurean*, 41.

The rest of the novel focuses mainly on Marius's ideas. He discovers in the teachings of the pre-Socratic philosopher Heraclitus (fl. c. 500 BCE) that the "impression of permanence or fixity in things" is "false."[17] The world, consciousness, and language are like the fire of which Heraclitus thought everything is composed. But this rejection of fixity is only a "first . . . merely negative step." It seems "to make all fixed knowledge impossible . . . [and] the momentary, sensible apprehension of the individual the only standard of what is or is not," but, mischievously appropriating the vocabulary of Comte's Positivism, Pater describes Marius discovering "a large positive system of almost religious philosophy,"[18] and recognizing in the "'perpetual flux' of things and of souls," a return, not of past experience, but of "orderly, intelligible relationships . . . ordinances of the divine reason, maintained through the changes of the phenomenal world" and disclosing "a principle of sanity, of reality there."[19]

Pater is notorious for trying, notably in the essay on "style," "to bring literature . . . under those conditions, by conformity to which music takes rank as the typically perfect art," but he also insisted that "over and above . . . colour and mystic perfume and . . . reasonable structure"—the merely aesthetic—great literature "finds its logical, its architectural place, in the great structure of human life." The principle of sanity in art, logic, and language, in mind and life, is not the fixity of things, meanings, or values, not "truth," scientific, philosophical, or moral ("Nothing is true"), but of exact "relationships . . . wrought out in and through the series of their mutations."[20]

This is Hamilton's line. He and Pater agree that relationships of form, "maintained through the changes of the phenomenal world," unite mind and external reality. The same patterns of difference, recurring in sensation, reason, passion, desire, language, and the arts, bring

17. Pater, *Marius the Epicurean*, 106.

18. Pater, *Marius the Epicurean*, 107.

19. Pater, *Marius the Epicurean*, 107–8.

20. Pater, *Essays on Literature and Art*, 77–78.

the world, art, and mind into unity. If Marius *is*, it is not because he thinks, but because he sees, and what he sees and remembers are not fixed images or essences, but "orderly relationships," patterns of difference. Thus "visible objects" are capable of "conforming the seer to themselves" because the mind can preserve formal relations of shape, texture, and color in its own complex operations. All this is in deft opposition to Mill, and specifically to Mill's definition of "Matter . . . [as] a Permanent Possibility of Sensation."[21] Only those "heavy with wine," Pater writes quoting from Heraclitus, attribute to "the phenomena of experience a durability which does not really belong to them"[22]—only the inebriated imagine that *anything* in sensation is permanent.

This mischievous rebuke conceals some tough thinking. Admittedly, Pater's assertion of the value of formal relations in a deterministic universe is an ingenious and consoling story. But that story is founded upon rigorous analysis of how mind and world *might* interact. There is, however, a debility in his outlook, which is revealed in his numerous references to Newman (more respectful but no less ironic than his references to Mill). By cultivating a "sense of conscious powers external" to daily life and passing judgment on it, the traditional religion of Rome effects in Marius "a powerful current of feeling and observance" to which Pater provocatively gives the name "*conscience*."[23] Of many passages in Newman expressing such ideas, the following is particularly relevant:

> Conscience is the essential principle and sanction of Religion in the mind. Conscience implies a relation between the soul and a something exterior, and that, moreover, superior to itself; a relation to an excellence which it does not possess, and to a tribunal over which it has no power . . . Here, then, at once, we have the elements of a religious system; for what is Religion but the system of relations existing between us and a Supreme Power, claiming our habitual obedience . . . ?[24]

21. Mill, *Examination of Sir William Hamilton's Philosophy*, 183.

22. Pater, *Marius the Epicurean*, 105–6.

23. Pater, *Marius the Epicurean*, 3.

24. Newman, *University Sermons*, 19.

Later, Marius asks himself of the synthesis of paganisms that he professes, "What really were its claims as a theory of practice, of the sympathies that determine practice? It had been a theory, avowedly, of loss and gain ... of an economy ... What did it lose, or cause one to lose?"[25] These references to Newman's novel *Loss and Gain* (1848) and to his principle of "economy" are deliberate. When the Epicureans of Cyrene are condemned as "faulty economists"[26] who, with "a little more of ... not unreasonable 'assent,' ... might have profited by a hundred services to their culture,"[27] the reference is to Newman's *An Essay in Aid of a Grammar of Assent* (1870). Marius is called the wiser "economist"; his experiences are like conversion to Catholicism from a narrow, nonconformist sect. Participating in a world system, a "wonderful order, actually in possession of human life," he even feels the need to limit his own freedom "in concession to ... that great crowd of admirable spirits" who engage in the pursuit of this grand vision: "he would be ... mistaken in his estimate of values, of loss and gain, and untrue to the well-considered economy of life which he had brought with him to Rome ... if he did not make that concession."[28]

Pater uses Newman's term "economy" to express the ways in which patterns of difference in Marius's world are distinct and yet capable of combination. But the ultimate effect of the references to *Loss and Gain* in *Marius the Epicurean* is to discriminate between incompatible views. Both novels describe a young man's absorption into Catholicism, but Newman's protagonist is committed to conversion before meeting a single believing Catholic; his decision "has been entirely the working of [his] own mind."[29] He does not even enter a Catholic Church until his conversion. Marius's experience is the reverse. Through the second great friend of his life, the Chris-

25. Pater, *Marius the Epicurean*, 221.
26. Pater, *Marius the Epicurean*, 217.
27. Pater, *Marius the Epicurean*, 218.
28. Pater, *Marius the Epicurean*, 221.
29. Newman, *Loss and Gain*, 370.

tian Cornelius, he is introduced to Catholic worship in the house of the beautiful widow Cecilia, without entertaining a single Christian idea. Impressed by the harmony of belief and feeling in the life and liturgy of a Christian household, by its *forms,* he never enquires into Christian *beliefs.* At the end of the novel, he is mistakenly imprisoned with a group of Christians, and out of natural affection persuades the guard that the non-Christian among the prisoners is Cornelius, not himself. Later, when he too is released because he is dying, the country people, thinking that he has been baptized, give him Communion, anoint him, and bury him as a martyr. But he is a martyr only to friendship.

The title of the chapter relating these events is "Anima Naturaliter Christiana" ("A Naturally Christian Soul"). As Pater well knew, however, Christians believe that the soul cannot be "naturally" Christian, but requires "supernatural" grace—in the Catholic tradition, Baptism—and adult Baptism requires the recitation of the Creed. But in his essay on Coleridge, Pater places "all that is desirable in the world" and "sympathetic to its laws" in "trenchant" opposition to the dogmatic spirit[30]—that is, to creeds—"Nothing is true." Marius never looks beyond this life; his "deeper wisdom," "with a sense of economy, with a jealous estimate of gain and loss, [is] to use life, not as the means to some problematic end, but, as far as might be, from dying hour to dying hour, an end in itself a kind of music, all-sufficing to the duly trained ear, even as it died out on the air."[31] Cornelius's ongoing life becomes for the dying Marius a sign of "permanent protest... against any wholly mechanical and disheartening theory of [humanity] and its conditions."[32] Positivism and empiricism won't be left ruling the roost after his death; Catholicism will remain to make things uncomfortable for them and this is all the future life Marius desires.

30. Pater, *Essays on Literature and Art,* 19.
31. Pater, *Marius the Epicurean,* 379.
32. Pater, *Marius the Epicurean,* 381.

This modest resistance to empiricism clarifies the limits of Pater's "Decadence." Pater affirms "the unity, the strict identity with itself of the apprehending mind." He also attributes unity to human utterance and the logical process of its construction. But he holds back from specific belief and action, and also from *Jouissance*. From time to time, Marius gazes at young men exercising, but he only gets into Flavian's bed when the latter is dying, and he only *looks* at Cecilia whom he contemplates marrying. He engages only with vision or *theoria*. He values "economies" while avoiding beliefs. Entranced by the beauties of the Catholic *langue* ("language"), he shies away from engagement with its specific *paroles* (utterances), the dogmatic principle. All the mind has to do is to see itself seeing. Marius does not believe or disbelieve: he has others do that for him. "In a philosophy of immediate consciousness," Paul Ricoeur writes, "the subject is first of all a knowing subject, ... a look directed at a spectacle; in such a philosophy the spectacle is the same as the mirage of self in the mirror things."[33]

As Oscar Wilde (1854–1900) noted in the "De Profundis" letter he wrote from prison to Lord Alfred Douglas (1870–1945):

> Marius is little more than a spectator: an ideal spectator indeed, and one to whom it is given "to contemplate the spectacle of life with appropriate emotions," ... yet a spectator merely, and perhaps a little too much occupied with the comeliness of the vessels of the Sanctuary to notice that it is the Sanctuary of Sorrow that he his gazing at.[34]

It is to Wilde that we must turn for an engagement with the paradoxes of atheism that reaches beyond *theoria*, beyond mere seeing. In *The Picture of Dorian Gray* (1890), Wilde takes his own bearings on relativism. In the opening chapters, a painter, Basil Hallward, and a young aristocrat, Lord Henry Wotton, compete for the attentions of the young and beautiful Dorian Gray. Basil paints his portrait, and Lord Henry declares Dorian's beauty to be "higher ... than Ge-

33. Ricoeur, *Rule of Metaphor*, 379.
34. Wilde, *Letters*, 476.

nius"—the "visible symbol" of "a new Hedonism." He begins, "some day, when you are old and wrinkled and ugly," and ends, "Youth! Youth! There is absolutely nothing in the world but youth."[35] At this, Dorian declares that he would give his soul to remain young and for the portrait to grow old and ugly in his place. This, of course, happens. Dorian locks the portrait away, and remains, to all appearances, as young as the day it was painted. Only the picture decays.

More importantly, Dorian surrenders to Lord Henry's influence. He ceases to "think his natural thoughts or burn with his natural passions ... His sins, if there are such things as sins, are borrowed. He becomes an echo of [Lord Henry's] music." Every "impulse that we strive to strangle," Lord Henry tells him, "broods in the mind, and poisons us ... The only way to get rid of temptation is to yield to it."[36] Lord Henry announces that he can "sympathise with everything, except suffering,"[37] and when Dorian falls in and out of love (or affects to) with the actress Sybil Vane, and she kills herself, he discourages Dorian from becoming involved. Tragedies, he observes,

> "hurt us by their crude violence ... Sometimes, however, a tragedy that possesses artistic elements of beauty crosses our lives ... Suddenly we find that we are no longer the actors, but the spectators of the play. Or rather we are both. We watch ourselves, and the mere wonder of the spectacle enthralls us ... Some one has killed herself for love of you. I wish that I had ever had that experience ... The people who have adored me ... have always insisted on living on ... That awful memory of woman! ... what an utter intellectual stagnation it reveals! ..."
>
> "I must sow poppies in my garden," sighed Dorian.
>
> "There is no necessity," rejoined his companion. "Life has always poppies in her hands. Of course, now and then things linger."[38]

Later, like Marius, Dorian becomes obsessed with a book, the classic text of Decadence, *À rebours* (1884) by Joris-Karl Huysmans

35. *Picture of Dorian Gray*, in Wilde, *Works*, 31–32.
36. Wilde, *Works*, 29.
37. Wilde, *Works*, 44.
38. Wilde, *Works*, 84–85.

(1848–1907), a gift from Lord Henry, from which he learns to look "on evil simply as a mode through which he could realise his conception of the beautiful."[39] Basil tries to believe that Dorian's enduring beauty is the index of a beautiful soul, but he provokes Dorian into showing him the portrait, after which Dorian feels compelled to murder him, blackmailing another friend into disposing of the body. The friend then kills himself. Later, Sybil's brother discovers the identity of his sister's betrayer but is accidentally killed by a houseguest of Dorian's. Lord Henry's response to this accident is characteristic. He regrets that the death was accidental. He would "like to know some one who had committed a real murder."[40] As of course he does.

Dorian, then, is Lord Henry's "own creation,"[41] and, like Pater's artist, Lord Henry "moves over his work, calculating the tenderest tone, and restraining the subtlest curve."[42]

> Talking to [Dorian] was like playing upon an exquisite violin ... To project one's soul into some gracious form, and let it tarry there for a moment; to hear one's own intellectual views echoed back to one with all the added music of passion and youth; to convey one's temperament into another as though it were a subtle fluid or strange perfume; there was a real joy in that.[43]

The process, however, is a two-way one. To "influence a person is to give him one's own soul."[44] In seeking "to dominate"[45] Dorian, Lord Henry transfers his own "soul," the form of his life, to the younger man, who then transfers it to the portrait. Each thereby strives to "become the spectator of [his] own life," and so "escape the suffering of life."[46] We are still in the domain of seeing, of *theoria*.

But how can this unrealistic story suggest anything about reali-

39. Wilde, *Works*, 115.
40. Wilde, *Works*, 155.
41. Wilde, *Works*, 55.
42. Pater, *Essays on Literature and Art*, 17.
43. Pater, *Essays on Literature and Art*, 41.
44. Pater, *Essays on Literature and Art*, 28.
45. Pater, *Essays on Literature and Art*, 41.
46. Pater, *Essays on Literature and Art*, 91.

ty? Wilde's answer is clear. The conventions of realism, according to Pater, depend on a nonrelativized notion of the ego, "simple, permanent, reliable, and of one essence."[47] Fiction based on it and naturalistic description—Millian naturalism in effect—is, to quote from Wilde's essay, "The Decay of Lying" (1889), "a complete failure."[48] "No great artist sees things as they really are." ("Nothing is true.") The Japanese people in Japanese art are "the deliberate self-conscious creation of certain individual artists . . . Hokusai or Hokkei."[49] What matters is form. With a significantly different emphasis than Pater's, Wilde writes in "The Critic as Artist" (1890),

> Forms are the food of faith, cried Newman on one of those great moments of sincerity that make us admire and know the man. He was right, though he may not have known how terribly right he was. The Creeds are believed, not because they are rational, but because they are repeated. Yes; Form is everything. It is the secret of life.[50]

Newman had, perhaps, clearer ideas about the relative effectiveness of reason and repetition in inculcating faith than Wilde gives him credit for. What matters, for Wilde, however, is form, which alone connects the mind with the world. It "is in the brain," he writes in "The Decay of Lying," "that the poppy is red," but in "that vital connection between form and substance, on which Mr. Pater insists,"[51] especially in fiction, there are not copies of experience, but equivalences: "abstract . . . ideal modes of art, such as architecture or music,"[52] express current sensibility without engaging in crude realism, but in all its other modes, Art is detached from "the moral and social conditions that surround it." It "has an independent life, just as Thought has."[53] It is "the supreme reality, and life," Wilde wrote

47. Pater, *Essays on Literature and Art*, 112.
48. Wilde, *Works*, 918.
49. Wilde, *Works*, 927.
50. Wilde, *Works*, 991.
51. Wilde, *Works*, 926.
52. Wilde, *Works*, 926–27.
53. Wilde, *Works*, 930.

from prison, "a mere mode of fiction,"[54] which is why, in *The Picture of Dorian Gray*, Lord Henry aspires to write "a novel ... as lovely as a Persian carpet, and as unreal."[55]

"The Preface" to *The Picture of Dorian Gray*, "The Decay of Lying" (1889), and "The Critic as Artist" flaunt these ideas. The creation of "beautiful things," "The Preface" declares, reveals neither ethical principles nor realistic images, but "the perfect use of an imperfect medium," and a critic, who translates "into ... a new material his impression of beautiful things,"[56] is also an artist. "The Critic as Artist" also represents criticism as "creative."[57] And just as music and architecture conceal and reveal the social conditions that they express, so authentic art and criticism "conceal the artist" and reveal him. The "only portraits in which one believes," Wilde writes in "The Decay of Lying," "are portraits in which there is very little of the sitter and a great deal of the artist";[58] criticism is "the record of one's own soul,"[59] and "a mode of autobiography"—but only at the level of form. Basil's picture registers not Dorian's beauty but Basil's affinity with it. The critic puts his own "soul" on record, not the work he is criticizing, and a portrait "painted with feeling is a portrait of the artist, not of the sitter."[60] Similarly, Dorian's life, which includes the hidden portrait, conceals and expresses Lord Henry's.

But the effects of art are not limited to artist and subject. "The one characteristic of a beautiful form," Wilde writes in "The Critic as Artist," "is that one can put into it whatever one wishes, and see in it whatever one chooses to see."[61] So the readers of *The Picture of Dorian Gray* may discover in it representations of its characters,

54. Wilde, *Letters*, 466.
55. Wilde, *Works*, 45.
56. Wilde, *Works*, 17.
57. Wilde, *Works*, 965.
58. Wilde, *Works*, 928.
59. Wilde, *Works*, 966.
60. Wilde, *Works*, 21.
61. Wilde, *Works*, 969.

its author, and *themselves*. As "The Preface" puts it, "Those who go beneath the surface do so at their peril ... It is the spectator, and not life, that art really mirrors."[62] Every reading of Wilde's fantasy incites its readers to reformulate their desires and reconstitute their "souls."

The implications of this relativist aesthetic become apparent if we compare desire in Wilde's novel with desire in Pater's. Marius becomes a research assistant to the philosophical emperor, Marcus Aurelius, whose fastidious Stoicism chimes with his own Epicureanism. The question examined in the novel is why "natural Christianity" can and should repress first-century Stoicism and nineteenth-century Empiricism. Marius finds his answer in the amphitheater. The games no longer present criminals in the role of Icarus, plunging into the arena to be devoured by a pack of bears, nor are they skinned alive like the impious Marsyas, but the spectacle is brutal enough, and Aurelius countenances it with his presence. And it is this "tolerance," Marius feels, which marks the emperor as "his inferior ... on the question of righteousness ... He at least, the humble follower of the bodily eye" is "aware of a fierce opposition of real good and evil around him." As a consequence of Aurelius's tolerance, Christians are tortured to death in Lyons "on the responsibility of the emperor."[63] So how does the pagan Stoicism of Aurelius differ from the Christian Epicureanism of Marius? Both are stories, the fictional carapaces by which identity resists incipient meaninglessness. Yet in the "fierce opposition of ... good and evil," Marius claims to have discovered some sort of absolute, namely, "righteousness." In effect, he cannot follow his "Nothing is true" with its corollary: "everything is permitted."

Wilde, by contrast, proclaimed himself "a born antinomian,"[64] and never stopped questioning whether "there are such things as

62. Wilde, *Works*, 17.
63. Pater, *Marius the Epicurean*, 355.
64. Wilde, *Letters*, 468.

sins." In "The Preface," he declares that there is "no such thing as a moral or immoral book" or "ethical sympathies" in art: the "artist expresses everything,"[65] and the reader has also to refrain from "ethical sympathies," as drugs, sex both straight and gay, gratuitous violence, and the callous ditching of sexual partners are all implicitly sanctioned. Chapter 11, which bridges the eighteen years between the death of Sybil Vane and the novel's melodramatic conclusion, constructs an anatomy of Decadent desire. Dorian indulges (like Marius) in the rituals of Catholicism, and "for a season" (like Pater), in "the materialistic doctrines of the Darwinismus movement ... the conception of the absolute dependence of the spirit on certain physical conditions, morbid or healthy, normal or diseased."[66] He studies perfumes, musical instruments (his collection includes "the mysterious futuparis [a sacred flute] of the Rio Negro Indians, that women are not allowed to look at, and that even youths may not see till they have been subjected to fasting and scourging ... and flutes of human bones such as Alfonso de Ovalle heard in Chile"),[67] jewels (as objects and as the source of tales of exquisite self-indulgence), embroideries, tapestries, and church vestments. He moves between "dreadful places" near the London docks, a "villa that he ... shared at Trouville with Lord Henry," and a "little white walled-in house at Algiers."[68] He is entranced by Huysman's descriptions of "Tiberius, in a garden at Capri, reading the shameful books of Elephantis," of Caligula carousing with jockeys, of Domitian peering "through a clear emerald at the red shambles of the Circus," and of a series of Renaissance atrocities including "the young Cardinal Archbishop of Florence, child and minion of Sixtus IV ... who ... gilded [sic] a boy that he might serve at [a] feast as Ganymede or Hylas."[69] There is

65. Wilde, *Works*, 17.
66. Wilde, *Works*, 106.
67. Wilde, *Works*, 107.
68. Wilde, *Works*, 111.
69. Wilde, *Works*, 114.

no fierce opposition of real good and evil here, no limit to "the ultimate realization of the artistic life," which, even in the Circus, Wilde tells Douglas, "is simply self-development."[70] Artistically for Lord Henry, Dorian, and Wilde himself, Marcus Aurelius and Domitian are equally admissible.

Where this leads is suggested in the conversation in which Lord Henry declares that he "can sympathise with everything, except suffering." He says this to impress Dorian, and as part of a discussion about good works among the poor. Slum life, he declares, "is the problem of slavery, and we try to solve it by amusing the slaves."[71] This clearly alludes to the comparison of poverty and slavery in "The Soul of Man under Socialism" (1890), where Wilde condemns the rich for trying "to solve the problem of poverty … by keeping the poor alive; or, in a very advanced school, by amusing the poor … Just as the worst slave-owners" effectively concealed the evil of slavery by being "kind to their slaves … so, in the present state of things in England, the people who do the most harm are the people who try to do the most good."[72] This is not the standard radical argument against charity and reform. At its heart is the claim that the goal of Socialism is not justice but pleasure. Socialism would "relieve us from that sordid necessity of living for others." The obvious target here is "Altruism"—the central ethical principle of Mill, Comte, and George Eliot—which Wilde dismisses as "unhealthy and exaggerated." But he also subverts conventional Christianity. The "new world," he writes, will replace the injunction "Know thyself" with "the message of Christ to man … 'Be thyself.'"[73] The central Christian commandment is "Individualism", by which authentic love of self replaces self-sacrificial love of others.

"Individualism" thus extends the goal of self-development from

70. Wilde, *Works*, 476.
71. Wilde, *Works*, 44.
72. Wilde, *Works*, 1018.
73. Wilde, *Works*, 1024.

the artist to humanity. "At present," Wilde argues, "in consequence of the existence of private property, a great many people ... develop a certain limited amount of Individualism."[74] But private property imposes dreary duties on the well-off; "its possession ... is a bore ... In the interest of the rich we must get rid of it." The "best" among the poor "are ungrateful, discontented, disobedient, and rebellious."[75] If wealth were evenly distributed, "family life" would be annihilated, "marriage in its present form would disappear," and everyone could "lead a Christlike life ... [by being] perfectly and absolutely himself," and realizing "the perfection of the soul that is within him."[76] While heartily *approving* of "agitators" as "meddling people, who come down to some perfectly contented class of the community and sow the seeds of discontent among them,"[77] Wilde prefers "Art" as "a disturbing and disintegrating force,"[78] though he also recognizes that "the classics" can become "means of checking the progress of Art" by degrading them "into authorities."[79] Consequently, "there is much more to be said in favour of the physical force of the public than there is in favour of the public's opinion."[80] Either way, there is a need "to reconstruct society," something that even Christ never attempted: "the Individualism he preached ... could be realised only through pain and solitude."[81] With Socialism and science, however, "the modern world ... proposes to do away with" both. "What it aims at is an Individualism expressing itself through joy."[82]

But perhaps "The Soul of Man under Socialism" is less and more than it seems. It was published first in the *Fortnightly Review* in the

74. Wilde, *Works*, 1019.
75. Wilde, *Works*, 1020.
76. Wilde, *Works*, 1025.
77. Wilde, *Works*, 1021.
78. Wilde, *Works*, 1030.
79. Wilde, *Works*, 1031.
80. Wilde, *Works*, 1033.
81. Wilde, *Works*, 1041.
82. Wilde, *Works*, 1042–43.

same year as *The Picture of Dorian Gray*, and then in a decoratively bound volume with fashionably large print—hardly designed for circulation among the laboring poor, in whose lives, Wilde observes, "there is no grace of manner, or charm of speech, or civilisation or culture, or refinement in pleasures, or joy of life."[83] There is no reason to doubt his belief that "Socialism ... will lead to Individualism."[84] The problem is his implicit acknowledgment that the reverse is not the case, that Individualism will *not* lead to Socialism. As a public and concealed (or half-concealed) individualist, Wilde will certainly not do so. The cause of Socialism needs agitators and paving stones, but the "note of the perfect personality is not rebellion, but peace."[85] Wilde's primary commitment is thus to individualism. In "The Soul of Man under Socialism," the poor disappear and the antagonism of public opinion and art is examined at length. "Socialism" can therefore seem to be no more than an aspect of Wilde's current self-presentation, the public, paradoxical face of his Decadence, a mask, like, if more knowing than, the "Altruism" and "righteousness" of the do-gooders, and the cynically coded manners and morals of "Society." It is Wilde's way of participating in collective mendacity by telling the truth.

In the work of Wilde, then, relativism, qualified by the conviction that formal relations can be transferred between different "economies," including those of the mind, sounds a menacing note of social and political subversion that can perhaps be best accounted for in the excitement Lord Henry induces in his listeners. Like Lord Darlington in Wilde's play *Lady Windermere's Fan* (1892), Lord Goring in *An Ideal Husband* (1895), and the corrupt Lord Illingworth in *A Woman of No Importance* (1893), Lord Henry offers his audience the pleasures of privileged bad faith. Wilde offered the same sort

83. Wilde, *Works*, 1019.
84. Wilde, *Works*, 1019.
85. Wilde, *Works*, 1023.

of excitement to his contemporaries both in his writings and in the insanely self-destructive self-indulgence, which led to his imprisonment for gross indecency at the instigation of Douglas's bullying father, the Marquess of Queensbury, and which he would then record in the famous letter to Douglas.

The bond between Lord Henry, his auditors (some ostensibly shocked, others gracefully amused), and the do-gooders in the East End is, of course, that society is *not* going to be reconstructed. In a brilliantly different register, Wilde makes the same point in *The Importance of Being Earnest* (1895), but it is implicit even in the awkward parts of *The Picture of Dorian Gray*. The film-noir world of Sybil, her disreputable mother, her vulgar Jewish manager, and her virtuous brother, the murder of Basil, and Dorian's last flirtation with a virginal country girl are all glaringly shallow and functional. The shallower a scene in *The Picture of Dorian Gray*, the clearer its message. We need not care for these people. The only way to get rid of injustice is to enjoy it.

And society, far from being weakened by witty exposures of its mendacities, is covertly strengthened by them. They lure minds toward the Real. *The Picture of Dorian Gray* follows relativism to its core, exposing and celebrating the void around which stories and values hectically circulate. George Eliot wills and wills to will, closing her eyes and hanging on in full knowledge of the abyss. Pater gazes, but Wilde, in his novel, teasingly suggests that it might be quite wonderful to leap into it. Yet far from weakening the social bond, glamorous pariahs, like Lord Henry and Wilde himself, immeasurably strengthen it, bringing people into that intimate engagement with the void that is at once foundational and just an effect of disjunction, social and personal, in lives perilously adjacent to it.

At the beginning of *The Picture of Dorian Gray*, Dorian is eager to be recognized as a clever, beautiful man of the world, which means he seeks to will as the world wills. That is why he submits to Lord Henry. Lord Henry introduces him to Desire as a series of objects:

a musical instrument made of human bones, a rare gemstone, a perfume, a drug, a new sexual partner, as if to divert his attention from Desire as such, freed from particular attachments and disclosed as precisely blind—the blind life, blind death, blind Nothing—around which George Eliot wills to will. So, imitating Lord Henry, Dorian gets by on substitutes, and though these finally disappoint, there is always something else to move on to, from the stale fumes of a low opium den to fresh clouds of incense at solemn High Mass. Lord Henry's thought experiment with Dorian thus discloses the logic of their situation. In their last exchange, before Dorian retreats to the secret room, stabs the picture, and destroys himself, Lord Henry tells him that "Art . . . annihilates the desire to act. It is superbly sterile."[86] But it is not just Art of which this is said. Throughout both the novel and the essays, Art manifests the formal qualities of Soul, and Soul is constituted by internalizing the formal qualities of Art. In this final exchange, Lord Henry insists that Dorian's certainty that there is "a soul in each one of us" is as illusory as the notion that Art is fruitful. "The things one feels absolutely certain about are never true."[87] He has projected (what he likes to think of as) his own soul into Dorian. When Dorian stabs the picture, it is really Lord Henry who has lost both his "soul" and the object of his desire, Dorian himself. The object has ceased to matter. Lord Henry now has and is "Nothing."

But what does this "Nothing" amount to? We learn a great deal about it in the last conversation. Lord Henry speaks of his divorce—his wife has run away with a man who "played Chopin exquisitely."[88] We encounter her only once, when Dorian calls on her husband only to be greeted by "a shrill voice"—"only his wife" is how she describes herself.[89] Her dresses look "as if they had been designed in a rage,

86. Wilde, *Works*, 163.
87. Wilde, *Works*, 161.
88. Wilde, *Works*, 159.
89. Wilde, *Works*, 47.

and put on in a tempest. She was," we are told, "usually in love with somebody, and, as her passion was never returned, she kept all her illusions." She haunts churches. She tells Dorian that Lord Henry has seventeen or eighteen photographs of him; she notices a remark of his that originated with her husband—whose views she only knows by hearing his friends repeat them—but she is keen to match his epigrams. "I like Wagner's music... It is so loud one can talk the whole time without other people hearing what one says." Nevertheless, she adores and is frightened by music. She has a "sudden silly laugh," and when Lord Henry appears, she flits out of the room, "looking like a bird of paradise that has been out all night in the rain."[90] The description is cruel, particularly in the light of Lord Henry's later viciously ambiguous remark to Dorian, after Sybil Vane's death, about the "awful memory of woman."

That is also the occasion when he remarks, apropos of forgetting, that "now and then things linger." As indeed they do, for both these conversations are evoked in the final exchange with Dorian, in which the real nature of Lord Henry's desire is disclosed. The first paragraph of the novel describes "the rich colour of roses ... the heavy scent of lilac ... the more delicate perfume of the pink-flowering thorn" (18); a little further on, we again read how "the heavy lilac-blooms, with their clustering stars moved to and fro in the languid air" (21); later, Lord Henry finds Dorian "burying his face in the great cool lilac-blossoms, feverishly drinking in their perfume as if it had been wine" (30); and when he concludes his rhapsody about the new Hedonism and the preeminence of youth, Dorian, like the sinless Adam confronted with the fallen Eve in *Paradise Lost*, drops the lilac he is carrying. Eighteen years later, in almost the last words he speaks to Dorian, Lord Henry says:

> Life is not governed by will or intention. Life is a question of nerves, and fibres, and slowly built-up cells in which thought hides itself and passion

90. Wilde, *Works*, 48.

has its dreams. You may fancy yourself safe, and think yourself strong. But a chance tone of colour ... a particular perfume ... a cadence from a piece of music that you had ceased to play—I tell you Dorian, that it is on things like these that our lives depend ... There are moments when the odour of *lilas blancs* passes suddenly across me, and I have to live the strangest month of my life over again.[91]

We know exactly what month that was. And the crucial word in the speech is "safe." When he smells white lilac, Lord Henry, the wit, the careless gay adulterer, the individualist, is swept from the safe ensemble of desirable things, desirable bodies, and desirable "souls" toward the intoxication of unconditional surrender. It is the point at which even he fails.

We know that point also, and most of us—all of us perhaps—fear it as the incompleteness and instability inhering in all the systems of understanding and desiring based on relativities, on the ways that this, that, and the other seem to us to differ, as they sustain our everyday functioning. Languages, for example, form around the patterns of difference in the sounds we make, but as sounds, as vibrations in the air, they enclose not "meanings" but nothing. And as Pater, Wilde, and Lord Henry so happily proclaim, all our so-called knowledge, all our "raw feels," all our thoughts, all our desires, constructed as they are out of patterns of difference, also enclose Nothing, nonbeing, *really*. So long as I function as a human being in such relativities, I am content to let the world to tell me what to want, but this means, Jacques Lacan declares, that I cannot "aim at being whole."[92] So what is this "I" that might *have* such an aim? "I am," Lacan says—and so Lord Henry is—"a place" from which it is possible to grasp that the "universe is a flaw in the purity of Non-Being." This "place," called *Jouissance*, is neither the shallow, ultimately deceptive systems of difference nor Nothing, the purity of Non-Being. It is rather the moment, the place, the shudder of their conjunction, where "Noth-

91. Wilde, *Works*, 163.

92. Lacan, *Écrits*, 287.

ing is true; everything is permitted," and "whose absence," declares Lacan, "would render the universe vain."[93] To be grasped as Nothing, therefore, the purity of Non-Being "needs" the shock of an invasive something—in Lord Henry's case, the smell of white lilac and Dorian's corpse, "withered, wrinkled, and loathsome."[94] We may therefore think of Dorian not as a person in his own right, but first as Lord Henry's fantasy, but when Dorian becomes a loathsome corpse, as the "something" through which "Nothing," as both *Jouissance* and the utterly abhorrent, leaps upon Lord Henry and upon us. This represents a remarkable and violent advance on Pater's attenuated pleasure in a mere "equivalent for the sense of freedom."

If Wilde's engagement with relativism had stopped here, at *The Picture of Dorian Gray*, or even at *The Importance of Being Earnest*, he would only have been interesting, not great. It was his destiny, however, or more probably his choice, in challenging Queensbury in the law courts, to become himself a symbol as central and disturbing as the corpse of Dorian Gray.

In a famous passage in the letter to Douglas, he writes:

> Everything about my tragedy has been hideous, mean, repellent, lacking in style. Our very dress makes us grotesques. We are the zanies of sorrow. We are clowns whose hearts are broken. We are especially designed to appeal to the sense of humour. On November 13th 1895 I was brought down here from London. From two o'clock till half-past two on that day I had to stand on the centre platform of Clapham Junction in convict dress and handcuffed, for the world to look at. I had been taken out of the Hospital Ward without a moment's notice being given me. Of all possible objects I was the most grotesque. When people saw me they laughed. Each train as it came up swelled the audience. Nothing could exceed their amusement. That was of course before they knew who I was. As soon as they had been informed they laughed still more. For half an hour I stood there in the grey November rain surrounded by a jeering mob. For a year after that was done to me I wept every day at the same hour for the same space of time.[95]

93. Lacan, *Écrits*, 317.

94. Wilde, *Works*, 167.

95. Wilde, *Letters*, 490–91.

Wilde's disaster enabled a social and legal elite, most of whom had experienced and colluded with the sadistic, pederastic rites of passage of English public schools, universities, and the armed services, as well as the customary sexual license of Society, to affirm their solidarity with the mass of the nation by constituting Wilde as the something nearest Nothing for all to see and relish—a far cry from the gay priestly voyeurism of *Marius the Epicurean.*

The weakness in Wilde's writing here should not be overlooked. Its "style" indicates that even after his ritual expulsion from the world, he still needs to register his difference from the world in the world's terms. He may have been "lacking in style" on the station platform, but not (he hopes) when he recalls it in writing. Nevertheless, his humiliation made it possible for him, in the letter to Douglas and in his letters to the *Daily Chronicle* on the cruelties of prison life, to make assertions from the heart of a still unqualified relativism that have significance beyond anything else in his writing. The letter to Douglas admittedly contains some silly passages:

> wherever there is a romantic movement in Art, there somehow, and under some form, is Christ or the soul of Christ. He is in *Romeo and Juliet,* in the *Winter's Tale,* in Provençal poetry, in "The Ancient Mariner," in "*La Belle Dame sans Merci,*" and in Chatterton's "Ballad of Charity."[96]

Nevertheless, it is on "Christ" that Wilde centers his important thinking—not the Christ of orthodox theology, and certainly not the comfortable Christ of higher criticism, but a first-century Jew who spoke both Aramaic and Greek (as Irish and English were spoken in the Irish countryside) and whose very words Wilde believed were recorded in the Greek Testament that he read daily in his cell.

According to Wilde, this "young Galilean peasant" imagined

> that he could bear on his own shoulders the burden of the entire world: all that had been already done and suffered: the sins of Nero, of Cæsar Borgia, of Alexander VI, and of him who was Emperor of Rome and Priest of the

96. Wilde, *Letters,* 482.

> Sun; the sufferings of those whose name is Legion and whose dwelling is among tombs, oppressed nationalities, factory children, people in prison, outcasts, those who were dumb under oppression, and whose silence is heard only of God: and not only imagining this but actually achieving it, so that at the present moment all who come in contact with his personality, even though they may neither bow to his altar nor kneel before his priest, yet somehow find that the ugliness of their sins is taken away and the beauty of their sorrow revealed to them.[97]

The Christ of Wilde's vision even reaches beyond the reach of Art.

> To the artist, expression is the only mode under which he can conceive of life at all. To him what is dumb is dead. But to Christ it was not so. With a width and wonder of imagination, that fills one almost with awe, he took the entire world of the inarticulate, the voiceless world of pain, as his kingdom, and made himself its eternal mouthpiece. Those of whom I have spoken ... he chose as his brothers. He sought to become eyes to the blind, ears to the deaf, and a cry on the lips of those whose tongue had been tied.[98]

This is not unrelated to the role that Wilde adopted after his release from prison in his letters to the *Daily Chronicle* about children sent to prison for trapping rabbits (Wilde got their fine paid and they were released)[99] and about a mentally disturbed soldier named Prince, whose prison number was A.2.11. He was serving six months, was "treated as if he was shamming," and received twenty-four lashes with a birch rod. Wilde saw him in the exercise yard the day after he had been flogged:

> his weak, ugly wretched face bloated by tears and hysteria almost beyond recognition ... It was my last Sunday in prison, a perfectly lovely day ... and there, in the beautiful sunlight, walked this poor creature—made once in the image of God—grinning like an ape, and making with his hands the most frantic gestures, as though he was playing in the air on some invisible stringed instrument, or arranging and dealing counters in some curious game. All the while these hysterical tears, without which none of us ever saw him, were

97. Wilde, *Letters*, 477.
98. Wilde, *Letters*, 481.
99. See Wilde, *Letters*, 554.

making soiled runnels on his white swollen face. The hideous and deliberate grace of his gestures made him like an antic. He was a living grotesque.[100]

Again, and inappropriately, Wilde's writing here is self-consciously fine. Prisoner A.2.11 is different from the shabby beggars and battered prostitutes lurking in the background of Dorian's nightlife. He is different too from the convict exposed to public derision at Clapham Junction. His is a tragedy from which elements of beauty are entirely absent, and there is no question in his case of getting rid of injustice by enjoying it. Instead, Wilde confronts Prince's suffering with the virtue of *misericordia* or, as MacIntyre puts it, "grief or sorrow over someone else's distress," someone who is "afflicted by some considerable evil, especially when it is not the immediate outcome of the afflicted individual's choices . . . just insofar as one understands the other's distress as one's own."[101] Wilde had felt what it was like to be so near the hell of nothingness, around which all meaning is constructed, when he became an object of gleeful excitement for those who jeered at him as he stood "on the centre platform of Clapham Junction in convict dress and handcuffed," but Prince seems to have entered it. When Wilde saw him on that last Sunday, he recognized that Prince's "mischances could have been [his own]."[102] The objective correlative of George Eliot's "vortex" of the will is Prince, A.2.11.

Pater's relativism reaches a terminus in the "righteousness" that Marius feels when confronted by the detachment of Marcus Aurelius in the Circus. His gaze stops short at the emperor. Wilde's stops at the face of a man who has been birched. Wilde remained an antinomian to his dying day (though he died a Catholic). Nevertheless, "even after" Prince was finally denied all opportunity of locating himself within any mental or social order, even after he was flogged a second time,[103] the man remained inarticulate and voiceless, but for

100. Wilde, *Letters*, 573.
101. MacIntyre, *Dependent Rational Animals*, 124–25.
102. MacIntyre, *Dependent Rational Animals*, 101.
103. See Wilde, *Letters*, 587.

Wilde absolute and irreducible. A.2.11 had lost his socially constructed "identity," but he could not be reduced to "the place from which 'The universe is a flaw in the purity of Non-Being' is vociferated." Prince is a person. The cognitive vacuum in which the self is lodged has become for Wilde the arena of virtue, of *misericordia*. Prince cannot be excluded from the *theoria* of opium-free atheism or from the place called *Jouissance*.

3

"What Have the Gods to Do with My Bridge!"

RUDYARD KIPLING'S "NAKED WORDS AND MEAN"

"He who would stir us now by fiction," Wilde writes in "The Critic as Artist," "must either give us an entirely new background, or reveal to us the soul of man in its innermost workings." The former, he continues,

> is for the moment being done for us by Mr. Rudyard Kipling. As one turns over the pages of his *Plain Tales from the Hills,* one feels as if one were seated under a palm-tree reading life by superb flashes of vulgarity. The bright colours of the bazaars dazzle one's eyes. The jaded, second-rate Anglo-Indians are in exquisite incongruity with their surroundings. The mere lack of style in the story-teller gives an odd journalistic realism to what he tells us. From the point of view of literature Mr. Kipling is a genius who drops his aspirates. From the point of view of life, he ... knows vulgarity ... its essence and its seriousness. He is our first authority on the second-rate, and has seen marvelous things through keyholes, and his backgrounds are real works of art.[1]

1. Wilde, *Works,* 993–94.

Like Wilde, Rudyard Kipling (1865–1936) was a philosophical relativist, an admirer of Pater, and an opponent of Mill, an intellectual, who thought far more seriously about race and religion than he is commonly given credit for. He had strong views on the government of India—favoring pragmatic respect for local custom and culture over the liberal theorizing of Lord Macaulay (1800–1859) and Mill. He was interested in comparative religion, and this affected his thinking about race. His writings deserve more exact attention than a reluctant admirer like Wilde was willing to give them.[2]

Unlike Wilde, he inhabited a vulgar world in which aspirates were dropped, people governed, and work done. And by avoiding "style," Kipling could give vulgar notions their head before subverting them. It is to Wilde's credit, however, that he recognized Kipling's "genius," the "seriousness" of his vulgarity. In fact, as a thinker, Kipling was as exact as Pater and as antinomian as Wilde. He was (in fiction) the first writer not only to explore syncretism in religion, but also to discover the emptiness at its heart, and therefore at the heart of the imperialist project he is often, wrongly, represented as arrogantly supporting. In evidence, I offer "A Song of the English" (a sequence of nine poems), published in 1893, and the short story "The Bridge-Builders," published as part of *The Day's Work* in 1898.

"A Song of the English"[3] addresses its readers as "we"—often a sign that invisible social, moral, and political assumptions—an ideology—are in play. The tone of the introductory poem seems resonantly orthodox. Its rhetoric is drawn from the Authorized Version of the Bible, and its cadences from the choral traditions of the Church of England (the word "sealed" is accented "sealèd"). It asserts that "the Lord our God Most High" is judge of the English as a people, precisely as he was Judge over Israel. But, like Israel, the English have sinned:

2. The best and deftly nuanced account of Kipling's thinking, especially on the topics of race and imperialism, is Hagiiouannu, *The Man Who Would Be Kipling*.

3. Kipling, *Seven Seas*, 1–17.

Yea, though we sinned—and our rulers went from righteousness—
Deep in all dishonour though we stained our garments' hem,
Oh, be ye not dismayed,
Though we stumbled and we strayed,
We were led by evil counsellors—the Lord shall deal with them!

The English, again like Israel, are urged not to whore with visions but to hold to the "Faith" sealed by their Fathers, and to "pay" the Lord with heart and sword lest punishment fall on their children.

But they are also urged to make "*sure to each his own / That he reap where he hath sown,*" and to maintain "*the peace among Our peoples.*" The Children of Israel—as they joyfully remind themselves throughout the Scriptures—reaped where they had *not* sown when the Promised Land was granted them by the outstretched hand of God. After the fall of the kingdoms of Israel and Judah, however, they also became a conquered people. The Assyrians, the Medes, the Babylonians, the Persians, the Greeks, and the Romans also do the Lord's will, even if, not being the Lord's People, they are "without the Law."

Another nonbiblical note marks this first poem—"*Clear the land of evil, drive the road and bridge the ford.*" The poem's concluding stanza is both assertive and cautious:

Hear now a song—a song of broken interludes—
A song of little cunning; of a singer nothing worth.
Through the naked words and mean
May ye see the truth between,
As the singer knew and touched it in the ends of all the Earth!

Subsequent poems deal with the history of the imperial enterprise, the sea, lighthouses, dead sailors, land explorers, Drake (linked to freemasonry, a favorite topic of Kipling's), and cable-laying—the latter touching briefly on the high Victorian theme[4] of worldwide unity:

4. See, e.g., Tennyson's "Locksley Hall":

For I dipt into the future, far as human eye could see,
Saw the Vision of the world, and all the wonder that would be;

> Hush! Men talk to-day o'er the waste of the ultimate slime,
> And a new Word runs between: whispering, "Let us be one!"

In the penultimate poem, the cities of the empire sing as sons to their Mother. This maternal image is taken up in the final poem, "England's Answer," introducing a note of paganism at odds with the patriarchal, monotheistic Old Testament ethos of the sequence as a whole. The themes are now "The Blood" and the Race rather than the biblical "seed." "England's Answer" ends:

> Stand to your work and be wise—certain of sword and pen,
> Who are neither children nor Gods, but men in the world of men!

This prophetic imperialism and seemingly vulgar patriotism evoke the cultural situation in which Kipling wrote "Recessional" for Queen Victoria's Jubilee of 1897 and "The White Man's Burden" on the United States' acquisition of the Philippine Islands, in 1899. Kipling's is a heroic, practical vision for a nonwordy, self-confident people, for whom pride of race and country are honorable emotions. "A Song of the English" is not anti-intellectual, but it is about action and power rather than thought and system.

But it is also more enigmatic than its tone might lead one to expect. The first poem calls on a Chosen People to obey a transcendent Law and Lawgiver, yet it reverses biblical themes and suggests that truth is only to be found "between" the "naked words and mean." In the last poem, Law is no longer given by God. It is not even made by the Mother but by the Sons, by "men in a world of men." This

---

> Saw the heavens filled with commerce, argosies of magic sails,
> Pilots of the purple twilight, dropping down with costly bales;
>
> . . .
>
> Far along the world-wide whisper of the south wind rushing warm,
> With the standards of the peoples plunging through the thunder storm;
>
> Till the war-drum throbb'd no longer, and the battle-flags were hurled
> In the Parliament of man, the Federation of the world.

Tennyson, *Poetical Works*, 10. See also 26n17.

suggests a "liberal" model of imperial authority (the adult "sons" thus emancipated, however, are of "The Blood"), but the ending also seems at odds with the celebration of the God of History and Law, with which the sequence opens. God is not mentioned in "England's Answer." These hidden meanings generate a tension in "A Song of the English" that informs all Kipling's best writing. On the one hand, the appetite for a secured identity, world order, and honest, manly endeavor—the Lord will *deal* with evil counsellors—is vigorously legitimized as a condition of building bridges and laying cables. But these assertions of heroic identity are accompanied by a tough-minded, potentially nihilistic relativism that Kipling was to develop more fully in "The Bridge-Builders."

Even in "The Deep-Sea Cables," this shifting literary ground is unsettling. The flickering and fluttering words that pass across "the waste of the ultimate slime" are contrasted with an ancient ocean world "that has neither voice nor feet." The electric telegraph has "wakened the timeless Things" and "killed their father Time" (9–10). There are suggestions of patricidal desecration in technology, even of triviality, which run counter to the work's overt self-celebration. The note of blasphemy marks the most optimistic line in the poem: "And a new Word runs between: whispering, 'Let us be one!'" Just as the Law of "the Lord our God Most High" is transformed into law made by "men in a world of men," so the "Word," with its capitalized initial letter, telegraphed along the ocean bed, replaces the Word that was in the beginning with God and was God. The truth to be discerned between the mean and naked words of "A Song of the English" doesn't quite fit its heroic grandiloquence of image and rhythm, both biblical and pagan-imperialist.

"A Song of the English" sets the scene for "The Bridge-Builders" in two respects. First, it illuminates the story's central character, "Findlayson, of the Public Works Department."[5] Findlayson speaks, in

5. Kipling, *Day's Work*, 7.

the words of "A Song," "*After the use of the English, in straight-flung words and few*" (17), and he has undertaken to "*Clear the land of evil, drive the road and bridge the ford.*" But it is also the story of Findlayson's opium-induced encounter with a relativized and relativizing text of the world with radical implications for both his and the reader's sense of identity, and inviting questions about the social order from which those identities are derived and the self-assertive "we" of "A Song of the English."

Findlayson's identity at the beginning of the story reflects an ideology of personal rectitude and progressive imperialism. An engineer, he has spent three years managing the construction of "the great Kashi Bridge over the Ganges ... Now, in less than three months, if all went well, His Excellency the Viceroy would open the bridge in state, an archbishop would bless it, the first train-load of soldiers would come over it, and there would be speeches." Findlayson expects to be made a Companion of the Indian Empire (CIE), though he dreams of being made a Companion of the Star of India (CSI). After all, he has designed a truss and a bolted shoe bearing his name. His bridge carries a railway line, a cart road, and red-brick towers "loopholed for musketry and pierced for big guns." The native laborers toil in his view, the "raw earth-ends ... crawling and alive with hundreds upon hundreds of tiny asses climbing out of the yawning borrow-pit with sackfuls of stuff." Barely conscious of the hundreds of riveters who "swarmed about the lattice side-work and the iron roof of the railway-line, hung from invisible staging under the bellies of the girders, clustered round the throats of the piers, and rode on the overhang of the footpath stanchions," he and his young assistant, Hitchcock, agree that the bridge is not "half a bad job for two men."[6]

The vocabulary—"crawled," "swarmed," "hung," "clustered"—by which the Indian workers are seen as ants or worker-bees evidently

6. Kipling, *Day's Work*, 8–9.

reflects the Englishmen's mind-set. That of the narrator is more difficult to place, an effect of the lack of "style" in the storytelling. His account of how two Englishmen casually take the credit for work that has been done by thousands is affectionately ironic: there *is* a sense in which they alone deserve credit for the bridge, yet there is no suggestion of discomfort with their sense of themselves as "men" in a special and honorable sense. But being a "man" is not just a matter of being male, adult, British, and of a certain class. Manhood is a condition Hitchcock has had to earn. When selected by Findlayson, he was "rather a colt," "chosen because of his rawness to break to [Findlayson's] own needs," a young horse, in effect, under training in the arena. He has apparently moved from being an untrained male animal into full human adulthood, a process that involved his being "appointed a magistrate of the third class with whipping powers, for the better government of the community."[7] He has learnt to wield these powers temperately—though, presumably, there was a coltish rawness in his first exercise of them.

But the manhood of Findlayson and Hitchcock differentiates them from more than their Indian workforce: there is also an imperial civil service, which knows nothing of "work"—"borrow-pits," "lattice side-work," "footpath stanchions" (Kipling infuses his "vulgar" technical vocabulary with ideological panache)—and consequently falls short of full manhood. Civil servants add two feet to the width of the bridge "under the impression that bridges were cut out of paper." (This is perhaps why the Mother in "A Song of the English" wishes her Sons to make laws without reference back to her.) Bureaucratic-commercial interests put pressure in Findlayson to accept "a rather doubtful consignment" and engage in "careful, polite obstruction" when he rejects it. (Hitchcock has to dash to London at his own and Findlayson's expense to use his influence to put things right.) Findlayson has internalized notions of responsibility and the

7. Kipling, *Day's Work*, 10.

expectation of judgment at a level altogether different from the scrutiny that results in a CIE after his name, or even a division between sheep and goats at the Second Coming.

And so, with the less than "manly" imperial administration on one side, native labor on the other, and with his bridge before him, Findlayson engages in "a long, long reverie" that covers "storm, sudden freshets, death in every manner and shape, violent and awful rage against red tape … drought, sanitation, finance, birth, wedding, burial, and riot in the village of twenty warring castes." He holds himself accountable, if not (with any theological explicitness) to God, then at least to the forum of his own heart. An implied education system has fitted him for leadership and mentoring young Hitchcock, whom he has initiated into manhood. Kipling invites his readers to see Findlayson as greater than his perception of himself. He is the self-effacing hero of an imperialist epic—Achilles, perhaps, in the *Iliad*—with Hitchcock as his armor bearer.

At this point, a third character is introduced: "so the bridge was two men's work—unless one counted Peroo, as Peroo certainly counted himself."[8] Peroo has also been shaped by an imperial system that has made him both a man of his own people, "a Lascar, a Kharva from Bulsar," and a *déraciné* cosmopolitan, "familiar with every port between Oakhampton and London … [who has] risen to the rank of serang on the British India boats." Like Findlayson, he can work on his own (four hours at the top of a crane fixing a loose plate). He, too, has a natural aptitude for engineering ("No piece of iron was so big or so badly placed that Peroo could not devise a tackle to lift it—a loose-ended, sagging arrangement, rigged with a scandalous amount of talking but perfectly equal to the work in hand.") And he is a leader of men: "He controlled his own gang of tacklemen—mysterious relatives from Kutch Mandvi gathered month by month and tried to the uppermost. No consideration of

8. Kipling, *Day's Work*, 11.

family or kin allowed Peroo to keep weak hands or a giddy head on the pay-roll":[9] his personal honor is the honor of the bridge, and "for Peroo and his people . . . honour and credit . . . are better than life."[10] Unlike Findlayson's, Peroo's ramshackle work will never be given a name. It stands to the truss and the shoe as an oral retelling of a traditional tale stands to a finished short story by a future winner of the Nobel Prize. Language for Peroo is fluid and fleeting. It does not fix or define—it performs. "He would interrupt the field-councils of Findlayson and Hitchcock without fear, till his wonderful English, or his still more wonderful lingua-franca, half Portuguese and half Malay, ran out and he was forced to take string and show knots that he would recommend."[11]

Compared with his ostensible attitude to the two Englishmen, the attitude of the narrator to Peroo is, at this stage, more difficult to place—an expert storyteller does not disclose his hand too soon. Peroo's initial role is disruptive and slightly comic—he punctures the (always innocent) self-importance of the two Englishmen. Nevertheless, he merits respect. Findlayson smiles when Peroo expresses his anxiety about the way in which the bridge impedes the flow of the river (he prefers "sus-sus-pen-sheen bridges that fly from bank to bank"),[12] and uses the word "we"—"we have put the river into a dock"[13]—but the reader suspects Findlayson will learn from Peroo before the tale is told. However, Findlayson's slight moral myopia does not remove him from the moral center of the tale. The narrator's strategy is to encourage the reader to anticipate and learn from a story about a passage in Findlayson's biography. If anything is to be learned from Peroo, therefore, it will be on the same terms as Findlayson learns from him. Findlayson is central to the story and Peroo

9. Kipling, *Day's Work*, 12.
10. Kipling, *Day's Work*, 17.
11. Kipling, *Day's Work*, 11–12.
12. Kipling, *Day's Work*, 13.
13. Kipling, *Day's Work*, 14.

is not, if only because the story itself is addressed to men (and perhaps to women) of "The Blood," not to Peroo and his kind. This is reflected in some of the terms used about him ("Peroo descended by a rope, ape-fashion").[14]

The first disruption of these expectations occurs when news comes that heavy rains and imminent flooding will put the bridge, the careers of the Englishmen, and the honor of all the bridge builders in jeopardy. Here, surely, is an epic situation in which the themes of "manliness," self-control, and the difficulty of distributing roles between people of different races can be developed, and in which Findlayson will experience the epiphany that will complete his formation as a "man" and surprise and enlighten the reader. At the very least, a moment of supreme testing seems imminent, because Hitchcock has to look after things on the opposite bank, and Findlayson is left alone with Peroo.

But expectations are again frustrated. When the crisis comes, there is no heroic work to be done. The courage, skill, leadership of the modern, technically educated hero and his exotic companion are at a discount. Religion, on the other hand, becomes, unexpectedly, important. It has been an amusing part of the background. The archbishop's proposed blessing is deftly ludicrous. In his career as a sailor, Peroo has been "unaffected by port missions or those creeds which are thrust upon sailors by agencies along the Thames' bank,"[15] his spirituality being eclectic and unstable. In London, he prayed to the dome of St. Paul's and "the first time he went into the engine-room of a steamer, when he was a boy, he prayed to the low-press cylinder." "Not half a bad thing to pray to, either," Findlayson remarks[16]—Findlayson is, obviously, a Church of England man of advanced views. On land, Peroo usually worships Shiva, but at sea, or on the bridge, the orders of the first mate or of Findlayson take

14. Kipling, *Day's Work*, 13.
15. Kipling, *Day's Work*, 12.
16. Kipling, *Day's Work*, 13.

precedence over dietary and other observances. Nevertheless, he has bullied a priest, "who had been chosen as ghostly counsellor by two generations of sea-rovers,"[17] to travel a thousand miles inland to serve as holy man to his Lascars, and changed the object of his devotions to the river, whom Peroo now worships as Mother Gunga. (Kipling's view of these matters is indicated, perhaps, in the mildly ironic, faintly papist term "ghostly counsellor," for an obviously "unmanly" Hindoo priest.) Nevertheless, and despite identifying the bridge with his own honor, Peroo professes to be upset that Mother Gunga is "in irons." (There are similar suggestions that technology may be blasphemous in "The Deep-Sea Cables.") Asked by Findlayson how much of this he believes in his heart, Peroo replies:

> All that our priest says. London is London, Sahib. Sydney is Sydney, and Port Darwin is Port Darwin. Also Mother Gunga is Mother Gunga, and when I come back to her banks I know this and worship. In London I did poojah to the big temple by the river for the sake of the God within. . . . Yes, I will not take the cushions in the dinghy.[18]

Findlayson and Peroo are worried about the same thing—will the bridge withstand the pressures building up on it?—but their differing perceptions of this anxiety disclose the gap between their worldviews. Findlayson could explain his concerns in terms of what he believes about bridges and the forces to which they are subject according to physical laws. But what is the relation, for Peroo, between expression and belief when he represents the same problem in terms of an outraged goddess whom he has only intermittently worshipped? What does he really mean by claiming to accept the teaching authority of his priest when he also calls him "son of a pig"[19] and threatens to whip him when he flees from the river instead of praying to Mother Gunga? What does "belief" mean, if it varies according to time and place? Again, what is the difference between doing "poo-

17. Kipling, *Day's Work*, 12.
18. Kipling, *Day's Work*, 14.
19. Kipling, *Day's Work*, 22.

jah" to St. Paul's in London, and knowing, in the river's presence, that "Mother Gunga is Mother Gunga"? The complexities of Peroo's casually delivered reply suggest relations between mind-set and utterance, between individual and ideology, different from those implicit in Findlayson's question.

Superficially, Peroo seems the more difficult to understand. The differences between his polytheistic and Western monotheistic culture need to be considered (though Kipling's respectful representations elsewhere of Islamic thought and practice are a warning against too hasty conclusions on this point). Peroo, moreover, is a special case—the fluidity of his identity and thinking is an historical accident—not many Lascars, nor Europeans, have crossed the racial, cultural, and class barriers that he has crossed.

But Findlayson's sheer obviousness may be equally significant. His practical Englishness, as against Peroo's cultural diffuseness, and his solitariness compared with Peroo's gregariousness—it is interesting that young Hitchcock went to London to sort out the doubtful consignment—suggest reserve, shyness even, but with hidden strengths as well as vulnerabilities. As the storm approaches, the two forms of life that each man embodies are going to be compared and tested.

Peroo is relaxed. He laughs when Findlayson refuses to leave the bridge, declaring, "Now we are in the hands of the Gods." (Kipling's use of an initial capital letter here is significant—"A Song of the English" repeatedly uses the same coercive device to reify and reverence key ideas such as "The Blood.") Findlayson is hungry, and Peroo unwisely gives him some opium to stave off hunger pangs during a long night. In his drugged state, Findlayson's reactions when some boats break loose are misjudged, and he and Peroo are swept downstream in a boat, facing imminent death, until by chance they are beached on an "island of last year's indigo crop"[20] in the middle of which is a Hindoo shrine. Here they spend the night, in what we

20. Kipling, *Day's Work*, 25.

may suppose is an opium dream, listening to a conversation between the Gods of India, who are debating the bridge's survival, their own identity, and the ultimate destiny of the universe.

The first arrival, Shiva, whom Peroo usually worships on land ("a huge and dripping Brahminee Bull shouldered his way under the tree"),[21] is quite as tangible and unproblematic as Findlayson and Peroo's: "The two men stumbled, heavy-limbed and heavy-eyed, over the ashes of a brick-set cooking-place." Findlayson acknowledges the Bull's presence: "Here be more beside ourselves," said Findlayson. (Kipling gives his characters archaic forms of English when they are not speaking in English.) Peroo tells him that their companions are the Gods, the drugged Findlayson believes him, and when Mother Gunga herself arrives, in the form of a crocodile ("the blunt-nosed, ford-haunting Mugger of the Ganges"), and protests that the bridge still stands after the floods, Findlayson says to himself, "My bridge . . . What have the Gods to do with my bridge!"[22] At one level, then, as a drug-induced illusion, the vision that Findlayson encounters on the little island is no more than a narrative device for bridging the gap between vulgar realism and the devices and rhetoric appropriate to representing the supernatural. But it is not just that—as an experience *shared* by the two men, it is also "real."

The Gods first discuss the bridge and try to persuade Mother Gunga that its surviving the storm would be unimportant. The fleeting work of human hands, it is insignificant "as the Gods count that which men call time."[23] When Shiva suggests that the Gods of the intruders taught them how to make railways, his companions laugh; such Gods are parvenus—"Tomorrow their Gods will die."[24] But Ganesh, the Elephant God of Good Luck, notes how well his money lenders have done in the process. Still, he dismisses all human effort

21. Kipling, *Day's Work*, 26.
22. Kipling, *Day's Work*, 27.
23. Kipling, *Day's Work*, 29.
24. Kipling, *Day's Work*, 30.

as "the sifting of a little dirt. Let the dirt dig in the dirt if it pleases the dirt."

So much for Findlayson's bridge-building epos, and for an identity determined by it. The discussion then moves on to the identities of the Gods themselves. Indra, the Buck, claims to be both the God and the Prophet of Islam. Kali, the Tigress and wife of Shiva, is also both "the Woman whom we know as hewn twelve-armed"[25] and the Woman the strangers call Mary. The story has moved from the instability of human identity to that of entire cultural (or religious) systems within which all human identities are constructed. The implications for ideology of comparative religion are bearing down upon the text.

The debate enters its final phase with the arrival of Krishna. Beautiful and beloved, Krishna is received with deference by his fellow Gods, but he tells them what they do not wish to hear. Shiva was wrong. The transformation of the world, as represented by the bridge, is not the work of Gods "one or three—man or woman," but "men in the world of men." "They move, and not the Gods of the bridge-builders."[26] And the result will be the extinction of the Gods themselves, who only exist in the worship accorded to them. Krishna assumes that he alone will survive, "so long as maiden and man meet together or the spring follows the winter rains … but … the beginning of the end is born already. The fire-carriages shout the names of new Gods that are not the old under new names."

At this point, a Westernized understanding of scientific and technological development displacing the superstition-laden cultures of the past seems to be emerging. Hearing Krishna's speech, Peroo whispers to Findlayson, "This I have not heard before … And yet sometimes, when I oiled the brasses in the engine-room of the Goorkha, I have wondered if our priests were so wise—so wise."

25. Kipling, *Day's Work*, 32.
26. Kipling, *Day's Work*, 37.

And with wonderful ambiguity he adds: "The day is coming, Sahib. They will be gone by the morning." Although the last two sentences refer to the imminence of the dawn and the disappearance of the present spectacle, they sound a distinctly progressive note: modern technology heralds the twilight of the Gods and a new world for human kind. Krishna, however, does not have the final word. Indra the Buck-God, reminds him of "the Riddle of the Gods. When Brahm ceases to dream, the Heavens and the Hells and Earth disappear . . . The Gods change, beloved—all save One."[27] Complacently, Krishna thinks he is the One, and Indra allows him to do so, though clearly the reference is to Brahm: "Brahm dreams—and till He wakes the Gods die not."

The day dawns, the Gods disappear, Peroo and Findlayson find themselves suffering from cold and cramp, the aftereffects of opium, and Kipling's tale takes its last twist. Findlayson has "forgotten much,"[28] and Peroo is astonished to find that this includes both events before they reached the island and the conversation of the Gods—everything has been reduced in Findlayson's mind to a fever dream of "beasts and men talking." Thus the hero of the story's opening phase has not apparently advanced in self-knowledge, but has seemingly learned nothing and appears actually stupid beside Peroo. Peroo's interpretation of this is equally unexpected—he sees Findlayson's forgetfulness as showing what Indra meant when he said that the Gods die when Brahm ceases to dream—the Gods cease when human thinking ceases: Brahm is human consciousness, not a transcendent reality nor even the ground of our being. Peroo has a dim memory of recalling this once before, when he nearly drowned, and he now looks forward to whipping his guru when he meets him "for talking riddles which are no riddles."[29] Findlayson and Peroo

27. Kipling, *Day's Work*, 38.
28. Kipling, *Day's Work*, 39.
29. Kipling, *Day's Work*, 40.

are quickly rescued—Hitchcock has persuaded a local native prince to search for them on his private steam launch—and the story concludes with Findlayson relieved that his bridge has survived, the prince hurrying back to a Hindoo temple ritual that he calls a "dambore,"[30] and Peroo contemplating the exercise of his personal whipping powers with "two feet of partially untwisted wire-rope" on the back of his dishonest guru.

What is to be made of "The Bridge-Builders"? By the end of the story, Peroo has disclosed a lively intelligence while Findlayson has not. On the steamboat, Findlayson is uneasy, unable to follow what Peroo tells him, indeed unable to look at him. Peroo stares "curiously at Findlayson's back, [as] the white man looked across the flood." It may be a mistake, however, to dismiss Findlayson as too stupid to see what Peroo has seen. Perhaps he is alert to the danger of what "A Song" calls "*Whoring . . . with visions.*" Perhaps he only fails to put his memories into words because he does not need to, according to "the use of the English." What have India's Gods to do with him, if his bridge is itself one of those new Gods that Krishna warns his fellow-Gods about, and that are not the old Gods under different names? If Findlayson worships anything it is the bridge, and if he has learnt anything from the flood it is that the Findlayson truss and the Findlayson shoe, CIEs and CSIs are not what matter. What matters, what makes Findlayson Findlayson, is not words but work: the bridge is there. Neither he nor it needs the support of story—he is content, therefore, to allow visions of the night to lapse into incoherence.

If this is a possible reading of the final stages of the narrative, it becomes more difficult to see Findlayson's identity as exclusively constituted in words or even nonverbal signs. Findlayson is Findlayson, not by virtue of anything explicitly signified, not as a story told by and about him, but by virtue of his work. Kipling was directly

30. Kipling, *Day's Work*, 42.

or indirectly influenced by Thomas Carlyle (1795–1881): Findlayson may be a latter-day Brindley, the silent, illiterate, heroic constructor of canals in Carlyle's *Past and Present* (1843). The reader, in effect, looks (with Peroo) at the back of a man who is *not* passively constituted by his "ideas," his culture, or his heredity. Findlayson and his bridge stand together, just as, sooner or later, they will disappear as the Gods will disappear.[31] Whether this is enough (for Findlayson, for Kipling, for the reader) is unclear.

Peroo, on the other hand, despite his need to use knots instead of speech, is confirmed as a man of words just as Findlayson is a man without them. The distinctive form of Peroo's manhood, moreover, is disclosed in his ability to speak about the relativities that Findlayson fails to remember, to grasp that ideology is constituted by the consciousnesses that it constitutes, and is extinguished when they are extinguished: people and their Gods are conditions of each other's being. Peroo has come to understand the "textuality" of the world and that "there is nothing outside the text"—the Gods constitute systems of meaning for the living but have nothing to offer the dead. In death, Brahm ceases to dream.

Nevertheless, Peroo also registers the insight that words are not everything. The recognition that he articulates so fluently, and that should extinguish his sense of himself—he now has nothing to believe in, whereas Findlayson still has his bridge—is precisely what brings out something fundamental in his makeup. Peroo moves himself out of the naively doctrinaire religious ideologies of his tradition into the demanding and always provisional reality disclosed in the conversation of the Gods. Grammatically, he is the subject who constitutes his own worldview, who constructs himself as willing to will, and grasps the utility of doing so.

31. Although the bridge may be regarded as a Great Action in Aristotle's sense, its status is not decisively endorsed any more than Findlayson's status as the hero of an epos. See Markovits, *Crisis of Action*.

His mental life is Nietzschean. In *Thus Spoke Zarathustra: First Part,* Nietzsche writes of the three metamorphoses of the spirit—into a camel that may be associated with Mill, "the strong reverent spirit that would bear much,"[32] into a lion who confronts the dragon's ancient "Thou shalt" with his own "I will" and says "a sacred "No" even to duty," and finally into a child:

> But say, my brothers, what can the child do that even the lion could not do? Why must the preying lion still become a child? The child is innocence and forgetting, a new beginning, a game, a self-propelled wheel, a first movement, a sacred "Yes." For ... the spirit now wills his own will, and he who had been lost to the world now conquers his own world.[33]

Peroo has passed through all three phases with persistence and guile. He has worked as a camel on ship and bridge; as a lion, he has rejected the taboos of his tradition; finally, on the night of the flood, he becomes a child—"creates new values," "wills his own will," decides to flog his guru, not for failing to pray to Mother Gunga but for pretending to. In building a bridge between tradition and modernity, the illiterate Kharva from Bulsar persists "even after" his story, and therefore his "I," have been expunged.

Peroo is a bridge builder in another sense. The (for Kipling not uncharacteristic) *Jouissance* of a wire-whipped guru with which the story concludes puts Peroo into the same frame as Hitchcock. I suggested earlier that the assumption, in the opening phase of the story, that Findlayson's perceptions are what matter derives from the powerful suggestion, in the way the tale is told and the manner of its publication, that the anticipated reader, being of "The Blood," belongs to Findlayson's world, not Peroo's. In the event, however, such readers have either to map themselves onto Peroo's experience or remain stuck inside the wordless amnesia of Findlayson, who puts Peroo completely out of his head as the story concludes.

32. Nietzsche, *Portable Nietzsche,* 137.
33. Nietzsche, *Portable Nietzsche,* 139.

Legitimate as this may be (perhaps) for Findlayson, it cannot have been so for the story's original readership. As readers of a work, not of the sword but the pen, they were expected to find meaning in the whole narrative, including Peroo. Peroo's perspective is all they are left with. It would seem, then, that it is the Englishman, Findlayson, who functions as a means in this narrative scheme, as a bridge between the putative reader's mind-set and the story's real protagonist, who, alien and dark-skinned, might at first have seemed merely one of the "new-caught sullen peoples, Half devil and half child" of "The White Man's Burden,"[34] but who ends up not only with a third-class magistrate's whipping powers but also as the story's Nietzschean child and exemplary guru.

Kipling's attitudes were overtly racist. But then the author of such morally complex novels as *Little Dorrit* and *Great Expectations* was in life an abuser of his wife, an adulterer, and a grossly insensitive father. Kipling's treatment of race and class was not *simply* reactionary, as attentive reading of his greatest Indian stories will disclose. He repeatedly maneuvers his readers into adopting a "native" perspective. In *Kim* (1901), they find themselves respecting a fat, self-important, half-Westernized Bengali, the kind of figure Kipling elsewhere represents with uninhibited derision. At least in "The Bridge-Builders," as in a poem such as "The Ballad of East and West" (1889), the reader is confronted with a "native" who is also a "man," and so challenging imperialist self-assurance. The measure of "the white man's" fitness to govern a subject people is his capacity to relate to men of the caliber of Peroo. And this cannot be dissociated from a capacity to learn from them about the transvaluation of values.

For what Peroo has to tell the people of "The Blood" who read *The Day's Work* is that racial issues are more complicated than civil servants, soldiers, or journalists make them seem. The debate between the Gods, which he alone holds in his head when the story

34. Kipling, *Works*, 323.

ends, has limitless application, not only to Christianity even in its purest "English" form—note the telling Trinitarian reference to Gods "one or three"—but also to everything else the reader may hold dear also. The implications of the Gods' debate go beyond the comforting nineteenth-century idea that the "divine" is the "human" after all. They encompass all aspects of the human, including "A Song of the English," England as Mother, her Sons as guardians and makers of Law, even, in the end, "The Blood" itself. These are your Gods, o' England, and like the idols of the faithless Israelites, they are no more than Brahm's dream, just stories for the Empire to live by.

G. K. Chesterton (1874–1936) is almost certainly thinking of "The Bridge-Builders" when he recalls a Hindu tradition "that gods as well as men are only the dreams of Brahma; and will perish when Brahma wakes." Appalled by this idea, he describes what it would be like to live through Findlayson's experience, "to plunge into the elephantine extravagance of Brahmin cosmology" and to "feel a shudder going through the veil of things, the many-handed creators, and the throned and haloed animals and all the network of entangled stars and rulers of the night, as the awful eyes of Brahma open like dawn upon the death of all."[35] It is only in that half second, when the veil of things and their obliteration are in conjunction, that atheism is fully grasped.

Findlayson turns his back on such thoughts, but Peroo takes them to heart: the fate of all values, his own as well as those of Kipling's readers, is obliteration. He imagines Brahm playing Freud's game of *fort da* not with its mother but with the universe for the last time, and sees, perhaps, what Lord Henry saw when they discovered the body of Dorian Gray. Yet, somehow, "even after," at the heart of the void that really is "Nothing!," and not as a victim like Prince, nor as movement of *misericordia* like Wilde, but coolly, quietly, as an intelligent and whole human being, Peroo persists. Somehow atheism must account for its own heroes and their capacity to will to will.

35. Chesterton, *Everlasting Man*, 110.

Kipling's understanding of what is involved in Relativism seems to me stronger and less inhibited than anyone else's. In the popular mind, he may be known as a reactionary imperialist; this reputation is not undeserved. But in his writing, he is much less subject to ideology than Mill, Pater, or even Wilde. He alone could approach (with Peroo) the foundational void without panic. This may be partly due to the desolations of his childhood, and to the intimate multicultural and multilingual experiences of his life in India, England, and the United States. But it is not unconnected either with the fact that he had no style and wrote short stories. He seems not to have needed words, words, words as much as most people do, least of all to make something of himself. Nevertheless, he used his "naked words and mean" to create great stories, great because they devour not only their characters but their readers also.

4

"What's God Got to Do with Pig-Killing?"

WHY THOMAS HARDY STOPPED WRITING NOVELS

Jude the Obscure, the last novel written by Thomas Hardy, was first published as a bowdlerized serial in *Harper's Magazine* from December 1894 to November 1895. A partially restored text appeared in 1895, and the novel was published with many emendations in various editions until Hardy's death. For the remaining thirty-three years of his life, he published only short stories and poems. Hardy implies that this had something to do with the controversy the novel's publication aroused. It seems to me to be rather that the novel exposes the mind of Hardy at the end of its tether.

It can be read as a social novel dealing with topics of great contemporary interest—divorce, an educational system closed to the poor, and the emotional power and intellectual weakness of Christianity, all of which bear down on the eponymous Jude Fawley and the schoolmaster Richard Phillotson, from the opening scene in which the eleven-year-old Jude bids farewell to his ambitious teacher to the novel's disastrous conclusion. Both are social misfits, both struggling, self-taught intellectuals, obsessed with the issue with which the novel is also *structurally* concerned, namely, the place of values in the system of things. They are united as rivals in love for Jude's cousin, Sue Bridehead, sensitive, febrile, highly intelligent but emotionally and sexually insecure, whose marriage to Phillotson is a disaster, and who (in her fashion) is in love with Jude, just as Jude, though in love with Sue, can never escape from his powerful, sexually, and socially uninhibited wife, Arabella, the only one of the four central characters who is not an introspective intellectual.

There is thus a complex interweaving of the varying ideas and insights of the characters and those of the writer. A characteristic passage describes the sixteen-year-old Jude painfully teaching himself Greek and Latin in the hope of following Phillotson to Christminster (Oxford) and a clerical career. After making bread deliveries for his great-aunt Drusilla by horse and cart, he stumbles through Horace's *Hymn to Apollo* as the horse makes its own way home. He stops the horse and kneels by the roadside:

> The horse stood still till he had finished the hymn, which Jude repeated under the sway of a polytheistic fantasy that he would never have thought of humouring in broad daylight.
>
> Reaching home he mused over his curious superstition, innate or acquired, in doing this.[1]

By and large, the narrative here stays with Jude's point of view. Two phrases, however—"the sway of a polytheistic fantasy" and "innate or acquired"—are not accessible to a sixteen-year-old country boy. Comte had claimed that "polytheistic" tendencies characterized the "adolescent" phase of human development in the individual and "the race," and the question of innate and acquired characteristics was central to debates about evolution. Jude would seem to illustrate the first hypothesis and the second unresolved problem. In his maturity, he will be introduced to both ways of thinking, first by Sue, then through his own reading. Near the end of his life, he will declare,

1. Hardy, *Jude the Obscure*, 28.

"The theologians, the apologists, and their kin the metaphysicians, the high-handed statesmen, and others, no longer interest me."[2] The reference to "theologians ... and their kin the metaphysicians" suggests that the mature Jude has read his Comte. Jude thus embodies the very ideas he assimilates. This mingling of the perspectives of Hardy's main characters and those of the novel's intellectual hinterland does not privilege either, however. The worldviews to which the narrator alludes are a measure against which the experience of the characters may be judged, but that experience tests the adequacy of their worldviews and those of the age.

This applies especially to the biological determinism that repeatedly overrides the "higher" aspirations of Hardy's characters. Learning his trade as a stonemason, Jude, not yet twenty years old, surveys his reading in classical literature, the Greek New Testament, and ancient and modern history. Graduation, ordination, and high office in the Church seem to be within his grasp: "Yes," he muses, "Christminster shall be my Alma Mater; and I shall be her beloved son, in whom she shall be well pleased." A group of young women are washing the chitterlings of a slaughtered barrow-pig, and one of them—Arabella—throws the animal's penis at him. She is "fine, dark-eyed ... not exactly handsome, but capable of passing as such, despite some coarseness of skin and fibre." Jude picks her out "in commonplace obedience to conjunctive orders from headquarters, unconsciously received by unfortunate young men when the last intention of their lives is to be occupied with the feminine."[3]

For Hardy, the "real" world of desire, work, and endurance, rooted in the countryside but carried by the laboring poor into the towns, often has the measure of theological, philosophical, or even scientific "theory." Speaking of Christminster, for example, a carter remarks to the boy Jude:

2. Hardy, *Jude the Obscure*, 380.

3. Hardy, *Jude the Obscure*, 33–34.

O—they never look at anything that folks like we can understand ... On'y foreign tongues used in the days of the Tower of Babel, when no two families spoke alike. They read that sort of thing as fast as a nighthawk will whir. "Tis all learning there; nothing but learning, except religion. And that's learning too, for I never could understand it. Yes; 'tis a serious-minded place. Not but there are wenches in the streets o' nights."[4]

An inn is described as "one of the great palpitating centres of Christminster life"[5] in contrast to the colleges—"It seemed impossible that modern thought could house itself in such decrepit and superseded chambers."[6]

Arabella embodies this ancient groundedness. Sexually and practically uninhibited, strong and shrewd, and more ready to take control of her destiny than any of the other characters in the novel, she seduces Jude, feigns pregnancy, wears false hair, and tricks him into marriage. The collapse of their marriage is precipitated by his soft-hearted botching of the slaughter of a pig. When at last the pig dies, and Jude thanks God, the exasperated Arabella retorts, "What's God got to do with such a messy job as pig-killing, I should like to know! ... Poor folks must live."[7] She moves into the city, travels to Australia, and bigamously marries a man called Cartlett. Some years later, after she has walked out on Cartlett also, she again meets Jude. Jude suggests they sort out their situation. "O bother arranging!" Arabella replies. "I'm not going to arrange anything."[8] Instead, they spend the night together. But when Cartlett follows her from Australia, she arranges matters after all, inveigling Jude into divorcing her so that she can marry Cartlett. Later she knows at a glance that Jude and Sue are not married, that he is "charmed by her" but that "she don't know what love is—at least what I call love."[9]

4. Hardy, *Jude the Obscure*, 18.
5. Hardy, *Jude the Obscure*, 171.
6. Hardy, *Jude the Obscure*, 73.
7. Hardy, *Jude the Obscure*, 59.
8. Hardy, *Jude the Obscure*, 174.
9. Hardy, *Jude the Obscure*, 282–3.

But there is another side to Arabella. Hardy's comments on her "coarseness of skin and fibre," and his use of the semiscientific term "fibre" imply a characteristically nineteenth-century distinction between a "lower" animal and a "higher," spiritual, condition. And whereas Jude can *think* about what happens to them—

> There seemed to him, vaguely and dimly, something wrong in a social ritual which made necessary a cancelling of well-formed schemes involving years of thought and labour, of foregoing a man's opportunity of showing himself superior to the lower animals . . . because of a momentary surprise by a new and transitory instinct which had in it nothing of the nature of a vice, and could be only at the most called a weakness[10]

—Arabella is as helpless sexually as he is. Before seducing him, she exclaims, "I shall go mad if I can't give myself to him altogether!"[11] Years later, her feelings have not changed. Cartlett dies, she becomes religious, sees Jude again, and her religion evaporates. "Pooh!" she says to her companion. "I know as well as you what I should do; only I don't do it." She still wants Jude. "He's more mine than hers!"[12]

The high-minded Richard Phillotson is different. "Be a good boy, remember; and be kind to animals and birds, and read all you can,"[13] he tells the young Jude in the novel's opening scene. When they meet again, he is "a spare and thoughtful personage of five-and-forty, with a thin-lipped, somewhat refined mouth, a slightly stooping habit."[14] Courting Sue when she becomes his apprentice teacher, he fails to detect the passionlessness with which she drifts into an understanding. Nor does he see that her consenting to marry him after her expulsion from college is in part because she can't think of what else she might do. (In play also, of course, are her disquieting feelings about Jude and the complexities of her response to him.)

10. Hardy, *Jude the Obscure*, 56.
11. Hardy, *Jude the Obscure*, 44.
12. Hardy, *Jude the Obscure*, 304.
13. Hardy, *Jude the Obscure*, 4.
14. Hardy, *Jude the Obscure*, 96.

Richard, however, has a deeper problem. Talking to Jude and Sue, their great-aunt Drusilla says of Richard, "there be certain men here and there that no woman of any niceness can stomach. I should have said he was one."[15] Sue runs out of the room to weep. A man must be sexually stupid not to detect such feelings in a potential partner.

Richard is a "theoretical" man, a thought experiment in "advanced thinking." He has liberal views about women. "He's as good to me as a man can be," Sue tells Jude, "and gives me perfect liberty—which elderly husbands don't do in general."[16] As their relationship deteriorates, he agrees to their sleeping apart and then to her leaving him to join Jude: "it is wrong," he says, "to … torture a fellow-creature any longer," and that "it is not an ignoble, merely animal, feeling between" them.[17] But a perverse aspect of his high-mindedness is apparent in his defiance of respectable opinion in permitting Sue to leave him, an action that makes it impossible to divorce her. His subsequent refusal to resign quietly from his teaching post, and his insistence on defending himself at a public meeting, are painfully self-defeating. His only supporters are disreputable itinerants "who frequented the numerous fairs and markets held up and down Wessex." The meeting concludes in a farcical rough-house, and Richard ends up regretting "that he had not resigned when called upon, and [goes] home so ill that next morning he [cannot] leave his bed."[18] It seems that Richard's moral sensitivity (his *misericordia*) and his principles (his Millian liberalism) arise less from moral seriousness than from innately embodied failure.

But the liberal thought experiment may fail for a deeper reason. After the widowed Arabella's encounter, years later, with the pregnant Sue at a cake stall, Arabella meets Richard on the road and tells him that Sue and Jude weren't lovers at the time of the divorce (he

15. Hardy, *Jude the Obscure*, 183.

16. Hardy, *Jude the Obscure*, 181.

17. Hardy, *Jude the Obscure*, 222–23.

18. Hardy, *Jude the Obscure*, 240.

had canceled the condoning of her supposed adultery by inviting her to return to him).

"Still—she wanted to go," he said.

"Yes. But you shouldn't have let her . . . *I* shouldn't have let her go! I should have kept her chained on—her spirit for kicking would have broke soon enough! . . . Well; she's got her deserts now."

"Yes," said Phillotson, with biting sadness. "Cruelty is the law pervading all nature and society; and we can't get out of it if we would!"

"Well—don't you forget to try it next time, old man."[19]

But if "Cruelty is the law pervading all nature and society," where does that leave Richard's emancipated liberalism and his *misericordia*?

And where does it leave Jude and Sue? In 1912, Hardy added a "Postscript" to the "Preface to the First Edition," in which he reports an "experienced" German reviewer describing Sue as

> the first delineation in fiction of the woman who was coming into notice in her thousands every year—the woman of the feminist movement—the slight, pale "bachelor" girl—the intellectualized, emancipated bundle of nerves that modern conditions were producing, mainly in cities as yet . . . The regret of this critic was that the portrait of the newcomer had been left to be drawn by a man, and was not done by one of her own sex, who would never have allowed her to break down at the end.[20]

Hardy does not endorse this judgment, but neither does he explain why he "allowed her to break down at the end."

How, for example, should Sue's sexual feelings and conduct be interpreted? When Jude meets her in Christminster, she seems to him "pretty, liquid-eyed, light-footed."[21] She is "artless and natural,"[22] "so vibrant" that everything she does seems "to have its source in feeling."[23] Her work in a shop dealing in religious books and objects

19. Hardy, *Jude the Obscure*, 306–7.
20. Hardy, *Jude the Obscure*, xlvi.
21. Hardy, *Jude the Obscure*, 86.
22. Hardy, *Jude the Obscure*, 93.
23. Hardy, *Jude the Obscure*, 96.

means nothing to her. But what is the significance of her impulsive purchase of two large "classical" statues, of Venus and Apollo, which leads to her dismissal? Is "paganism" an aspect of modernity? When she takes a group of children to see a model of Jerusalem in the time of Christ and meets Jude there, she is not impressed. "There was nothing first-rate about the place, or people," she tells him.[24] Emancipated from family pressures, she seems well equipped to make her own way in the world, eager for, and capable of, self-emancipation, as the German reviewer suggested.

But her response to Jude's defense of the exhibition is telling: "she was silent, for she was easily repressed." Her later acceptance of Richard's attentions, while at the same time cultivating a close relation with Jude, suggests that she will be as inadequate an example of feminism as Richard is of liberalism. As she and Jude set out on her day's holiday from training college, they are put into an empty compartment by a guard who thinks they are lovers. "That's a good intention wasted!" Sue says. Jude thinks "the remark unnecessarily cruel, and partly untrue."[25] Either Sue has as little insight into the feelings of others as Richard, or she really is "cruel." They miss the return train and spend the night with a country couple, but sleep apart.

Her subsequent escape from the college in the middle of the night to Jude's lodgings, where she changes into his Sunday suit while her clothes dry, is equally ambivalent. He remarks that she does not "talk like a girl"; she explains that she has read "most of the Greek and Latin classics through translations, and other books too ... Lamprière, Catullus, Martial, Juvenal, Lucian, Beaumont and Fletcher, Boccaccio, Scarron, De Brantôme, Sterne, De Foe, Smollett, Fielding, Shakespeare, the Bible and other such." She says she has no "fear of men ... —almost as one of their own sex."[26] For fif-

24. Hardy, *Jude the Obscure*, 100.
25. Hardy, *Jude the Obscure*, 130.
26. Hardy, *Jude the Obscure*, 141.

teen months she lived with a young graduate, and when he died, she felt guilty about not agreeing to be his lover. He was "the most irreligious man" Sue ever knew, "and the most moral,"[27] and approved of her scheme of rearranging the New Testament "in chronological order"—something Jude regards as sacrilege.[28] Of pious interpretations of the Song of Solomon, Sue declares that "people have no right to falsify the Bible. I *hate* such humbug as could plaster over with ecclesiastical abstractions such ecstatic, natural, human love." Yet when Jude, quoting the Song of Solomon, tells her, "You know *you* are the fairest among women to me," she, "with the softest note of severity," tells him "not to say it now," and they shake hands "like cronies in a tavern." They fall asleep in separate chairs. When Jude wakes at six o'clock, Sue sleeps on "inside his great-coat, looking warm as a new bun and boyish as a Ganymedes,"[29] the beautiful youth that the besotted Zeus made his cupbearer.

Later she maneuvers Jude into agreeing to "give her away" when she marries Richard. Before the marriage service, she inspects the church, holding Jude's arm "almost as if she loved him." When they walk down the aisle together, they are "precisely like a couple just married." "I like to do things like this," Sue remarks, "in the delicate voice of an epicure of the emotions," and when Jude protests, she exclaims, "I promised never to vex you ... My curiosity to hunt up a new sensation always leads me into these scrapes."[30] These are not the words of *any* "slight, pale 'bachelor' girl," but those that an aesthete like Oscar Wilde's Lord Henry Wotton. One can't help feeling that the German critic saw something important in Sue and yet failed really to understand her.

27. Hardy, *Jude the Obscure*, 144.

28. Hardy, *Jude the Obscure*, 145.

29. Hardy, *Jude the Obscure*, 146.

30. Hardy, *Jude the Obscure*, 165–66. It is interesting to think of women like Sue, feminist aesthetes with a particular refinement of nervous development, being among the readers Hardy was consciously writing for. See Dames, *Physiology of the Novel*, Part One.

Soon after her marriage to Richard, her feelings of revulsion toward him lead, as we have seen, to their sleeping apart. Sitting up late one night, Richard mechanically goes up to the bedroom they formerly shared. Sue springs out of bed and leaps out of the window. Her "condoned" union with Jude follows. They meet at Melchester station, and Jude tells her he has booked their room in a hotel at Aldbrickham. "I thought you might do it," Sue says, "But I didn't mean that," and she adds "smilingly" that he has "no right" to ask whether she has changed her mind—she cannot "be quite candid about the mystery of her heart."[31] They go to another hotel and take separate rooms. Initially, Jude does not recognize that Sue's is the one in which he slept with Arabella. Sue finds out about this from a chambermaid. Jude explains that at the time he thought Sue and Richard were "on good terms." Sue replies:

> No, I wasn't, Jude. O how can you think so! And you have taken me in, even if you didn't intend to ... Was it this room? Yes it was—I see by your look it was! I won't have it for mine! O it was treacherous to have her again! *I* jumped out of the window!

Jude points out that Arabella was still legally his wife. "I am not to approach you," he protests, "nor anybody else!" Sue replies:

> "O don't you *understand* my feeling! *Why* don't you. Why are you so gross? *I* jumped out of the window!"
>
> "Jumped out of the window?"
>
> "I can't explain!"[32]

Jude must understand what Sue can't explain, and he does—"a little." The gaps between her opinions, her feelings, her words, and her actions can't be put into words. This makes impossible demands on Jude and the reader, yet it is also what makes Jude love her, and what makes her a fascinating fictional personality.

31. Hardy, *Jude the Obscure*, 230–23.
32. Hardy, *Jude the Obscure*, 234–35.

> Looking at his loved one as she appeared to him now, in his tender thought the sweetest and most disinterested comrade that he had ever had, living largely in vivid imaginings, so ethereal a creature that her spirit could be seen trembling through her limbs, he felt heartily ashamed of his earthiness in Arabella's company. There was something rude and immoral in thrusting these recent facts of his life upon the mind of one who, to him, was so uncarnate as to seem at times impossible as a human wife to an average man.[33]

It is easy to miss the subtleties in this unmannered prose. Expressions like "as she *appeared* to him now" and "who, *to him*, was so uncarnate" are important.

Arabella's perspective on her differs markedly from his. As soon as she sees Jude and Sue together, Arabella realizes that they haven't had sex. With both divorces made absolute, Arabella, now legally married to Cartlett, arrives unexpectedly to have a talk with Jude, but Jude is out. Sue guesses who she is, and is convinced that she has come to seduce Jude. Jude insists on meeting Arabella, to Sue's considerable distress. The next morning, Sue herself goes to see Arabella and is "wicked enough" to wish Jude could see Arabella's "frowsiness" in the morning, but then rejects this "meanly sexual emotion." Arabella assumes that Sue calls herself "Mrs Fawley." Sue indignantly denies it. "O I thought you might have," Arabella says, "even if he's not really yours." "I don't know what you mean," Sue replies. "He's mine, if you come to that." "He wasn't yesterday." Sue blushes and asks how Arabella knows. "From your manner when you talked to me at the door," Arabella answers. "Well, my dear, you've been quick about it, and I expect my visit last night helped it on—ha-ha! But I don't want to take him from you." She urges Sue to marry Jude. "Life with a man is more business-like after it, and money matters work better."[34] So is jealousy, rather than "ecstatic, natural, human love," the reason for Sue's acceptance of Jude as her lover? And who is really the more emancipated of the two women?

33. Hardy, *Jude the Obscure*, 179–80.

34. Hardy, *Jude the Obscure*, 258–59.

And what about Jude? A self-educated countryman and skilled craftsman, moving out of traditional peasant life into and then beyond late nineteenth-century intellectual culture, he is a *type*, like the heroes of *Alton Locke* (1850) by Charles Kingsley (1819–75) or *Felix Holt, the Radical* (1866) by George Eliot. He embodies his time, and his experiences disclose its shortcomings. He is a victim of a class-based educational system, outdated marriage laws, a repressive sexual culture, and exploitative employment practices. He is different from Alton Locke and Felix Holt, however, because he less overtly manifests the authorial viewpoint. "Christminster shall be my Alma Mater," he tells himself, before Arabella throws the pizzle at him; "and I shall be her beloved son, in whom she shall be well pleased." His misuse of the words of the voice from heaven, which are addressed to Jesus in the Transfiguration scenes in the New Testament, whether conscious or not, points toward his future freethinking, wholly beyond his adolescent mind. The moment of mutual sexual awareness in Jude and Arabella is vividly natural, yet we are also given a detached view of it. Calling sex "a *new and transitory* influence" on a young man not yet twenty years old points to assumptions about adolescent masculinity that seem odd in today's culture. Has Jude never been in thrall to lust before?

Like many of his predecessors in fiction, he turns to drink. But his way of looking at things is broader and bleaker than theirs. Even in youth, it is not just his times but "the terrestrial scheme" that presses upon him:

> Growing up brought responsibilities, he found ... Nature's logic was too horrid for him to care for ... As you got older ... you were seized with a short of shuddering ... All around you there seemed to be something glaring, garish, rattling, and the noises and glares hit upon the little cell of your life, and shook it and warped it.[35]

35. Hardy, *Jude the Obscure*, 12.

He is drawn to religion by this felt confusion and by an idealism grounded in his "higher" natural gifts. Then along comes Arabella, and he encounters the "lower" impulses of his nature. What were his plans, after all? "Dreams about books, and degrees, and impossible fellowships."[36] After Arabella's desertion, the religious impulse is revived: "a religion of some sort seems a necessity" to him, "and not only a luxury of the emotional and leisured classes";[37] a cathedral service in Christminster provides an "anchorage for his thoughts,"[38] though he is also dreaming about his cousin Sue, to whom he has yet to introduce himself. His letter to the Heads of Colleges inquiring about admission, and the single reply he receives advising him to stick to his calling as a stonemason, expose the educational elitism that has relevance to this day. He gets drunk and humiliatingly recites the Nicene Creed in Latin in a pub. His adolescent dream "in which an abstract figure, more or less himself, was ... making his calling and election sure in the paradise of the learned"[39] apparently extinguished, he returns to Marygreen; thinks "what a poor Christ he made," his mind filled with "the hell of conscious failure both in ambition and love"; and learns from the curate there that he might receive ordination without a university degree, provided he avoids "strong drink."[40] He cannot escape from his fantasies.

His problem, however, is not drink but love. Marriage to Sue after divorce would prevent his being ordained. There are also the difficulties of her feelings about him, and the self-division in himself—in Sue's words, between "relations based on animal desire" and the "wide field of strong attachment where desire plays, at least a secondary part."[41] During their nighttime talk after Sue's flight

36. Hardy, *Jude the Obscure*, 51.

37. Hardy, *Jude the Obscure*, 85.

38. Hardy, *Jude the Obscure*, 86.

39. Hardy, *Jude the Obscure*, 106–7.

40. Hardy, *Jude the Obscure*, 118–19.

41. Hardy, *Jude the Obscure*, 160.

from the college, he confesses to his love for her—they agree that she has been unaware of this, though perhaps not all Hardy's readers are convinced—and she looks away "as if afraid she might forgive him" (and yield to him?). "By every law of nature and sex," Hardy writes, "a kiss was the only rejoinder that fitted the mood and the moment, under the suasion of which Sue's undemonstrative regard of him might conceivably have changed its temperature,"[42] but Jude does not act. Neither does he tell her about his marriage. The barriers between them are not all of Sue's making. When he does tell her about Arabella, Sue protests: she has allowed him to love her "just out of charity—and all the time—O it is perfectly damnable how things are!" The next moment, she supposes Arabella to be "a very pretty woman" and then mocks his religious beliefs: "Your theories are not so advanced as your practice."[43] Later, Jude accepts that "he was a man of too many passions to make a good clergyman," though the flesh "might not always be victorious" over the spirit.[44] For a second time, his aspirations have been checked by a woman. "Is it . . . that women are to blame," he asks himself, "or is it the artificial system of things, under which the normal sex-impulses are turned into devilish domestic gins and springes to noose and hold back those who want to progress?"[45] Would then a "natural system of things" be the answer?

Jude's susceptibilities distinguish his engagement with late nineteenth-century intellectual life from Sue's. Her reading provides her not with a sense of self and the world, but with ad hoc proof-texts in argument, as when she pleads with Richard for his consent to her living with Jude. "She, or he," she tells him, "'who lets the world, or his own portion of it, choose his plan of life for him, has no need of any other faculty than the ape-like one of imitation.' J. S. Mill's

42. Hardy, *Jude the Obscure*, 151.

43. Hardy, *Jude the Obscure*, 159.

44. Hardy, *Jude the Obscure*, 185.

45. Hardy, *Jude the Obscure*, 209.

words, those are. I have been reading them up." At this poor Richard moans, "What do I care about J. S. Mill!" (an ironic echo, perhaps, of Arabella's "What's God got to do with such a messy job as pig-killing!"). Their conversation continues in the farcical series of notes carried from one to the other by the children they are teaching, in one of which Sue writes, "I don't want to be respectable. To produce 'Human development in its richest diversity' (to quote your Humboldt) is to my mind far above respectability," and in another, "No poor woman has ever wished more than I that Eve had not fallen, so that (as the primitive Christians believed) some harmless mode of vegetation might have peopled Paradise."[46] Defeated by Sue's persistence, Richard consents to the ending of their sexual relationship. Ideas and their authors matter differently to Jude. Arriving in Christminster, he becomes intensely conscious of great minds haunting the place, of the great divines and theologians (Bishop Ken, John Wesley, and the Tractarians—Newman, Keble and Pusey), of poets (Ben Jonson, Browning, and Swinburne), of essayists (Addison and Arnold), of a politician (Peel), and even of the spokesman of Enlightenment skepticism (Gibbon).[47] Later, having advanced from the religiosity of his young manhood, and feeling that his ambitions have been diverted by his sexual life, he is led to burning his theological books:

> It was nearly one o'clock in the morning before the leaves, covers, and binding of Jeremy Taylor, Butler, Doddridge, Paley, Pusey, Newman, and the rest had gone to ashes; but the night was quiet, and as he turned and turned the paper shreds with the fork, the sense of being no longer a hypocrite to himself afforded his mind a relief which gave him calm.[48]

Jude internalizes his reading as Sue does not, and casts it out as he develops intellectually.

46. Hardy, *Jude the Obscure*, 216.
47. Hardy, *Jude the Obscure*, 75n403.
48. Hardy, *Jude the Obscure*, 209–10.

The further trouble haunting Jude's relation with Sue is "bad blood." According to their great-aunt Drusilla, "The Fawleys were not made for wedlock. There's sommat in our blood that won't take kindly to the notion of being bound to do what we do readily enough if not bound"[49]—witness the failure of the marriages of Sue and Jude's parents. An ancestor was "hanged and gibbetted" for burglary, though he only broke into the house where his separated wife was living to obtain the body of their dead child so that he could bury it with his own family.[50] This inheritance is not just a matter of peasant superstition. The modern-minded Jude is troubled by the thought that "marriage with a blood-relation would duplicate the adverse conditions."[51] This expectation that things cannot turn out well for him and Sue because of their biological inheritance is part of the pervasive feeling in the narrative that they are destined for tragedy.

The final phase of the novel involves a fifth character, Father Time. To understand Father Time, not so much as a character but (to put it fantastically) as a cosmic portent, I place in evidence two of Hardy's poems. The first, "Hap," is dated 1866, twenty-eight years before the first version of *Jude the Obscure* was published, and the second, "A Philosophical Fantasy," was finished thirty-six years later, in 1926, but begun in 1920.

"Hap" is a celebrated expression of mid-Victorian atheism, and of the tragic pessimism present in all Hardy's writings.

Hap

If but some vengeful god would call me
From up the sky, and laugh: "Thou suffering thing,
Know that thy sorrow is my ecstasy,
That thy love's loss is my hate's profiting!"

49. Hardy, *Jude the Obscure*, 65.
50. Hardy, *Jude the Obscure*, 272.
51. Hardy, *Jude the Obscure*, 84.

Then would I bear it, clench myself, and die,
Steeled by the sense of ire unmerited;
Half-eased in that a Powerfuller than I
Had willed and meted me the tears I shed.

But not so. How arrives it joy lies slain,
And why unblooms the best hope ever sown?
—Crass Causality obstructs the sun and rain,
And dicing Time for gladness casts a moan . . .
These purblind Doomsters had as readily strown
Blisses about my pilgrimage as pain.[52]

Among Victorian poets, only Robert Browning (1812–89) matches Hardy's antilyrical awkwardness ("would call me," "my hate's profiting," "a Powerfuller," "unblooms the best hope ever sown," "strown/ Blisses"). But whereas a Browning poem presents an energetic pursuit of hard, complex truthfulness about human life as it is, Hardy's antilyricism enforces an uncompromising despair, a dogged resistance to any consolation about cosmic reality. "Hap" could stand as the epigraph of nearly all Hardy's fictions before *Jude the Obscure*, and indeed for the latter as far as I have considered it: "dicing Time" is chance, "Crass Causality" is necessity—the axes of biological determinism—the headquarters from which "conjunctive orders" are issued is indifferent to the well-being of its subordinates, but it has, if not purposes, then a direction, Comte's or Spencer's or Darwin's.

"A Philosophical Fantasy"[53] dismantles even this stern picture. It derives from Hardy's interest in Giacomo Leopardi (1798–1837), especially the latter's "Dialogue between Nature and an Icelander" (1824), and summarizes ideas that were given fuller expression in the only long work completed by Hardy after *Jude the Obscure*: *The Dynasts*, a poetic drama, published between 1904 and 1908. It is prefaced by an epigraph: "Milton . . . made God argue —Walter Bagehot." The "God" and principal speaker of Hardy's poem, how-

52. Hardy, *Collected Poems*, 7.

53. Hardy, *Collected Poems*, 852–56.

ever, is not the dark figure of "the Father" in Milton's *Paradise Lost*, but is addressed or self-described as "Causer," "sir or Madam," or "It" (the latter is agreed on, since "God" is not bothered about names or gender). "It" is also described as "dream-projected," "blind force persisting," "Aimless."

The tone adopted by "It" is gracelessly anti-Miltonic. As Milton represents him, the Father ends the opening exchange between the Son and himself before the angels in heaven as follows:

> Meanwhile
> The world shall burn, and from her ashes spring
> New heaven and earth, wherein the just shall dwell,
> And after all their tribulation long
> See golden days, fruitful of golden deeds,
> With joy and love triumphing, and fair truth.
> Then thou thy royal sceptre shalt lay by,
> For regal sceptre then no more shall need,
> God shall be all in all. But all ye gods,
> Adore him, who to compass all this dies,
> Adore the Son, and honour him as me.
> (III 333–43)

Hardy's "It" has a different way with words:

> Well, if thou wilt, then, ask me:
> To answer will not task me:
> I've a response, I doubt not,
> And quite agree to flout not
> Thy question, if of reason,
> Albeit not quite in season:
> A universe to marshal,
> What god can give but partial
> Eye to frail earth—life-shotten
> Ere long, extinct, forgotten! . . .

No verse could be less dignified or further removed from Miltonic eloquence than these seven-syllable couplets (stumbling one syllable short of the more usual, if still informal eight) that squeeze the structure of the English sentence and rely on two-syllable rhymes, including "ask me" / "task me" and "life-shotten" / "begotten"; "shotten" is normally used of herring that have just spawned and are not for cooking. Hardy's "It" gives only passing attention to an unappetizing Darwinian earth that spawns life like a fish and is then extinguished and forgotten.

The interviewer of "It"—whom for convenience I will call "Hardy"—suggests that the world has not fulfilled "It"'s original intention. Human vanity prompts such questions, "It" replies. Nor does "It" mind being regarded as a human fantasy; only the "witless" and "weak" would imagine that

> *Man's* shape must needs resemble
> Mine, that makes the zodiacs tremble!

But "It" promises to meet "Hardy" or a later representative early in his next creation, or maybe the one after that, rather as God is supposed to have met Adam in his garden—even though "in timeless truth," "It" declares, Adam never existed. "It" claims to be a lover of procrastination—

> To use the words in thy sense
> Which have no hold on my sense.

Language, according to "It," cannot encompass reality—meaning depends on where and what you are. Judeo-Christian myths are nonsense; "Hardy" may speak "Of the world's sore situation," but "It" has no sense of "the Fall," which symbolically gave rise to that soreness, and "no sense" either of "moral features,"

> Or of ethical endeavour,
> Or of justice to Earth's creatures,
> Of how right from wrong to sever:
> Let these be as men learn such;
> For me I don't discern such,
> And—real enough I daresay—
> I know them but by hearsay

As something time hath rendered
Out of substance I engendered,
Time, too, being a condition
Beyond my recognition.

Time is no more real to "It" than language, morality, or justice. The main topic—"Hardy's" notion of "unfulfilled intention" in the universe—is therefore meaningless also, since intention implies time. "Being unconscious of my doings," "It" has been neither unkind nor loving "to human tribes," just mindless. Nevertheless, "It" promises to explain to the successor of "Hardy":

What thing it was befell me . . .
And acted to compel me
By that purposeless propension
Which is mine, and not intention,
Along lines of least resistance,
Or, in brief, unsensed persistence,
That saddens thy existence
To think my so-called scheming
Not that of my first dreaming.

Though it is hard to see how, in light of all this, "It" can promise anything, "Hardy"'s successor may eventually grasp what compelled "It" to yield to the "*purposeless propension*," mindless drive, which brought the world and its successors into being, which "It" declares "is mine," and which, having begun in unreason, any world's outcomes must be in principle unknowable, and, except in the rough approximations of improvised language, unstateable. If crass causality is to be understood as "information" that is *in practice* undecodeable (like the alleged effect of a butterfly's wings on the weather a continent away), purposeless propension is completely random, mere "noise," *in principle* undecodeable, literally nothing. Headquarters? What headquarters?

Chance and necessity—"Hap"—underpin Hardy's novels prior to *Jude the Obscure*. The novelist and critic Tim Parks has written about the "accumulation of coincidences" in *The Return of the Native* (1878).

> It's not that Hardy is such a poor writer that he needs to use elements of chance to move his stories on: rather, he tosses them in mad abundance to create a situation where no one is responsible but everyone can blame everyone else—as well as themselves and the weather and destiny and witchcraft and Victorian bigotry and more or less anything you care to mention.[54]

The result is catastrophic misery and death for all the main characters, except—gratuitously—for two, who get married and live happily ever after. *The Return of the Native,* in other words, is "Hap" in three volumes.

Crass causality also operates in *Jude the Obscure*—in the events that lead to Sue's expulsion from college, or Richard's disastrous defiance of public opinion about his separation from Sue, or Jude's accidental choice of the hotel, or the widowed Arabella's meetings with Sue and Richard on the same afternoon. Crass causality continues to operate in the final stages of the novel. Nevertheless, Hardy is much less reliant in *Jude the Obscure* on the kind of elaborate accumulation of coincidences described by Parks. Something far more troubling is at work.

The final stage of the novel begins with the introduction of Father Time. Sue and Arabella's first meeting not only prompts Sue to have sex with Jude but also results in Jude's being told (later by letter) that he and Arabella have a son, who has been living with his grandparents in Australia but has now been shipped back to England. Married to Cartlett, Arabella wants Jude and Sue to look after the boy, and they agree. Sue subsequently has two children of her own. She and Jude are twice on the verge of marrying but pull back in distaste. Instead they travel to London, and Sue returns wearing a ring. But their irregular union and Jude's frail health put them un-

54. Parks, "Bitten by an Adder," 12.

der financial and social pressure. Moving from place to place, they arrive in Christminster on a rainy day. Sue is pregnant again. Jude, still obsessed with his youthful dreams, insists on watching an academic procession. Late in the day, they can only find lodgings for Sue and the children—Jude sleeps in a pub. Sue impulsively admits to her landlord's wife that she and Jude aren't married, and she is told she must quit the lodgings in the morning. Her stepson asks her why things are so difficult for them. Sue explains that children are not popular in lodgings. Next day, she leaves the children in the house as she tries to find new accommodation. In her absence, the boy hangs his two siblings from door handles and then himself. His infamous suicide note explains: "*Done because we are too meny.*"[55] Faced with this horror, Sue miscarries. Filled with sorrow and guilt, she insists that she must return to Richard. They remarry, but at first sleep apart. Though she still finds Richard physically repellant, however, she forces herself to have sex with him. Jude turns to drink and is manipulated into remarrying Arabella, who is still obsessed with him: "his long lashes, dark brows and curly black hair and beard" have a strong appeal for "a woman of rank passion."[56] But his health is broken; Arabella tires of nursing him and goes off to enjoy the spectacle of college boat races. She returns to find him dead, but she goes back to the festivities without telling anyone. She meets up with a wandering quack doctor, easily twice her age, and decides to make the best of things by becoming his woman.

Darwinian evolution is terribly illustrated in these events. Admittedly, the "fittest" (presumably Jude and Arabella) do not pass on their genes, while the sexually ambivalent Sue, "ethereal, fine-nerved, sensitive . . . quite unfitted by temperament and instinct to fulfil the conditions of the matrimonial relation,"[57] and the sexually

55. Hardy, *Jude the Obscure*, 325.
56. Hardy, *Jude the Obscure*, 367.
57. Hardy, *Jude the Obscure*, 210.

repellant Richard may well do so. At one point, Sue even thinks that having children may be "presumptuous."[58] Darwinists would point out, however, that evolution is indifferent to particular cases, that the genetic inheritances that survive do so because of their fitness over the long term, but this would be no comfort to Hardy because genetically sidetracked human beings are just as conscious as genetically successful ones. Pain and pleasure are mere tools in the evolutionary process, yet for human beings they alone (in the broadest terms) are what count.

In this context, "temperament"—and especially its inherited component—is also a complex mix of chance and necessity. Once Sue accepts Jude as her lover, they show "that tender attention to each other which the shyest can scarcely disguise,"[59] in spite of Arabella's contempt for it—"silly fools—like two children!"[60] But the sexual tension between them never goes away. After the catastrophe, Jude tells Sue, "Your natural instincts are perfectly healthy; not quite so impassioned, perhaps, as I could wish; but good, and dear and pure ... you are absolutely the most ethereal, least sensual woman I ever knew to exist without sexlessness."[61] The overall quality of their relationship seems to be the novel's highest value, however, a wonderful mix of what chance and necessity can realize at the human level. What is distinctive in their relationship is suggested by Hardy's description of them as being "like cronies in a tavern" and in Jude's description of Sue as the "sweetest and most disinterested comrade" and "my curious little comrade."[62] The modern reader may bridle at Jude's calling Sue "little"—"jealous little Sue,"[63] "Now we are right again, aren't we little girl!"[64] but Jude only addresses

58. Hardy, *Jude the Obscure*, 301.
59. Hardy, *Jude the Obscure*, 281.
60. Hardy, *Jude the Obscure*, 284.
61. Hardy, *Jude the Obscure*, 333.
62. Hardy, *Jude the Obscure*, 264.
63. Hardy, *Jude the Obscure*, 268.
64. Hardy, *Jude the Obscure*, 292.

Sue like this after they have become lovers, such expressions, used by both sexes, being a customary way of signaling sexual intimacy. In the eyes of Arabella, and of the narrator, *both* lovers seem childlike. The point being made is that the richest part of their relationship, their life as comrades and cronies, is independent of sexual desire—there is much, much more to it than biological imperatives. That is why it is not just a question of Hardy's allowing Sue, as an emerging "type" of womanhood, "to break down at the end," appalling as that breakdown is. What is destroyed is not "the slight, pale "bachelor girl"—the intellectualized, emancipated bundle of nerves," but a special, highly significant *relationship*. And to understand the significance (or lack of it) of that destruction, its precipitation by Jude and Arabella's son needs to be examined.

"Father Time," sometimes shortened to "Time," tells Jude and Sue that he was never christened because "if I died in damnation, 'twould save the expense of a Christian funeral!" "We'll have him christened," Jude says, "the day we are married"[65]—but they never are. Father Time travels by himself from Australia, and Arabella puts him on a train in London with the key to his baggage round his neck and his ticket stuck in his hat. Other passengers are amused by the antics of a kitten. Time, however, regards the kitten "with saucer eyes, as if to say: 'All laughing comes from misapprehension. Rightly looked at there is no laughable thing under the sun.'"[66] In his final conversation with Sue, he asks her why people have children if they "make so much trouble." It "is a law of nature," Sue tells him. Time is sadly aware that Sue isn't his real mother and that he has troubled everyone. He wishes he "hadn't been born"—unwanted children, he says, "should be killed directly, before their souls come to 'em." When he hears that Jude and Sue are expecting another child, he cries out: "O you don't care, you don't care! ... How *ever* could you

65. Hardy, *Jude the Obscure*, 270.

66. Hardy, *Jude the Obscure*, 265–66.

mother, be so wicked and cruel as this ... 'tis done o' purpose!—'tis—'tis!"[67]

The modern reader may be tempted to "diagnose" Time, to put him on some sort of "spectrum." In fact, two "diagnoses" are offered for the reader's consideration, both of their period, both based on rudimentary evolutionary theory, and neither endorsed by the author. Sue suggests "that these preternaturally old boys almost always come from new countries,"[68] and after the tragedy, when Sue blames herself for not being frank with the child about how babies come to be "expected," Jude says,

> No ... It was his nature to do it. The doctor says there are such boys springing up amongst us—boys of a sort unknown in the last generation—the outcome of new views of life. They seem to see all its terrors before they are old enough to have staying power to resist them. He says it is the beginning of the coming universal wish not to live. He's an advanced man, the doctor.[69]

Sufficiently advanced to have anticipated the Freudian "death wish"? We are not told, of course, *how* "new views of life" might produce new kinds of children.

But the question is not whether boys like Time exist in the "modern" world but why he is made the agent of a catastrophe so gratuitously horrible that it destroys Sue as a rational, sensitive woman, as a "comrade." There might seem to be more "convincing" ways in which Time might have brought about the deaths of the children, either accidentally or on purpose—drowning them and himself in the river, for example. Such would be the kind of expected outcome in a novel written on the lines of *The Return of the Native*, in which crass causality operates as the decisive trigger of tragedy. Father Time and his terrible act seem to be something else. He is a deliberate, a willful

67. Hardy, *Jude the Obscure*, 323.
68. Hardy, *Jude the Obscure*, 270.
69. Hardy, *Jude the Obscure*, 326.

choice by the narrator to construct extreme and random horror: that is what he *means*.

Hardy writes about Father Time with some eloquence. When the boy arrives at Aldbrickham station, he is directed to the street where Jude and Sue are living:

> The child fell into a steady mechanical creep which had in it an impersonal quality—the movement of the wave, or of the breeze, or of the cloud. He followed his directions literally, without an inquiring gaze at anything. Children begin with detail and learn up to the general; they begin with the contiguous and gradually comprehend the universal. The boy seemed to have begun with the generals of life, and never to have concerned himself with the particulars. To him the houses, the willow, the obscure fields beyond, were apparently regarded as human dwellings in the abstract, vegetation, and the wide dark world.[70]

Because Arabella and his grandparents have failed to educate the boy in "the particulars" of life, Jude and Sue do so, with only partial success. By the time he has his final conversation with Sue, his capacity for feeling emotion and for thoughtful expression of his opinions has developed considerably, but he is still strange. He is incapable, for example, of imagining what effect his killing of the children and himself will have on his parents.

The description of his dead body is important:

> The boy's face expressed the whole tale of their situation. On that little shape had converged all the inauspiciousness and shadow which had darkened the first union of Jude, and all the accidents, mistakes, fears, errors of the last. He was their nodal point, their focus, their expression in a single term. For the rashness of those parents he had groaned, for their ill assortment he had quaked, and for the misfortunes of these he had died.[71]

He is a victim first of Jude and Arabella's inappropriate marriage, then of "the misfortunes" of Jude and Sue's life together. But how? The words "inauspiciousness and shadow" are not "scientific." The

70. Hardy, *Jude the Obscure*, 267.
71. Hardy, *Jude the Obscure*, 326.

emphasis in "expressed" "tale," "nodal point," "focus," "expression in a single term" is on Time as a "sign" to be interpreted, not a "case" to be understood. In assuming that children "begin with detail" and only "gradually comprehend the universal," which was the standard "Associationist" theory of mental development, Hardy implies that Time's mental formation is *uncaused*. Just as "It" was to do in "A Philosophical Fantasy," the child's mind falls outside science without falling into religion or mysticism:

> He was Age masquerading as Juvenility, and doing it so badly that his real self showed through crevices. A ground swell from ancient years of night seemed now and then to lift the child in this his morning-life, when his face took a back view over some great Atlantic of time, and appeared not to care what it saw.[72]

Even after the intrusion of Father Time into the narrative, Hardy's readers are under pressure to continue reading *Jude the Obscure* as a narrative dominated by chance and necessity. The gloomy shared family history of Jude and Sue that in part accounts for their failure to marry, the marriage laws then prevailing—which Hardy claims in the "Postscript" of 1912 that he "used in great part as the tragic machinery of the tale"[73]—the class-based educational system, the sick Jude's obstinacy in watching the academic procession, Sue's impulsive confession, and the family's threatened homelessness are important in generating a context for Father Time's act. But they do *nothing* to account for it. It simply happens. Purposeless propension supersedes crass causality. Father Time, who could look at the "great Atlantic" of the past as if it were nothing, is himself nothing, an uncaused sport of nature—like "It" in "A Philosophical Fantasy" an improvised literary device, whose function is to personify the randomness, the core of nothing, which chance and necessity so usefully conceal.

72. Hardy, *Jude the Obscure*, 266.
73. Hardy, *Jude the Obscure*, xlv.

In his "Preface to the First Edition", Hardy describes the novel as "simply an endeavour to give shape and coherence to a series of seemings."[74] He has not laboriously and systematically recorded observable data in the manner of the "Naturalist" school of novelists. *Jude the Obscure* is not about the world as it *is*, but about how things *seem* to its author. Between 1895 and the final revised edition in 1928, he made numerous modifications, especially to the way Sue is presented. But like so much of what Hardy wrote about his own work, "an endeavor to give shape and coherence to a series of seemings" leaves the reader feeling that it would have been helpful if Hardy had explained himself more fully. What *sort* of "shape and coherence" does he have in mind, and how far does he think he has succeeded?

One thing seems clear. To have gone back to writing novels like *The Return of the Native, The Mayor of Casterbridge* (1886), or *Tess of the d'Urbervilles* (1891) would have implicitly signaled a repudiation of Father Time as a "seeming" in *Jude the Obscure.* On the other hand, purposeless propension, as a move beyond crass causality, could only figure once in Hardy's work *as a novelist.* He could continue to write poems and short stories illustrating the terrible beauties of chance and necessity, but the equivalent of Father Time in a later novel would have become predictable, and therefore just what purposeless propension is *not.* The move once made, the Hardyean novel had checkmated itself.

There is a film of Pablo Picasso (1881–1973) working on a painting on glass. The development of the design is recorded without interruption by a camera on the other side of the glass—the reversed image revealing the emerging composition as Picasso sees it. The logic of the buildup slowly reveals itself, but there comes a point at which (it seems) Picasso loses his way; the composition becomes confused, and suddenly a disfiguring streak is splashed across the glass, and the picture is abandoned and destroyed. Father Time and his de-

74. Hardy, *Jude the Obscure,* xliii.

struction of the children may be compared to that disfiguring streak, except of course that instead of abandoning his project, Hardy published it repeatedly, with corrections, for the remainder of his life. The streak becomes the point. Moreover, unlike the writers of other late nineteenth-century fiction, he has nothing to say about how we might live with nothing. For him it is simply there to be seen.

From the perspective (if it may be called such) of It, George Eliot's willing to will, Wilde's humiliation on the station platform, and the flogged Prince's mindless pawings of the air simply do not matter—nor does *Jouissance,* nor does *misericordia.* Is Hardy's dark *theoria* all we are left with?

Part II

The Grant of Freedom

My heart leaps up when I behold
A rainbow in the sky
—William Wordsworth

5

Writing and Freedom

> And you never know, captain
> You never know, not with what you might call
> metaphysical certainty, captain: our phenomenology
> is but limited, captain.
>
> —*David Jones, "The Lady of the Pool," The Anathemata*

Much has been written about freedom by philosophers, poets, and even scientists. And writing can also be where writers and readers discover freedom. Consider first some ideas developed by two prominent philosophers, then an anecdote about a great scientist, and finally samples of writing by a scientist and a poet.

Paul Ricoeur was a phenomenologist and an analytical philosopher. He came from a Protestant family and "bluntly" opposed "the school of suspicion" (Marx, Nietzsche, and Freud) with "the second faith ... that has undergone criticism."[1] His philosophy is based on "the Cogito," by which the mind is said to grasp itself in its own thinking, and on which, it is claimed, *after careful analysis*, "a final, ultimate foundation"[2] can and should be based. Describing the obscure workings of the mind that experiences nature is a precondition

1. Ricoeur, *Rule of Metaphor*, 28.
2. Ricoeur, *Oneself as Another*, 4.

of describing the obscure workings of nature, and this entails "the positing of the self."[3]

Ricoeur identifies two modes of certitude: "the certitude of the Cogito and the certitude of space."[4] He puts the latter "in brackets" while analyzing the former as an experience of autonomy. Consciousness, he asserts, does not disclose "a cluster of functions" that replaces a "central will,"[5] or "a mental physics in which succession of moments" is grasped "in terms of . . . causality."[6] Rather, "thought and movement . . . bring about an undecipherable unity, beyond effort"[7] observed in others and in the self. Freedom is a fact of consciousness and is bound up with the ability "to receive and approve values."[8] It occurs in the context of "desire," the involuntary, and "the fault."

Desire—wanting something whether or not you can get it—"fractures" the ego, but without it, willing would be mere process. Willing involves effort and culminates in a "*fiat*," which, "though it represents a discontinuity, springs from a certain continuity of voluntary experience."[9] The voluntary *requires* the involuntary, since without it the voluntary would be meaningless. The fault is darker, a vast domain,[10] "an absolute irrational,"[11] giving rise to "Reproach, suspicion, concupiscence, envy, hurt and grief . . . various names for chasing the wind." It leads to "bondage to the Passions—to *Nothing*," the latter being "an inexhaustible source of error,"[12] because it posits the freedom of indifference. Actions are said to exhibit the freedom

3. Ricoeur, *Rule of Metaphor*, 43.
4. Ricoeur, *Freedom and Nature*, 218.
5. Ricoeur, *Freedom and Nature*, 117.
6. Ricoeur, *Freedom and Nature*, 136.
7. Ricoeur, *Freedom and Nature*, 249.
8. Ricoeur, *Freedom and Nature*, 21.
9. Ricoeur, *Freedom and Nature*, 137.
10. Ricoeur, *Freedom and Nature*, 22.
11. Ricoeur, *Freedom and Nature*, 24.
12. Ricoeur, *Freedom and Nature*, 23.

of indifference when, after a complete description of a state of mind, it would make equal sense to say an agent decided to act or not to act,[13] and for Ricoeur, this is simply "risked choice," "default of adequate reason."[14] It eliminates "the very essence of motivation,"[15] replacing it with "the "bad infinite"" of passion.[16] By contrast, the freedom of spontaneity, unforced, motivated choosing, is "an infinite without disorder"[17] that "can 'incline without compelling'":[18] "the highest form of the will . . . has its reasons" and acts on them without coercion; "all choice is determined by its motives."[19]

Reflection before decision-making is "in principle endless"[20] and cannot be concluded straightforwardly by "determination by reasons."[21] Instead, "the indivisible mass of personality brings an enthusiasm and weight which no calculus and no dialogue can equal";[22] conclusions are reached by "the free vision of attention,"[23] a controlled shifting and holding of "the focus,"[24] which "reveals the 'I' in the *fiat*" and makes "the decision . . . a personal and direct achievement of the will which intervenes in order to tip the scales."[25] Suddenly, "my project is determinate, my reasons become determinate" in "the irruption of choice."[26] Provided "the term 'force'" is not modeled on "physical force,"[27] it applies to the "con-

13. See Myers, *Milton and Free Will*, 77.
14. Ricoeur, *Freedom and Nature*, 170.
15. Ricoeur, *Freedom and Nature*, 81.
16. Ricoeur, *Freedom and Nature*, 24.
17. Ricoeur, *Freedom and Nature*, 24.
18. Ricoeur, *Freedom and Nature*, 80.
19. Ricoeur, *Freedom and Nature*, 182.
20. Ricoeur, *Freedom and Nature*, 47.
21. Ricoeur, *Freedom and Nature*, 158.
22. Ricoeur, *Freedom and Nature*, 163.
23. Ricoeur, *Freedom and Nature*, 157.
24. Ricoeur, *Freedom and Nature*, 150.
25. Ricoeur, *Freedom and Nature*, 176.
26. Ricoeur, *Freedom and Nature*, 172.
27. Ricoeur, *Freedom and Nature*, 177.

trol over ... attention" that makes the *fiat* "a decision rather than a mental mechanism."[28] Though "there is no moment of freedom,"[29] consciousness "progresses simultaneously towards a judgment of preference and towards an act of election ... two different dimensions of the same concrete act."[30]

Freedom has to accommodate two other kinds of involuntariness, "character" and the unconscious. Character—"the set of lasting dispositions by which a person is recognized,"[31] "the 'what' of the 'who'"[32]—is an abiding given to which it is possible to *consent.* "A freedom situated by the fate of a character to which it consents becomes a destiny, a vocation."[33] The (Freudian) unconscious is "an obverse, a nether side" of consciousness, the site of "'something' issuing from the past... [and] oppressing consciousness."[34] It "does not think, does not perceive, does not remember, does not judge"[35] and therefore does not compromise "authentic awareness."[36] It contributes to mental disruption, but it "is not thought ... not body." It is not a memory, more "akin to habit."[37] "There is no *my* unconscious as there is *my* personality."[38] The unconscious is an "it"—Id.

Freedom for Ricoeur may have a lot to contend with but it is *there,* at the center of human self-awareness. "Freedom ... says NO in wresting itself from misfortune and absurdity."[39]

The American cognitive philosopher Daniel C. Dennett is chalk to Ricoeur's cheese. Ricoeur's thinking is infused with religious

28. Ricoeur, *Freedom and Nature,* 178.
29. Ricoeur, *Freedom and Nature,* 186.
30. Ricoeur, *Freedom and Nature,* 182.
31. Ricoeur, *Oneself as Another,* 121.
32. Ricoeur, *Oneself as Another,* 122.
33. Ricoeur, *Freedom and Nature,* 373.
34. Ricoeur, *Freedom and Nature,* 391.
35. Ricoeur, *Freedom and Nature,* 387.
36. Ricoeur, *Freedom and Nature,* 388.
37. Ricoeur, *Freedom and Nature,* 391.
38. Ricoeur, *Freedom and Nature,* 392.
39. Ricoeur, *Freedom and Nature,* 354.

intuitions; Dennett is "a good materialist, atheist Darwinian."[40] Ricoeur distinguishes between "the certitude of the Cogito and the certitude of space"; Dennett asks why anyone "should ... expect that *consciousness* would bifurcate the universe."[41] He regards philosophers who are serious about the "famous formulation 'what is it like?'"—the debate about which dates from Thomas Nagel's essay "What Is It Like to Be a Bat?" (1974)—as "an embarrassment."[42] The more important question is "how this marvelous treasure trove was possible."[43] It is not "nature," therefore, that "must be bracketed," but the "special subjective properties"[44] that phenomenologists prioritize. To "trace events to their ultimate causes" is to be "forced into reductionist views";[45] "the sole choreographer is physical law."[46] Its working in the brain "is ... hopelessly inscrutable"[47] and will remain so until the "sub-personal information structures and events" of the brain are aligned with clearly identified "mental states."[48] But though what it is *like* to intend, believe, or desire is unimportant, *imputed* or "*as-if*" "intentions," "beliefs," and "desires" have explanatory power: "*what for*" questions are important and can be answered independently of answers to "*how come*" questions.[49] DNA can be *read* as if it had a goal, reproduction,[50] and evolution as if it were a prolonged R&D (research and development) procedure. If you want to explain things, "the intentional stance works."[51]

Computers and brains are alike in some ways and not in others.

40. Dennett, *From Bacteria to Bach and Back*, 26.
41. Dennett, *From Bacteria to Bach and Back*, 15.
42. Dennett, *From Bacteria to Bach and Back*, 337.
43. Dennett, *From Bacteria to Bach and Back*, 364.
44. Dennett, *From Bacteria to Bach and Back*, 365.
45. Dennett, *Brainstorms*, 184.
46. Hofstadter and Dennett, *Mind's I*, 453.
47. Dennett, *Elbow Room*, 77.
48. Dennett, *From Bacteria to Bach and Back*, 367.
49. Dennett, *From Bacteria to Bach and Back*, 40.
50. Dennett, *Brainstorms*, 73.
51. Dennett, *Brainstorms*, 96.

"The brain is not a digital computer, but it is still a kind of computer."[52] Unlike existing serial computers, which execute one computation at a time, though at amazing speed, the brain operates a parallel computational array capable of executing "many millions of 'computations' simultaneously spread over [its] whole fabric."[53] You can't program a serial computer to analyze every possible future move early in a game of chess, but you can program it to use data-informed "bottom-up" procedures that are good enough to beat grand masters. Similarly, our brains can't process all the relevant data before making a decision, but they can process enough of them to give decisions a good chance of being good at the moment a built-in heuristic cutoff procedure shuts data-processing down and action follows. We "must relinquish control over the incomplete set of considerations on which we act."[54]

A major difference between animal and human brains is the "infestation" of the latter by "memes," behaviors that can be imitated. Memes "are transmitted perceptually, not genetically."[55] They are "mindless informational things that provoke coalitions of rebellious neurons to support them."[56] Like genes, they are "successful" provided they contribute to the reproductive effectiveness of their hosts (or are freeloaders). Some animal behavior (much birdsong, for instance) is memetic, but animal brains are limited as hosts to memes. Not so human brains. Early in the evolutionary process, a major advance occurred when one simple-cell organism was enclosed by another simple-cell organism to form the more complex eukaryotic cell, from which multicellular life evolved.[57] Similarly, when memes got inside human brains, "two largely independent legacies of R&D

52. Dennett, *Brainstorms*, 110.

53. Dennett, *Brainstorms*, 155.

54. Dennett, *Elbow Room*, 87.

55. Dennett, *From Bacteria to Bach and Back*, 206.

56. Dennett, *From Bacteria to Bach and Back*, 173.

57. Dennett, *From Bacteria to Bach and Back*, 8.

were united ... to create ... the *comprehending* mind."[58] Perhaps vocalizations and gestures ("pronounceable proto-words ... silent behavioral habits")[59] first entered human brains (as they enter parrot brains) "without belonging ... or being favored" by their hosts,[60] but, with the development of language, human intercommunication became diversified, meme-rich human beings could talk to themselves as well as to others and even engage in "a private, proprietary communication-control buffer that [created] opportunities for *guided* deception—and, coincidentally, opportunities for self-deception."[61] From this *human* consciousness emerged.

"Consciousness exists," Dennett declares, "but it is not what most folks think it is."[62] He dismisses the "Cartesian Theater" model—"the illusion that there is an inner eye ... and an inner ear,"[63] a homunculus monitoring current thoughts and experiences: "*all* the work done in the Cartesian Theater," he insists, "has to be broken up and distributed ... to lesser agencies in the brain."[64] What, then, does consciousness *do*? It is the site of what he calls "personal user-illusions." The cursor on a laptop screen clicks on an icon to open a file, though that is a partial version of what is really happening in the laptop. In a comparable way, "a system of user illusions ... [makes] *versions* of ... cognitive processes—otherwise ... imperceptible— ... accessible ... for purposes of communication."[65] I explain what I am doing with my computer by referring to the desktop icons. Similarly, I explain what I am doing with my life by referring to "icons" of consciousness. So, a "*first-person* point of view of [one's] own mind is not so different from [a] *second-person* point of view" of

58. Dennett, *From Bacteria to Bach and Back*, 389.
59. Dennett, *From Bacteria to Bach and Back*, 285.
60. Dennett, *From Bacteria to Bach and Back*, 122.
61. Dennett, *From Bacteria to Bach and Back*, 342.
62. Dennett, *From Bacteria to Bach and Back*, 223.
63. Dennett, *From Bacteria to Bach and Back*, 185.
64. Dennett, *From Bacteria to Bach and Back*, 353.
65. Dennett, *From Bacteria to Bach and Back*, 344.

someone else's.[66] And two minds are better than one. "Heterophenomenology is more accurate ... once you control for lying."[67]

Two experiences arise from this: the concepts of *free will* and the *self*. As I've pointed out, Dennett holds that a "heuristic" or *blind* shutdown procedure halts practical reasoning and precipitates action. Far from being "a personal power somehow isolated from physical causation," willing is the outcome of the work of those "lesser agencies in the brain" referred to earlier. At the same time, however, a "user-illusion" of *personal* decision-making and responsibility emerges. The arbitrary shutdown procedure is concealed and its consequences rationalized. Free agency is thus "in the same category with colors, opportunities, dollars, promises and love,"[68] part of an individual's "personal ontology"[69]—an illusion—but a *real* illusion, like a rainbow, something that is there even if it is not what you think it is.

For practical purposes, however, what you imagine free agency to be makes sense. Whenever people act without being subject to coercive external pressures, they act *accountably*, just as public bodies—corporations, police forces, and the military—do. *Real* free will, unlike Ricoeur's freedom of spontaneity, is the outcome of hidden computational functions, which consciousness *registers* as choosing. All living things, Dennett suggests, "from single cells to elephants," have "ontologies"—those aspects of themselves and their situation that are relevant to their life, their *Umwelt*. This includes "a rudimentary 'sense of self.'"[70] A human being's "ontology" includes families, money, food, cats, expectations, the taste of mushrooms—*and* an autonomous, accountable "me."

This is best understood "as a *center of narrative gravity* ... the au-

66. Dennett, *From Bacteria to Bach and Back*, 345.
67. Dennett, *From Bacteria to Bach and Back*, 351.
68. Dennett, *From Bacteria to Bach and Back*, 368.
69. Dennett, *From Bacteria to Bach and Back*, 369.
70. Dennett, *From Bacteria to Bach and Back*, 343.

thor of both deeds and words."[71] It is accessed through a "rather narrow and heavily edited channel"[72] best described in "a metaphorical idiom." The self is in effect a fictional character constructed to make the material of a life "into a single good story." People are "virtual persons" who spin stories about themselves, "weaving them like spiderwebs into self-protective strings of *narrative*,"[73] until, that is, the narrative begins to spin them. "I" am an autobiographical fiction that a computing brain tells about itself. That "I" don't "feel" like a computational system, and that my past does not seem like a computer-assembled story shows what a talented author is telling my tale. The divide between Ricoeur and Dennett is both striking and complicated.

Ricoeur rejects "a mental physics in which succession of moments" is grasped "in terms of . . . causality," and a "central will" is replaced by "a cluster of functions." But a Cognitive Philosopher could reasonably reply, "Determinism doesn't *operate* at the 'mental' level, but at the level of physical law," and consciousness could only function as it does if the physical operations sustaining it remained outside it. Ricoeur describes the unconscious as "vital, sexual, infantile, perhaps even ancestral," but his denial that this makes consciousness "only a disguise of its own unconscious"[74] (in effect a Freudian user illusion) is unargued. "The refusal to conceive of the unconscious as thinking," Ricoeur writes, "is a foregone conclusion of freedom itself,"[75] to which a Cognitive Philosopher could reply, "A foregone conclusion of physical law is that 'freedom' cannot have foregone conclusions." Ricoeur claims to confront the unconscious just "as Descartes confronted the great deceiver: I save myself by . . . the refusal to make my thought conform to something which is not

71. Dennett, *From Bacteria to Bach and Back*, 344.
72. Dennett, *From Bacteria to Bach and Back*, 346.
73. Dennett, *Consciousness Explained*, 417–18.
74. Ricoeur, *Freedom and Nature*, 401.
75. Ricoeur, *Freedom and Nature*, 386.

also conscious."[76] Both these assertions, however, look like grandstanding. Ricoeur insists that practical reasoning can be concluded by the "mastering of [a] process whose flux itself is radically involuntary,"[77] by "the free vision of attention,"[78] but by his own admission, "repression is a real exclusion which a phenomenology of the implicit or co-intended can never reach."[79] So there are occasions when "attention" *cannot* know the extent to which it is distorted by the dynamics of "repression." And if attention were always "free," how would "back-sliding" be possible? Isn't an impulse that "can 'incline' without compelling" simply a weak impulse? Ricoeur claims that "thought and movement ... bring about an undecipherable unity"; he writes of the "indivisible mass of personality which no calculus and no dialogue can equal," but this is to base his argument on ignorance and intellectual impotence. Cognitive Philosophers choose instead to analyze this alleged unity, and to suggest the kind of calculus that hard science may subject it to. Finally, Ricoeur designates "truthfulness" as "the threshold" of ethics.[80] But what if the "scientism" he dismisses is, for some, a basic truth, if it is *truthfulness* that motivates the Cognitive Philosopher to declare: "The 'ultimate foundation' of mental activity is material process. Here I stand. I can no other!'"?

In reply, a disciple of Ricoeur could challenge Dennett's critique of philosophers who represent consciousness as *bifurcating* the universe. For Ricoeur, it is not the *universe* that is bifurcated, but "the language of psychology and the language of physics,"[81] the "concepts of the Cogito and those of biology."[82] Dennett says little about

76. Ricoeur, *Freedom and Nature*, 403.
77. Ricoeur, *Freedom and Nature*, 152.
78. Ricoeur, *Freedom and Nature*, 157.
79. Ricoeur, *Rule of Metaphor*, 392.
80. Ricoeur, *Rule of Metaphor*, 280.
81. Ricoeur, *Freedom and Nature*, 68.
82. Ricoeur, *Freedom and Nature*, 420.

how language works, how nouns refer, and verbs relate to actions, as in "I follow her into the elevator"; "I follow her example"; "I follow her command"; "I follow her logic." I can *point* to her and to the elevator. I can *utter* her commands. Can I point to her logic, to "example," to myself? Dennett ignores the disciplines required by different orders of language.

He also underestimates his opponents' treatment of the Cogito. He suggests that it is only recently that an "*unconscious mind*" has ceased to be "seen as a contradiction in terms."[83] But Jeremiah, St. Paul, St. Augustine, St. Teresa of Avila, Descartes, Kant, and John Henry Newman all asserted the reality of the unconscious. It is the great Enlightenment philosophers—Locke, Hume, Kant (possibly), and Mill (certainly)—who denied it. Ricoeur holds that "phenomenology begins by a humiliation or wounding of the knowledge belonging to immediate consciousness."[84] He sees the body, "neither representation in me nor thing outside me," as "the ontic model for any conceivable [Freudian] unconscious."[85] Nor do Dennett's opponents envisage a "triumphant self," sovereign and "posited in abstraction as an invariable entity," "a homunculus" in a Cartesian Theater. On the contrary, Ricoeur sees the self as "inchoate, problematic," in "hesitation" yet called "to unity";[86] phenomenology, he claims, contests "the illusion of immediate self-knowledge";[87] it "begins by . . . a wounding of the knowledge belonging to immediate consciousness . . . though the Cogito is the starting point, you do not start from it";[88] it has to be found. He thinks the concept of the person "primitive," but this involves not "a second referent, distinct from the body, such as the Cartesian soul . . . but a single referent possessing two

83. Dennett, *From Bacteria to Bach and Back*, 100.
84. Ricoeur, *Rule of Metaphor*, 377.
85. Ricoeur, *Rule of Metaphor*, 382.
86. Ricoeur, *Freedom and Nature*, 140–41.
87. Ricoeur, *Rule of Metaphor*, 386.
88. Ricoeur, *Rule of Metaphor*, 377.

series of predicates: physical predicates and mental predicates."[89] To claim the body as one's own is to give the self a "logical force" that is "tied to utterance and not on the side of the 'thing.'"[90] The self cannot be pointed to alongside toast, coffee, and the Security Council of the United Nations.

Dennett envisages an alignment between mental states and structures in the brain. But this would have to be accounted for as well as observed. The weather determines the dials on a barometer, and similar dials can be used in controlling the temperature in my house. In each case the causal *direction* is crucial. Dennett would need to show that consciousness *never* determines events at the physical level. Also, he asserts that brains "execute many millions of 'computations' simultaneously," but says nothing about how these millions of computations are, or even might be, connected to form a single working system.

He relies on metaphors. Metaphysical or religious explanations are called "skyhooks"; "cranes" are sound ways of thinking, evolved by natural selection, "labor-saving products ... which have opened up Design Space for further cranes in an accelerating ... *cascade* of cranes"![91] He compares mistaken "assessments of our fellow humans—and of ourselves" to the ancient shell game in which an observer thinks a pea is under one shell when it is under another.[92] But the *sense* of a word in Dennett's usage is like the pea in the shell game. Consider the following statements:

> "Neurons ... are capable of self-organizing into teams that can take over important information handling work."[93]

89. Ricoeur, *Oneself as Another*, 33.
90. Ricoeur, *Oneself as Another*, 34.
91. Dennett, *From Bacteria to Bach and Back*, 379, my emphasis.
92. Dennett, *From Bacteria to Bach and Back*, 306.
93. Dennett, *From Bacteria to Bach and Back*, 163.

> "We can perform many ... *retrospectively* justifiable actions with only a vague conception of what we are up to ......sharpened by the self-attribution of reasons."[94]

> "All organisms from single cells to elephants, have a rudimentary 'sense of self.'"[95]

> "The evolution of memes provides the conditions for the evolution of a user interface that renders memes 'visible' to the 'self.'"[96]

> " ... among the things in our *Umwelt* ... are *ourselves*."[97]

> " ... the capacity to self-monitor, to subject the brain's patterns of reaction to yet another round ... of pattern discernment, that gives minds their breakthrough powers."[98]

Is there a meaning common to all these uses of "self"? Is Dennett himself playing the shell game? Or perhaps the meme "self" is playing the shell game in Dennett's prose: "once the infrastructure for culture has been designed and installed," he writes, "the possibility of parasitical memes exploiting that infrastructure is more or less guaranteed."[99]

While Dennett takes science seriously, "his tactics," he insists, are "those of an art."[100] There is no need, he writes, to be "afraid of a little metaphor."[101] He also endorses Freud's "championing of unconscious motivations."[102] But perhaps such motivations are at work both in his own use of metaphor and the stories he tells about him-

94. Dennett, *From Bacteria to Bach and Back*, 341.
95. Dennett, *From Bacteria to Bach and Back*, 343.
96. Dennett, *From Bacteria to Bach and Back*, 344.
97. Dennett, *From Bacteria to Bach and Back*, 356.
98. Dennett, *From Bacteria to Bach and Back*, 390.
99. Dennett, *From Bacteria to Bach and Back*, 217.
100. Dennett, *Elbow Room*, 3.
101. Dennett, *From Bacteria to Bach and Back*, 189.
102. Dennett, *From Bacteria to Bach and Back*, 100.

self, especially if Ricoeur is right in judging Freudian psychoanalysis to be true in the sense that history as opposed to empirical science can be true: “the analyst does not observe,” Ricoeur writes, “he interprets.”[103] Ricoeur points out that metaphor always conceals something; it “is nothing other than repression, and vice versa,”[104] a shell covering, or not covering, a pea; repression always dresses itself up in a figure of speech. “The mechanisms of the unconscious are not so much particular linguistic phenomena as they are paralinguistic distortions of ordinary language.”[105] The psychoanalytical “patient’s ‘story’” is told “in a field of speech ... hence the proper object of psychoanalysis is the effects of meaning—symptoms, delusions, illusions ... For the analyst, behavior is a segment of meaning.”[106] Psychoanalysis is thus *in-depth* heterophenomenology. Dennett’s failure to address the *possibility* of concealed distortion in his own writing, whether by manipulative memes or Freud’s unconscious or both, matches Ricoeur’s assumption that “the *fiat*” can master “the fault” and that it is enough simply to assert the mind’s “undecipherable unity.”

Does this mean that they are really saying the same thing? It can look like it. Like Dennett, Ricoeur perceives the self as narrative: “a theory of narrative,” he writes, “[contributes] to the constitution of the self.” The “concrete dialectic of selfhood and sameness ... attains its fullest development” “within the framework of narrative theory.”[107] The “narrative unity of a life ... [is] an unstable mixture of fabulation and actual experience.”[108] Again, if you reverse Ricoeur’s two statements, “choice *follows from* the final practical judgment” *and* “a practical judgment is final when choice *irrupts*,”[109] his version

103. Ricoeur, *Rule of Metaphor*, 365.
104. Ricoeur, *Rule of Metaphor*, 402.
105. Ricoeur, *Rule of Metaphor*, 404.
106. Ricoeur, *Rule of Metaphor*, 369.
107. Ricoeur, *Oneself as Another*, 114.
108. Ricoeur, *Oneself as Another*, 162.
109. Ricoeur, *Rule of Metaphor*, 181.

of willing looks much like Dennett's. When the heuristic cutoff function comes into play, choice follows! For his part, Dennett claims that imputed intentions, beliefs, and desires can explain behavior independently of the neurological underpinning that really drives it. But this argument depends on the *experience* of its validity, not on the neurological underpinnings of that experience. The intentional stance is a phenomenological construct through and through.

It is possible, then, that the difference between Ricoeur and Dennett is just a matter of style. Ricoeur's is a French manner of philosophizing characterized by the lofty abstract nouns and concretely metaphorical verbs; Dennett combines an eclectic scientific vocabulary with American demotic. They use the words "we" and "I" differently. Ricoeur's "we" is scholarly ("an immediate understanding of the voluntary and involuntary is what we have sought to elaborate first of all").[110] Or "we" can signify the philosophical community ("as we examine actual practice").[111] He uses "I" of the representative mind ("By communication with another, I have a different relation to a body"),[112] and rarely refers to himself except as author. Dennett's is an ebullient "I." He is present in his "we," though who else is in it varies. Sometimes it includes the whole human race ("We human beings"),[113] sometimes the scientific community ("We know that information about faces is somehow being processed"),[114] sometimes people who agree with him ("We are slowly shedding the habit of thinking that way"),[115] sometimes a tiny minority of human beings ("We send our children to universities").[116] His "you" can be jokily professorial ("bide your time ... instead of trying to

110. Ricoeur, *Rule of Metaphor*, 4.

111. Ricoeur, *Rule of Metaphor*, 13.

112. Ricoeur, *Rule of Metaphor*, 10.

113. Dennett, *From Bacteria to Bach and Back*, 70.

114. Dennett, *From Bacteria to Bach and Back*, 110.

115. Dennett, *From Bacteria to Bach and Back*, 100.

116. Dennett, *From Bacteria to Bach and Back*, 56.

derail my attempts at a calm, objective account of your premonitions").[117] Excluded are the sheep that are not of Dennett's fold, the Labelled ("pathetic bleats from the mouths of the Defenders"),[118] and the Misguided ("a frantic campaign of misbegotten criticism ... from scholars in the humanities and social sciences").[119] Different as their verbal manners may seem, however, Ricoeur and Dennett have, apparently, a similar aim: controlling their readers' thinking. The Hedgehog, Ricoeur, encloses himself in the stiff, pointed quills of Gallic power-speak; the Fox, Dennett, improvises expository tricks to suit the occasion. Both strategies are necessary because each is attempting to construct a systematic, potentially comprehensive description of minds in the world from an unargued base, Ricoeur from "the self as radical autonomy,"[120] Dennett from "physical law" and the computer mind, and each leaves the details to be filled in later. Are they describing the same curve, Ricoeur its concave aspect, Dennett its convex aspect?

Perhaps. But the difference between them is still significant. Dennett presents himself as a literary rather than a scientific writer, and the kind of literary critic best qualified to appraise his writing, he suggests, would be a practitioner of the so-called New Criticism that once dominated literary studies. There seem to be two reasons why he is drawn to New Criticism. First, just as he dissolves the self, and sidelines consciousness, so New Criticism ignored authors and their intentions. An author's personality and whether a work was written for money, to express a grievance, to flatter, even what a writer consciously *intended*, were irrelevant. Only the words on the page mattered. Second, New Critics believed they could identify a text's specific and unique significance. The critic, Dennett asserts, can "speak of what is true *in* [a] story ... the interpretation of fiction is undeniably doable."

117. Dennett, *From Bacteria to Bach and Back*, 20.
118. Dennett, *From Bacteria to Bach and Back*, 19.
119. Dennett, *From Bacteria to Bach and Back*, 210.
120. Ricoeur, *Rule of Metaphor*, 29.

Both the stories people tell about themselves and the world textually realized in a work of fiction, are, he claims, "stable" in the light of "the best, most coherent, reading of the text we can find."[121] Each of his own ingenious and often funny thought experiments, therefore, must have a definite meaning, and what is true in each of them can be definitively and uncontroversially accessed. New Criticism is no longer fashionable, and Dennett's own argument illustrates its weakness. Each of his fictional "I's" would need to fit the poems and stories that it reads or hears into its own story. Consequently, agreement between computational autobiographers about "the best and most coherent reading" of a computational poet or novelist could *not* be guaranteed. Once the self is perceived as the "chief fictional character" in a self-told tale, and consciousness points things out *about* oneself without accounting *for* them, relativism seems inescapable.

Ricoeur's view of literature is different. Literature for him is "a vast laboratory in which we experiment with estimations, evaluations, and judgments of approval and condemnation,"[122] a laboratory "for thought experiments in which the resources of variation encompassed by narrative identity are put to the test of narration."[123] But they don't have specifiable results. The "imaginative variations ... of literary fiction," Ricoeur writes, "concern ... selfhood in its dialectical relation to sameness."[124] A work of literature takes "its very existence as work" from the other, from the reader, "the mediation of [the reader] "being ... thoroughly constitutive of its meaning."[125] Ricoeur's position is thus the opposite of Dennett's. Dennett relativizes the human and pins down meaning. Ricoeur affirms the autonomous will and risks everything else. Neither is economical with truth.

Because Ricoeur and Dennett appeal to science and literature in

121. Dennett, *Consciousness Explained*, 81.
122. Ricoeur, *Oneself as Another*, 115.
123. Ricoeur, *Oneself as Another*, 148.
124. Ricoeur, *Oneself as Another*, 150.
125. Ricoeur, *Oneself as Another*, 156.

explaining their points of view, it is appropriate to test their arguments in the light of scientific and literary writing. I will also consider briefly an anecdote about the great Danish physicist Nils Bohr (1885–1962).

As an example of scientific writing, I quote the opening of a paper by Albert Einstein.

DO GRAVITATIONAL FIELDS PLAY AN ESSENTIAL PART IN THE STRUCTURE OF THE ELEMENTARY PARTICLES OF MATTER?

Neither the Newtonian nor the relativistic theory of gravitation has so far led to any advance in the theory of the constitution of matter. In view of this fact it will be shown in the following pages that there are reasons for thinking that the elementary formations which go to make up the atom are held together by gravitational forces.

1. Defects of the Present View

Great pains have been taken to elaborate a theory which will account for the equilibrium of the electricity constituting the electron. G. Mie, in particular, has devoted deep researches to this question. His theory, which has found considerable support among theoretical physicists, is based mainly on the introduction into the energy-tensor of supplementary terms depending on the components of the electro-dynamic potential, in addition to the energy terms of the Maxwell-Lorenz theory. These new terms, which in outside space are unimportant, are nevertheless effective in the interior of the electrons in maintaining equilibrium against the electric forces of repulsion.[126]

If you glanced at this before reading it, you would probably register that it is in English prose, and that it uses expressions like "the Newtonian ... theory of gravitation," "the energy-tensor of supplementary terms," and "the Maxwell-Lorenz theory." You would make a quick judgment about your ability to engage with such writing, about what doing so might be like, and about the value for you that it might have. You would then have given the quotation fuller attention or skipped it, possibly hoping that you would be able to follow the present discussion anyway.

The first, usually fleeting, connection one makes with a text is thus mainly related to the demands it seems to make on the mind. This I

126. Einstein, *Principle of Relativity*, 191.

call the general level of signification. This is in essence a judgment about language (*langue*), about what will be required of me to understand Einstein's terms, to respect them so as to follow his argument, and to prevent irrelevant associations from obstructing my attention. Because this is scientific writing, I will need to put aside my distaste for Newton's performance as Master of the Mint and my admiration for Gustave Mie (1868–1957) as an opponent of Nazism because they are irrelevant to Einstein's view of the structure of elementary particles, to the passage's specific level of signification (*parole*).

I think it possible *in principle* for an advanced Turing machine to be programmed to "understand" Einstein's text at this specific level. It might generate a text that brought this fragment of Einstein's thinking into relation with other texts in the field or even specify undetected problems or solutions to known problems. Einstein wrote in German, and I quote from a translation. One serial supercomputer programmed to process the German text and another one programmed to process the English version might produce the same results. The general level of signification, its *langue*, does not affect the meaning. I conclude that there is nothing in the specific meaning of Einstein's text, its *parole*, that is incompatible with Dennett's "computational" theory of mind.

But not all signification and communication is like this. Consider the following anecdote.

> Nils Bohr had a horse-shoe nailed over the door of his house. When a guest exclaimed, "surely you don't believe that will bring you luck," Bohr replied: "Of course, I don't. But they tell me it works whether you believe in it or not."

A brain that was *just* a parallel computer, no matter how many millions of computations it could perform simultaneously, could not adequately engage with this little story. Nor could New Criticism. Bohr may have signaled that he was making a gag, or perhaps he was charmingly naïve, or having fun with paradox, or making a serious philosophical point, or signaling annoyance with the question and the questioner. The possible intonations in the guest's exclamation and in Bohr's reply are without limit. And the more one dwells on this limitless variety, the more intriguing the anecdote becomes. Its infinite variety becomes its point, why one wants to repeat it, why I am repeating it. And as I think of myself as someone who sees all this, and, seeing it, relishes the prospect of sharing it with others, I *know* I am not merely telling myself a "story" about me as a user illusion. When I say, "I see!," I *am telling the truth about me*. As I think about Bohr and his horseshoe, I know that I am and that he was. To which a Cognitive Philosopher might reasonably respond, "But is this claim decipherable? Can you go *better* than Ricoeur?" I think I can.

A close student of Aristotle, Ricoeur examines what it means to say that an agent is "the principle" of an action—that the action *depends on* and doesn't just occur *in* the agent. Dennett would say that a biophysical complex such as a human being is an agent if an action arises *in* it, rather than being forced upon it, but Ricoeur requires the agent to be "a principle." He uses the formula "*A principle that is a self, a self that is a principle*" ("principle" being Aristotle's *arkhē*). He wants to say that "the ethical determination of the principle of action [the self] wins out over its physical determination."[127] But what might be involved in "winning out"? And what counts as adequate deliberation? (It should be borne in mind that what counts as deliberation for Ricoeur is not just articulated reasons and counter-reasons, but all the relevant insights, feelings, and habits embedded in the agent's character and experience.) A vast range of intelligent, responsible behavior can be described as adequately by Dennett as by Ricoeur. What is needed are examples of the self *winning out* "over its physical determination" precisely in the *way* it deliberates. This, I suggest, requires a thought experiment in which the self as a principle and a principle as the self move beyond the freedom of spontaneity into the freedom of indifference in which, contrary to

127. Ricoeur, *Oneself as Another*, 92.

Ricoeur and Descartes, there is no "default of adequate reason," no "bad infinite" but "an infinite without disorder" after all.

I offer a sonnet by Milton as my example of such a thought experiment.

> Lawrence of virtuous Father virtuous Son,
> Now that the Fields are dank, and ways are mire,
> Where shall we sometimes meet, and by the fire
> Help waste a sullen day; what can be won
> From the hard Season gaining: time will run
> On smoother, till Favonius re-inspire
>
> The frozen earth; and cloth in fresh attire
> The Lillie and Rose, that neither sowed nor spun.
> What neat repast shall feast us, light and choice
> Of Attic taste, with Wine, whence we may rise
> To hear the Lute well touched, or artful voice
> Warble immortal notes and Tuscan air?
> He who of those delights can judge, and spare
> To interpose them oft, is not unwise.[128]

Glancing at these lines for the first time, I would register that they are in English verse (some of Milton's sonnets are in Italian) and that there are references to "Favonius," "Attic," and "Tuscan." I would then make a quick judgment about my ability to engage with a poem using this sort of vocabulary, about what the experiences of doing so might be like, and about the value they might have for me. I might then decide to pass the poem over. Suppose, however, I decide to engage with Milton's specific meanings, what he "says." Doing this will confirm, modify, or disprove my preliminary judgments about the poem's general level of signification. One way or another, I will come into fuller contact with the poem, have a fuller sense of the specific input its interpretation requires. I may discover, for example, that it has religious implications that are not to my taste. Others might find it incompatible with their disapproval of drinking alcohol.

128. Milton, *Critical Edition of the Major Works*, 81.

It invites me to respond with different skills from those that enabled me to respond to the Einstein passage. Whereas in reading the Einstein passage it would be a serious mistake for me to dwell on what it was *like* for Mie to research "the equilibrium of the electricity constituting the electron," the sonnet, addressed to a young friend, Edward Lawrence, *requires* me to sense and savor what it would be *like* to feast on "a neat repast" of "Attic taste" and then to hear a Tuscan air sung to a "Lute well touched." In his posthumously published compendium of Protestant theology written in Latin, *De Doctrina Christiana* (1825), Milton praises "the discriminating enjoyment of food, clothing and all the civilized refinements of life, purchased with our honest earnings"[129] and identifies as virtues "COURTEOUSNESS ... [which] makes us affable and easily approachable,"[130] and "URBANITY [which] entails not only elegance and wit (of a decent kind) in conversation, but also the ability to discourse and to reply in an acute and apposite way."[131]

The two passages therefore require different relationships between the specific and general levels of signification. In Einstein, the general level simply establishes the conditions required for interpretation at the specific level. The specific level stands on its own. That is why the fact I quote from a text that has been translated from German is far less important than if I had chosen to discuss, say, a translation of one of Milton's Italian sonnets, the general level of which I could not with any fullness relate to in an English translation. In order to assimilate the specific meanings in the sonnet, I must not only exercise precisely indicated interpretative powers, but also let awareness of those powers coming into play modify my grasp of what is being suggested at the specific level. As in an experiment in quantum physics, in this experiment the observer is intrinsic to the data observed.

129. Milton, *Complete Prose Works*, 6:732.
130. Milton, *Complete Prose Works*, 6:769.
131. Milton, *Complete Prose Works*, 6:769–70.

This play in the sonnet between the specific and general levels of reading can be analyzed in detail. The eighth line, for example, assumes that I will recognize the reference to the Gospel According to Matthew (6:28)—"Consider the lilies of the field, how they grow; they neither toil nor spin"—and find the intrusion of a New Testament reference after the classical "Favonius" unexpected and possibly inappropriate, but nonetheless make sense of it. Again, the mild evocation of an erotic as well as a mystical tradition with the addition of the Rose to the Lillie makes a considerable difference to the words of Jesus in the Gospel. So too the return to pagan values in the reference to an Attic and not a Eucharist feast, to the singing of a Tuscan air, and to this-worldly immortality. The Einstein text requires skilled responses, but its sense ignores them—the sonnet different ones that feed into what it says.

The poem assumes my capacity to deal with its rhyme scheme. Irregular arrangements of the last six lines of a sonnet are common in Milton: in four of his sonnets besides this one, the return of a rhyme is delayed for four lines. In these other cases, however, the lines rhymed in this way are the ninth and the thirteenth, and the effect of disconnection is offset by a more easily remembered rhyme in the final line. But here the sense of connection established by the couplet rhyme in the twelfth and thirteenth lines is disrupted by the loosely connected rhyme at the end of the last line, which can seem lame and detached, an impression increased by the delayed pause after "judge," and the grammatically weak construction, "And spare / To interpose them oft," that follows it.

These effects of disconnection and inappropriateness are, presumably, meant to be overcome. The poem depends on my ability not only to discover consistency and integration in apparent inconsistency and disintegration, but also to allow the experience of this mental work to enrich the poem's specific meanings. Considerable rhythmical and grammatical emphasis, for example, is given to the word "judge." Appreciation of the skill with which this is done exemplifies what the word "judge" here actually means. To understand Milton's sense of "judgment," I must become conscious of myself judging how Milton manages the sonnet form. I must also pass judgment on the poem's mix of Humanist and Christian signs. I must endorse as well as understand them with respect both to the poem's specific meaning as modified by my experience of interpreting it, and to what experiencing those values means to me. The poem engages me as a thinking, conscious, and self-conscious being: to assimilate Milton's use of the word "judge," I must do some judging for myself and about myself.

The differences between interpreting "objective" and "literary" language are now clearer. The former, while dependent on an appropriately disciplined response signaled at the general level of meaning, preserves the autonomy of the specific level, while literary language exploits general signs at the specific level. So, of course, does everyday speech. We may therefore further define the language of literature by referring to pleasure and play: the child's pleasure in nonsense talk is a kind of ur-literature, the joke its most widespread form, the anecdote about Bohr a bald but pertinent example.

"Objective" and literary language also have a relation to values. In objective discourse, responsible reading requires accepting the autonomy of the specific level of signification. If I were a Nazi or a Stalinist, I would need to suppress my urge look for evidence of Jewish science or bourgeois decadence and focus on Einstein's argument as science. A reader of scientific literature can be motivated by jealousy, or the pursuit of power or prestige, or the need to remember before an exam, but interpreting objective language requires the elimination of such motives. Scientific reading requires a degree of self-control, bordering on the ethical and easily passing into it. A corresponding respect for the specific level of signification is assumed of the writer. The relationship between Einstein and his reader involves a mutual commitment to impersonality. This may involve a high level of mutual respect, but this has nothing to do with what

Einstein says about "the elementary formations which go to make up the atom" and is not evident in what he has written. The reverse is the case with literary reading. It begins in the value-free area of play between levels of signification, and moves, sometimes disruptively, into the area of values. It may incite the reader to make judgments about its own verbal strategies, like those that the young Lawrence is invited to make in Milton's sonnet. Thus the true poet may finally invite and require from the reader (or listener) a moral or aesthetic judgment about a problem involving an entire set of signs. Within the general structure or web of interpersonal activity, both science and literature create opportunities for responsible linguistic practice.

Yet they do so indirectly—through silence. The general level of signification is necessarily implicit, even when a text alludes to its own procedures. In his most famous novel, *Tom Jones* (1749), Henry Fielding (1707–54) repeatedly interrupts his story with addresses to the reader—each of the novel's eighteen Books is introduced by an often facetious but sometimes serious mini-essay—but these and other interruptions leave the reader with the extra tasks of grasping their implications as well as their meaning (particularly what attitude to adopt toward the author) and of making a judgment about the impact of those implications on his specific significations. Literature thus obeys the rule of being unable to supply the rules for its own interpretation. Even a flaunted rhetoric cannot explicitly invite critical responses to itself without ceasing to be itself. There is always a point at which readers are left to their own resources, and in some works this point is itself specific, as in the sonnet to Lawrence, which, out of respect for everything the word "judge" has to convey, has to be silent about the personal responsibilities its full appreciation requires.

Ricoeur is familiar with this excitement, tension, risk.

> Just when the work is separated off from its author, [he writes] its entire being is gathered up in the signification that the other grants it. For the author, the work as an index of individuality and not of universal vocation, is quite simply relegated to the ephemeral. The way the work has of taking its meaning,

> its very existence as work, only from the other [the reader] underscores the extraordinary precariousness of the relation between the work and the author, the mediation of the other being so thoroughly constitutive of its meaning.[132]

In the case of Milton's sonnet, however, it is the precariousness of the relation between the author and the *reader* that is crucial to the poem's meaning. I can respond to its explicit and implicit meanings, and form a judgment about the urbane courtesy of Milton's attitudes to his readers and in particular to Lawrence as one of them, what it means for Milton to remain silent about what he hopes from Lawrence and ourselves, even though his successful communication of all that the word "judge" can imply, when applied to civilized intercourse and entertainment, depends on our cooperation. The poem thus puts me into judicious contact with Milton's sense of my potentialities as guest and reader, and with his dependence on them. But my reaction to that reticence, as Ricoeur emphasizes, is unpredictable. I may resent Milton's failure to direct my responses in a way that I find aesthetically, morally, or even theologically necessary, or I may admire the technical skill with which he has avoided just such explicitness. Equally, I may react to the poem in ways that Milton might find distasteful, even corrupt. I may thus contain my judgment of the poem within the limits of propaganda or aestheticism or predisposition. But I can also make Milton's sense of my unpredictability another aspect of his meaning, part of what he silently yet precisely indicates he is allowing for. I can acknowledge a moral significance in his willingness to leave me to judge for myself (and Lawrence to judge for himself) even if I do so wrongly or inexpertly or even (as Milton might see it) corruptly, and I can see this too as integral to what the poem signifies. This goes beyond Milton's making the ends of his readers his own, beyond what Nagel calls "personal sympathy,"[133] though he also does this with great skill and sensitivity. It

132. Ricoeur, *Oneself as Another*, 156.

133. Nagel, *View from Nowhere*, 168.

allows for a reader who rejects that sympathy. It is by virtue of that silent, undemonstrative acceptance of the other, this grant of freedom to the reader without which the poem would not be what it is, that *Milton* is free. The precariousness of the relation between poet and the poem's reception is the site of the poet's strength of will. This "simultaneous accompanying,"[134] to use an expression of Ricoeur's, is, I suggest, anterior to all other ethical willing, that is, in the tradition of ethics that descends from Aristotle to Nagel and identifies "the relation among three concepts: the good life, the moral life, and the rational life."[135]

Encapsulated in the sonnet, therefore, is a principle of intimacy in separateness, an exact, entirely open authorial voluntariness, which I can value as a good and make my own. This openness is Milton's and not mine. His choice, that I should choose for myself, is specific and complete—it is in the poem; mine exists only as a possibility, but as a possibility, it is Milton's self-effacing gift to me. He invites me into the intimate, domestic world of his desires, hopes, and affections, yet, like a good host, he leaves me to myself, and in this self-effacement he becomes fully and movingly himself, manifesting all those facts of his powerful mind and damaged body that are simultaneously his wealth and his specific limitation as an acting person.

The sonnet to Lawrence thus contains necessarily implicit but exact traces of "involvement or participation with others in interpersonal human relationships."[136] This stands even if we adopt the New Critics' principle that Milton's poem may not be discussed as if the poet in the text and the man he is addressing were historical persons. The validity of what the poem points toward is not lessened by the events it apparently predicts and even the identity of its speaker being read as fictional. Fact or fiction, a precondition of its being read is its capacity to signal a relevant set of interpersonal attitudes that,

134. Ricoeur, *Oneself as Another*, 80.

135. Nagel, *View from Nowhere*, 193.

136. Strawson, *Freedom and Resentment*, 9.

as the means by which we can make sense of it, are logically independent of the sense it makes. Included in that set of attitudes is an ethical stance of considerable importance. Here we have the marks of a will—not being a New Critic or a strict Deconstructionist, I will call it Milton's—with a clearly apprehended object (the reader's freedom) that, as an object, cannot *determine* choice no matter how fully it is known. The more Milton's sensitivity and truthfulness unite to apprehend and value the reader's freedom as an end in itself, the more profoundly voluntary that sensitivity and truthfulness become, the more exemplary its manifestation of the freedom of indifference.

What is revealed, therefore, in "Lawrence of virtuous Father virtuous Son" is the mode of freedom that Ricoeur dismissed so decisively because "all choice is determined by its motives," and the freedom of indifference is supposed not to have any. But in acknowledging the freedom of his reader, in attuning his writing to it, and in making no attempt to survey the consequences of the restraint that Milton thus imposes on himself, Milton *unites* motive and freedom. He knows that he must either choose the reader's freedom as an end in itself without regard to consequences, or not choose it at all. He thus implicitly recognizes that his own freedom consists not in a choice between objects, but in making freedom itself, and specifically the freedom of Lawrence and his readers, his object. We are face-to-face with a principle that is a self and a self that is a principle, with freedom that is Milton, and Milton who is free.

6

What It's Like to Be a Person

"Identities," Selves, and Economies

Personhood is a tricky idea. It was first clarified in the Church councils that defined the doctrines of the Trinity and the Incarnation in the fourth century. The outcome after much complicated argument was that personhood was more than a matter of appearance or character. It was something you *were*. But it remains an elusive idea. As the twentieth-century priest, essayist, detective novelist, and translator Mgr. Ronald Knox (1888–1957) pointed out, "Human personality is indivisible ... A person cannot ... become more or less of a person." Yet human beings can become identified "first with this motive, then with that"; they can be "all over the place"; there can be "no unity to [their] moral being."[1] To many observers, therefore, it is not obvious that human personhood is indivisible, as scrutiny of three related terms—*identity*, *self*, and *economy*—makes clear.

First, *identity*. Well into the nineteenth century, children, lunatics, and wives were not considered persons by English law. Personhood was a condition lawyers prudently conceded to some of the people some of the time, but not to all of the people all of the time. It depended on your position in society; it was not something people

1. Knox, *God and the Atom*, 12.

were in themselves (though of course lawyers themselves were *always* persons, and according to the US Supreme Court, so are corporations). This idea is with us still. Some recent theorists have suggested that we are no more than we are *said* to be either in society, or when we invent our own personal histories, or both. This is what is commonly called "identity." I use quotation marks to distinguish it from *identity* meaning what someone *really is*—"Jesus Christ, super-star, who do you think that you really are?" "Identity" is a public matter, *identity* something ultimate, what uniquely I am. Acquiring "identity" in the first sense—the sense I am presently discussing—happens over time, and people would be in a pretty bad way if it didn't. It includes being given a name, and learning the languages and codes of one's world, seeing oneself as female or male, old or young, Irish, English, Scottish, Welsh, or American, Jew or Greek, slave or free, LGBT or straight. But it is not the same as being a person.

Nor is having a *self*. "Identity" is a matter of language. But there are lots of ways of being human that can't be netted by language, including some important, private sensations and what the Italian philosopher Antonio Rosmini (1797–1855) called "the fundamental feeling"[2] of our bodies. "Nothing," wrote the poet Gerard Manley Hopkins, "comes near this unspeakable stress of pitch, distinctiveness ... this selfbeing of my own. Nothing explains it or resembles it ... searching nature I taste self but at one tankard, that of my own being."[3] This comes nearer to my notion of the person than socially constructed "*identity*" does, but the taste of me is still not my complete being. I am more than that—I am more than I feel and think myself to be.

"Identity" and *selfhood* are both in Newman's sense *economies*—their coherence and truthfulness depend on and are limited by "initial conditions." Consider the five senses that contribute so much to self-experience. Since the eighteenth century, many philosophers believed, like Mill, that the mind was just consciousness and its con-

2. Rosmini, *New Essay on the Origin of Ideas*, 200–220.

3. Hopkins, *Poems and Prose*, 148.

tents, and they tried to identify the laws by which these experiences automatically associated together. The Romantic poet William Blake (1757–1827) hated this theory because it turned the mind into a passive machine, receiving signals from out there to be put in order according to fixed laws of association. He mocked it in "The Marriage of Heaven and Hell" as "a Ratio of the five senses,"[4] and he was right—the senses have their limitations.

Nowadays, it is scientists rather than poets who insist that the senses mislead us about the universe, with its black holes, fundamental particles, and bent time. Knox described "the world of the physicist" in Blakean terms as "rotating, coruscating, ebullient with paradox" and asked,

> How does an angelic intelligence see [a] lump of coal? Not lump-wise, we may be sure of that; such a view of it could only present itself to our terrestrial slowness of wit. But does the angel see a bunch of accidents inhering in a substance, or a stream of whirling electrons, or both, or something yet other, beyond all these?[5]

Or, as Blake put it,

> How do you know but ev'ry bird that cuts the airy way,
> Is an immense world of delight clos'd by your senses five?[6]

But if the senses limit our knowledge of the universe, they must also limit our knowledge of ourselves. On this basis, Blake was able to turn the notions of body and soul upside-down. Instead of thinking that the human being has no soul, only a body, or that the soul is a kind of ghost in a biological machine, Blake insisted that a human being is nothing *but* soul: "for that call'd Body is a portion of Soul discern'd by the five Senses, the chief inlets of Soul in this age,"[7] that aspect of the soul that can be seen, heard, smelt, tasted, and touched.

4. Blake, *Complete Writings*, 149.
5. Knox, *God and the Atom*, 63.
6. Blake, *Complete Writings*, 150.
7. Blake, *Complete Writings*, 150.

The senses then are one economy, giving limited information about the world and the individual. Language is another. Some things said in French cannot be translated into German. The translator of the Book of Ecclesiasticus was driven nearly to despair by the way the nuances of Hebrew were lost in Greek. But there are other languages besides the spoken ones, the languages of gesture, clothes, food—a lot is "said" in the way a scarf is knotted or a table is set. There are the languages of music, dance, painting, tattoos. And it is by means of these languages that variously constructed "identities"—gender, age, family, nationality, religion—are built up. Having an "identity"—or, frequently these days, having "identities," thinking of yourself and being recognized as masculine, or a Mormon, or an aunt, are also experiences, and each has a certain feel to it—feeds into the sense of self and vice versa. Economies often fuse together.

But though self and "identity" are mutually interactive, together they do not add up to the whole of me because no economy and no combination of economies can ever express the complete truth about anything—that is why Newman called them economies. And so, while "identity" and *selfhood* keep on developing and enriching each other, they are never the whole story. Beyond, behind, within, around them, there is the *person*, what I really am.

Being a Person

Or is there? Is there really a principle or *substance* or *arkhē* underlying, and giving indefeasible unity to, "identity" and *self*, as Knox alleged? Since the seventeenth century, philosophers have been suspicious of substances. Spinoza held that only one thing could properly be called a substance, namely, "God or nature."[8] For Locke, a person was just an ongoing consciousness irrespective of its underlying base, soul, or spirit—his argument has much in common with "brain-in-a-vat" and teletransportation thought experiments[9]—and

8. Spinoza, *Ethics and De Intellectus Emendatione*, 142.

9. See Locke, "Of Identity and Diversity" (Essay II xxvii), in *Essay of Human Nature.*

Hume held that human beings "are nothing but a bundle or collection of different perceptions, which succeed each other with an inconceivable rapidity, and are in a perpetual flux or movement."[10] If there was anything underneath, it was unknowable, but there probably wasn't. Many modern theorists agree with this: human beings are the unstable outcome of a bundle of information-processing and decision-making systems working semi-independently of each other, and there is no single command post from which the whole is seen and controlled. The idea of such a center is convenient but has no more reality than a physical object's center of gravity.[11] There is no captain on the bridge, no "little soul-captain" or "homunculus" in overall charge.[12] One illustration of the idea is the way our eyes work. Sight is not what it seems to be. If I hold out a playing card to one side while staring straight ahead, I can't tell whether the card is in a red suit or a black, though I can see when it is moving. I have no sense of how poor my peripheral vision is because my eyes "dart about in an incessant and largely unnoticed game of visual tag with the items of potential interest happening in [my] field of view."[13] Seeing is thus semiautonomous; its workings and indeed its effects on my actions are outside my knowledge and control. Most of us have no problem with this. But what if more "personal" aspects of behavior are playing incessant, largely unnoticed games of tag, and are directing our actions, this way and that, toward ends of which we are not aware? Worse, what if the mind has a design feature by which the body's biological game plan is concealed from consciousness? This would certainly threaten the notion of the person.

Sperm Wars: Infidelity, Sexual Conflict and Other Bedroom Battles, a book by Robin Baker, received a lot of publicity when it was published in 1996. In it Baker argues that much sexual behavior, male

10. David Hume, *Treatise of Human Nature*, 252.

11. See Dennett, *Consciousness Explained*, 429.

12. Dennett, *Consciousness Explained*, 14.

13. Dennett, *Consciousness Explained*, 54.

and female, can be explained in terms of competition inside a woman's body between the sperm of rival lovers. The woman may hasten home to her partner from her lover's bed, not to have an alibi or because she needs comfort and reassurance, but because her body "wants" to set up a competition between the lover's sperm and the partner's. The feelings she has, and her account of them, facilitate this process, but they don't account for it. Her sense of self and her identity are thus both lies that she is biologically programmed to invent. The body, we shouldn't be surprised to learn, has a mind of its own[14]—Dennett would say "minds" that together run the show.

To this I reply, what about Uriah the Hittite? Not the man himself, but how his story might strike a modern-minded reader of the Second Book of Samuel. He is summoned home by King David after David has impregnated Uriah's wife while Uriah was away fighting. According to the theory, Uriah's body's mind ought to direct him to sleep with Bathsheba as soon as possible, not (as he might think) because he loves her, nor even to satisfy his pent-up desires, but in order to give his sperm the best possible chance against the sperm of any other male who has made love to her in his absence. But for him, loyalty to David overrides any such biological programming, and he joins the soldiers guarding the king. So, even if biological programming determined the behavior of David and Bathsheba, perhaps Bathsheba's noble and unfortunate husband offers a counterexample. It is possible the biological programming was overridden by other algorithms in the Uriah system—determining his need to establish his "identity" in Israel, for example—he was, after all, a Hittite, but if he is a "person," then it is possible to offer another description of his behavior.

What do I mean by a *person*? My starting point is a claim by Rosmini that "The person resides in the will as the supreme active principle in an intelligent spirit, the principle to which all other powers

14. A sentence stolen from the redoubtable and much missed essayist, the late Jenny Diski (1947–2016); see *London Review of Books* 26, no. 21 (2014): 23.

are joined and to which they are subject."[15] "The person resides in the will." The will is not a yes/no lever in the mind, by which the "soul" controls the body, but, as Newman also argued, body, mind, and everything else operate as a whole. "It is the concrete being that reasons ... the whole man moves."[16] And it is the whole being that wills, that acts deliberately. Pope St. John Paul II made the same point in 1969 when he wrote: "action *reveals* the person, and we look at the person through ... action."[17]

Uriah is a person, therefore, insofar as his decision not to return to Bathsheba is not *necessarily* the outcome of a competition between forces within him, even if one of those forces is a special power called the will; if Uriah is a person, the whole human being opts to serve King David. We see the *person* in the action, just as we see the *person* in David's action when he later arranges Uriah's murder. St. John Paul II calls this "person-action unity": "human action" being more than "a sum of ... other dynamisms."[18] And it is to the possibility of such human action that the Christian Church has been dogmatically committed since the fourth century.

To sum up: first, a human being acquires an "identity" as a member of a society, which categorizes people in the numerous "languages" that constitute its culture. But that "identity" is not stable. It can be transformed or even lost. There are old men in night shelters who have used so many names and told so many stories about themselves that their "identities" are irretrievably obliterated. But that need not mean that they have ceased to be *acting persons.*

Second, a human being acquires a sense of *self,* in and through the unique mind-body mix each of us is. This sense of self is incommunicable. In *The Picture of Dorian Grey,* the smell of white lilac in the head and heart of Lord Henry Wotton belongs exclusively to him

15. Rosmini, *Philosophy of Right,* 80.

16. Newman, *Apologia pro Vita Sua,* 83.

17. Wojtyła, *Acting Person,* 11.

18. Wojtyła, *Acting Person,* 197.

and cannot be put into words, because words are shared between minds, and (perhaps mercifully) no one but Lord Henry can sip at the cup of his deeply decadent being. Like the sense of identity, the sense of self is constantly changing; it may wither in old age; it will finally be put out. But—or so some people believe—we will remain persons even when it is.

Finally, the word *person* itself. It has its origins in Christian dogma, and so it is more difficult to demonstrate that we are persons than that we have identities or a sense of self. Perhaps it is impossible to do so. All I have tried to do is clear up some common misconceptions about what the word implies, particularly the idea that I am "really" my soul, that my soul is "inside," or in some way controls, my body, and that it has a design feature called free will, a central control panel by which my life is finally governed. In place of this model, I offer the integral conception of Newman, Rosmini, and John Paul II, which I would sum up like this. The person is the whole damn shooting match: things "happen" in persons, it is true, as John Paul II is careful to remind us[19]—biological and social imperatives are not nonsense—but persons "act," and the sum of those "acts" discloses what they "are."

Light and Joy

In *The Prelude* (1805), William Wordsworth (1770–1850) writes of a baby "Nursed in his Mother's arms" and gathering "passion from his Mother's eye."

> Such feelings pass into his torpid life
> Like an awakening breeze, and hence his mind,
> Even in the first trial of its powers,
> Is prompt and watchful, eager to combine
> In one appearance, all the elements
> And parts of the same object, else detached

19. Wojtyła, *Acting Person*, 80ff.

And loth to coalesce . . .
In one beloved presence . . .
there exists
A virtue which irradiates and exalts
All objects through all intercourse of sense.
No outcast he, bewildered and depressed;
Along his infant veins are interfused
The gravitation and the filial bond
Of nature, that connect him with the world.
(II, 240, 243–50, 255–64)[20]

The infant mind discovers unity and order in the chaos of sensory experience. But why should it? It feels warm—fine. Is there any need to go beyond the feeling? Noises happen—but it is itself noisy; it can hear its own heartbeat. Why isn't the child's mind content to be its own universe? Why is some experience outside, *there*, objective? For Wordsworth, as for his collaborator and friend Samuel Taylor Coleridge, this movement of consciousness outside itself is the work of what Coleridge calls the "prime Agent of all human Perception," the primary imagination. The imagination, he maintains, "struggles to idealize and to unify" and is "a repetition in the finite mind of . . . the infinite I am."[21] The "primary imagination" is thus much like the "light" that Rosmini identifies as the prime agent of perception: "Every single sensation," Rosmini suggests, would end in itself if we did not also have a basic intuition, or "sense," of *being*,[22] which floods the mind with undifferentiated light, and in effect "irradiates and exalts / All objects through all intercourse of sense" and so enables us to turn sensations *in there* into objective, potentially universal ideas *out there*. This I take to be the foundational experience of personhood—light in the mind. It enables us to form concepts out of sensations.

Wordsworth links the early adventures of this light-filled mind

20. *The Prelude*, in Wordsworth, *Selected Works*.
21. Coleridge, *Biographia Literaria*, 2:202.
22. Rosmini, *Philosophy of Right*, 21.

with the baby's enjoyment of its mother's body. This gives the baby a sense that it *belongs* in the world *out there,* which it is trying to come to terms with. Intelligence needs the "awakening breeze" of emotion in order to grow properly, and for Wordsworth, the fundamental emotion is *joy*.

Blake had already expressed this idea in a vivid little poem about what it is like to be a baby:

Infant Joy

"I have no name:
"I am but two days old."
What shall I call thee:
"I happy am,
"Joy is my name."
Sweet joy befall thee!

Pretty joy!
Sweet joy but two days old,
Sweet joy I call thee:
Thou dost smile,
I sing the while,
Sweet joy befall thee![23]

A two-day-old baby cannot smile or speak—it has no sense of social identity, and its sense of self is surely rudimentary. But immediately after birth, before the cord is cut, if the birth has been a relatively untroubled one, it can lie on its mother's stomach, and exchange little noises with her, "converse" with her, for half an hour or more. This is why I agree with Blake that a baby feels not just warmth or milk, but joy—joy that in a light-filled world includes the beloved presence of a mother's body. And it has this capacity because it is a *person* and so is she.

Joy is one of the great rediscoveries of the Romantics—it is of course a major theme of the Scriptures—and I close this brief section on light and joy with *The Prelude*'s description of Wordsworth at five

23. Blake, *Complete Writings*, 118.

years of age playing by the lovely river that runs at the back of his childhood home in Cockermouth. This "fairest of all Rivers," he tells us,

> loved
> To blend his murmurs with my Nurse's song,
> And from his alder shades and rocky falls,
> And from his fords and shallows, sent a voice
> That flowed along my dreams . . .
> He was a Playmate whom we dearly loved.
> Oh! many a time have I, a five years' Child,
> A naked boy, in one delightful Rill,
> A little Mill-race severed from his stream,
> Made one long bathing of a summer's day . . .
> or coursed
> Over the sandy fields, leaping through groves
> Of yellow grunsel . . .
> as if I had been born
> On Indian plains and from my Mother's hut
> Had run abroad in wantonness, to sport,
> A naked Savage, in the thunder shower.
> (I, 272–76; 290–98; 301–4)

Glory and Disintegration

From light and joy I turn to another biblical theme—glory. Glory is *personal*. Animals may experience comfort and pleasure, even, perhaps, in the rarefied form of beauty. But glory requires a response only persons can manage. Consider Hopkins's poem "Hurrahing in Harvest":

> Summer ends now; now, barbarous in beauty, the stooks arise
> Around; up above, what wind-walks! what lovely behaviour
> Of silk-sack clouds! has wilder, willful-wavier
> Meal-drift moulded ever and melted across skies?
>
> I walk, I lift up, I lift up heart,
> Down all that glory in the heavens to glean our Saviour.[24]

24. Hopkins, *Poems and Prose*, 31.

Here, "down" is a verb. When Hopkins "downs" all that glory, he is an acting person. And when such acts are shared with others, they are immeasurably intensified. Whether it is an opening ceremony at the Olympic Games, or the cries of the audience when an opera is playing in *La Scala*, or the joy of the saints in Heaven, the experience of others "downing" glory makes it even more glorious. We begin as babies with light and joy; in the minds of some people, we will be complete when we cry out

> with the voice of a great multitude, like the sound of many waters and like the sound of mighty thunderpeals ... "Hallelujah! For the Lord our God the Almighty reigns. Let us rejoice and exult and give him the glory." (Rv 19:6–7)

But glory is also something individuals can have in themselves. In Wordsworth's poem "The Idiot Boy," a mother sends her idiot son on a pony to fetch the doctor for a sick neighbor whom she herself cannot leave. Johnny disappears into the night. The doctor does not come. The mother, frantic, leaves the sick woman to hunt for her boy. At last she finds him, making the "burr burr" noises that, with the hooting of the owlets, run through the poem. The sick woman recovers, and together they bring Johnny home. As they go, his mother asks him what he has been doing all this time:

> Now Johnny all night long had heard
> The owls in tuneful concert strive;
> No doubt too he the moon had seen
> For in the moonlight he had been
> From eight o'clock till five.
>
> And thus to Betty's question, he
> Made answer like a traveler bold,
> (His very words I give to you,)
> "The cock did crow to-whoo, to-whoo,
> And the sun did shine so cold."
> —Thus answered Johnny in his glory,
> And that was all his travel's story. (452–63)

As autobiography, Johnny's story is pretty thin, and those who contend that the narrative we spin for ourselves about ourselves, is, in the end, all we amount to would be hard pressed to see full personhood in Johnny; but for Betty, Johnny has been revealed in all his glory, and as long as Wordsworth's poems are read, it shall not be taken from him.

A more conventional example of glory occurs in the sixth book of Homer's *Odyssey*. The young Princess Nausicaa is playing with her maidens after doing the court's laundry in a limpid stream, and a badly thrown ball disturbs a naked shipwrecked sailor, begrimed with salt and the dead leaves under which he has been sleeping. He marches toward the young women and addresses the princess. On her orders, her maidens lay out some of clothes for him and modestly retire. The poem continues:

> Meanwhile great Odysseus in the river scrubbed the salt crust from the flesh of his back and broad shoulders and cleaned his hair of the frothy scum dried in it from the infertile sea. When he had so thoroughly washed and anointed himself smoothly and put on the clothes given him by the girl, then did Athene daughter of Zeus contrive to make him seem taller and stronger, and from his head she led down the curls of his hair in hyacinthine tendrils. As when some master craftsman … washes his silver work with molten gold … just so did the goddess gild his head and shoulders with nobility. Then he went far apart and sat down by the margin of the sea, radiant with graciousness and glory.[25]

Glory here is a divine gift, a grace, making Odysseus the object of Nausicaa's admiration and our own. This passage was undoubtedly in Milton's mind when he described the glory of the unfallen Adam and Eve in *Paradise Lost*:

> Two of far nobler shape erect and tall,
> Godlike erect, with native honour clad
> In naked Majesty seemed Lords of all,
> And worthier seemed, for in their looks Divine

25. Homer, *The Odyssey*, 90–91.

> The image of their glorious Maker shone…
> His fair large Front and Eye sublime declared
> Absolute rule; and Hyacinthine Locks
> Round from his parted forelock manly hung
> Clustering, but not beneath his shoulders broad:
> Her unadorned golden tresses wore
> Disheveled, but in wanton ringlets waved.
> (IV, 288–92; 300–306)

Unlike Odysseus, Adam and Eve are glorious when naked and devoid of glory when clothed.

The effect on Satan, through whose eyes we are seeing this glory, is terrible. First, he is speechless. Then he cries out:

> O Hell! what do mine eyes with grief behold,
> Into our room of bliss so high advanced.
> Creatures of other mold, earth-born perhaps,
> Not Spirits, yet to heavenly Spirits bright
> Little inferior; whom my thoughts pursue
> With wonder and could love, so lively shines
> In them Divine resemblance, and such grace
> The hand that formed them on their shape hath poured.
> (IV, 358–65)

With what is understood in psychoanalysis as ambivalence, Satan's thoughts *pursue* Adam/Eve with wonder. He *could* love them—and therefore does—not least because their "resemblance" to God is also their resemblance to what he once was. But he drives his love away because he has a problem with any glory that is not his own. The glory of Adam and Eve arouses a particularly intense hatred that is well known in psychoanalysis. As an angel ("sons of one great Sire" [VI, 95]), Satan was, and remains, a son of God. Adam is God's "youngest son" (III, 151). Satan's reaction to the image before him is like an elder sibling's furious hatred of a younger rival. That Eve is there as well as Adam does not weaken this suggestion, since "spirits when they please / Can either sex assume, or both" (I, 423–24). (And so, incidentally, can we—in Juliet Mitchell's words, "somewhere one is, psychically, both sexes."[26]) It is as if Satan were looking in a mirror and seeing not an image of himself/herself but that of the hated usurper.

But there is another layer to his rage. He is surely transferring onto Adam (and Eve) an older trauma. Placed, before his fall, high in the heavenly order—

> of the first,
> If not the first archangel, great in power,
> In favour and pre-eminence—

he was suddenly confronted with the existence of the real and only Son of God, a fact that had been concealed until that moment, a rival both older and younger than he, who was "that day / Honoured by his great father, and proclaimed / Messiah king anointed." This he "could not bear / Through pride that sight, and thought himself impaired … / Deep malice thence conceiving and disdain" (V, 659–66). Even worse, this newly revealed anointed Son would, on his own, drive Satan and his vast following out of Heaven, a fact that in Hell, and later in *Paradise Regained,* is never mentioned. As psychoanalysts would see it, for Satan, Adam and Eve are, with a vengeance, the return of the repressed. They confront Satan "with the *personal* difficulties that had stayed hidden because they were too unbearable to face."[27]

Glory, then, seems—*is*—fine so long as it is a grace, when the inner and the outer person match. Johnny, Odysseus, the Son of God, Adam, and Eve are integrated in glory. But by desiring to seem more than he knows himself to be, Satan loses touch with the integrity, the substantial unity that belongs to him as an acting person. Yet, paradoxically, only an acting person could make this move. Satan's "supreme active principle," the angelic equivalent of Newman's "whole man," opts for a false "identity," for bad faith, for self-alienated being. Person-action unity wills its own disunity in untruth. Hence the

26. Mitchell, "Love and Hate, Girl and Boy," 11.
27. Mitchell, "Love and Hate, Girl and Boy," 14 (my emphasis).

contradictions in Satan's scrutiny of his condition. He even addresses himself as someone else; in Knox's words, he is all over the place:

> Hadst thou the same free Will and Power to stand?
> Thou hadst: whom hast thou then or what to accuse
> But Heaven's free Love dealt equally to all?
> Be then his Love accursed, since love or hate,
> To me alike, it deals eternal woe.
> Nay cursed be thou; since against his thy will
> Chose freely what it now so justly rues.
> Me miserable! which way shall I fly
> Infinite wrath, and infinite despair?
> Which way I fly is Hell; myself am Hell;
> And in the lowest deep a lower deep
> Still threatening to devour me opens wide.
> (IV, 66–77)

But you don't have to be a fallen angel to turn self-destructively upon yourself. In the companion poem to "Infant Joy," Blake suggests that even a baby can do so, an observation also shared by psychoanalysts:

> Infant Sorrow
>
> My mother groan'd! my father wept
> Into the dangerous world I leapt:
> Helpless, naked, piping loud
> Like a fiend hid in a cloud.
> Struggling in my father's hands,
> Striving against swadling bands,
> Bound and weary I thought best
> To sulk upon my mother's breast.[28]

Secrecy and Reserve

Reading this poem, however, and the terrible speech of Milton's Satan, many people have an interesting reaction. Blake's sorrowful baby is more exciting than his joyful one, and Satan more intriguing than Odysseus. They have depth, an inner life people recognize. And

28. Blake, *Complete Writings*, 217.

a crucial feature of this inner life is its duplicity. Oh, what a tangled web we weave, when first we practice to deceive—and how interesting we become in the process.

Blake understood this. The poem printed after "Infant Sorrow" in *Songs of Innocence and Experience* is "A Poison Tree."

> I was angry with my friend:
> I told my wrath, my wrath did end.
> I was angry with my foe:
> I told it not, my wrath did grow.
>
> And I water'd it in fears,
> Night & morning with my tears;
> And I sunned it with smiles
> And with soft deceitful wiles.
>
> And it grew both day and night,
> Till it bore an apple bright;
> And my foe beheld it shine,
> And he knew that it was mine,
>
> And into my garden stole
> When the night had veil'd the pole:
> In the morning glad I see
> My foe outstretch'd beneath the tree.[29]

This is remarkably clever. The speaker not only deceives his foe, but he also calculates on the foe's stealing the poisoned apple by night despite the appearance of friendship between them. Each is assessing what it is like to be the other, until they can finally disclose themselves in actions based on those calculations. That is also what it is like to be a person.

The poem preceding "Infant Sorrow" is closely related to "A Poison Tree" and has even more disturbing implications:

29. Blake, *Complete Writings*, 218.

The Human Abstract

Pity would be no more
If we did not make somebody Poor;
And Mercy no more could be
If all were as happy as we.

And Mutual fear brings peace,
Till the selfish loves increase:
Then Cruelty knits a snare,
And spreads his baits with care.

He sits down with holy fears,
And waters the ground with tears;
Then Humility takes its root
Underneath his foot.

Soon spreads the dismal shade
Of Mystery over his head,
And the Catterpiller and Fly
Feed on the Mystery.

And it bears the fruit of Deceit,
Ruddy and sweet to eat;
And the Raven his nest has made
In its thickest shade.

The Gods of the earth and sea
Sought thro' Nature to find this Tree;
But their search was all in vain:
There grows one in the Human Brain.[30]

This is about the way people exploit other people's suffering for their own satisfaction. The deceit is shared—*we* make people poor—whole societies do this—and then *we* congratulate ourselves on feeling pity for *them*. The poem follows such shallow acts of collective self-deception into the complicated duplicitousness of the poison infecting not just the individual human person but the institutions and "ideologies" arising with them, which give us an "identity" we

30. Blake, *Complete Writings*, 217.

can feel (more or less) pleased with. But Blake doesn't allow us to take refuge in amorphous collective guilt; he homes in on the image of the tree of deceit growing in the individual mind.

Milton has the same message. One of the impressive things about the Hell scenes in *Paradise Lost* is the way the fallen angels enter into a collusive agreement to go along with Satan's half-truths, so that they can retell their personal stories in selective self-glorifying ways, giving themselves and each other false "identities." They organize themselves into focus groups for this purpose. Satan publicly flaunts his falsehoods while making a show of concealing them. He lies and knows his followers know he is lying, yet they ecstatically accept his lies, enrich them, and return them to him with thanks and adulation. The bad faith is shared, consciously and deliberately; it grows in each angelic brain and is relished as a lie that is working in and for all of them.

The First Book of *Paradise Lost* contains scenes that anticipate the compulsive horrors of a Nuremberg rally. Shared untruth unifies the devils in a communion almost as intense as that of saints glorifying God in the Book of Revelation. This is something we can also recognize. It really can be like this to be a person—to be in intimate communion with others in a lie—when there is a lot of money to be made, or a war to be fought, or fame to be enjoyed, or a university to be organized to turn a profit.

But what about this?

Memory

i

I nursed it in my bosom while it lived,
I hid it in my heart when it was dead;
In joy I sat alone, even so I grieved
Alone and nothing said.

I shut the door to face the naked truth,
I stood alone—I faced the truth alone,
Stripped bare of self-regard or forms or ruth
Till first and last were shown.

None knew the choice I made; I make it still.
None knew the choice I made and broke my heart,
Breaking my idol: I have braced my will
Once, chosen for once my part.

I broke it at a blow, I laid it cold,
Crushed in my deep heart where it used to live.
My heart dies inch by inch; the time grows old,
Grows old in which I grieve.

ii

I have a room whereunto no one enters
Save I myself alone:
There sits a blessed memory on a throne,
There my life centres.

While winter comes and goes—oh tedious comer!—
And while its nip-wind blows;
While bloom the bloodless lily and warm rose
Of lavish summer.

If any should force entrance he might see there
One buried yet not dead,
Before whose face I no more bow my head
Or bend my knee there;

But often in my worn life's autumn weather
I watch there with clear eyes,
And think there how it will be in Paradise
When we're together.[31]

This poem is by Christina Rossetti. Her secrecy is different from the corrupt innerness, both individual and collective, depicted by Milton and Blake. She discovers fullness of personal being in a reserved place, in memory, in her own interior life. Secrecy, suffering, and integrity unite.

Why is revealed in another poem also by Christina Rossetti, this time not in her own voice but in that of an ill-used artist's model.

31. Rossetti, *Works*, 93–95.

L.E.L.

Downstairs I laugh, I sport and jest with all
But in my solitary room above
I turn my face in silence to the wall;
My heart is breaking for a little love . . .

I deck myself with silks and jewelry,
I plume myself like any mated dove:
They praise my rustling show, and never see
My heart is breaking for a little love.[32]

If the world is locked into interpersonal structures of deceit, collusion, and abuse, personal reserve is a fundamental requirement of personal integrity, especially for victims. This was what made Newman so distrusted by his contemporaries—he wrote *Apologia pro Vita Sua* in defense of his right to reserve. But, though Newman most fully articulated the concept of reserve in the 1830s, the experience of interior wholeness, as a secret, is unsurprisingly most vividly expressed in the writings of nineteenth-century women. I therefore close this section with two witty poems by Emily Dickinson, about the two faces of secrecy—its deceitfulness and its integrity. They contain some satisfying echoes of the poems by Milton and Wordsworth considered above.

Sweet is the swamp with its secrets,
Until we meet a snake;
'Tis then we sigh for houses,
And our departure take

At that enthralling gallop
That only childhood knows.
A snake is summer's treason,
And guile is where it goes.

---

32. Rossetti, *Works*, 132.

The reticent volcano keeps
His never slumbering plan;
Confided are his projects pink
To no precarious man.

If nature will not tell the tale
Jehovah told to her,
Can human nature not survive
Without a listener?

Admonished by her buckled lips
Let every babbler be.
The only secret people keep
Is Immortality.[33]

Freedom and Peace

Significant to much of women's writing in the nineteenth century, as the poems of Christina Rossetti and the work of the Brontës and George Eliot attest, is its emphasis on centering and controlling the interior life, on what George Eliot in *Daniel Deronda* called "the royalty of discernment and resolve."[34] This is grist to my mill—I have (on good authority) identified as a person with the unity of the human being in action. But it is one thing to affirm with Newman that the whole human being moves, and another to suggest how the whole human being can move freely

I am talking here about what philosophers term full two-way freedom. Some accounts of freedom suggest that we are free insofar as external forces don't act on us coercively. I am free to walk, so long as I am not chained up. But there is a stronger version of freedom, in the words of Peter Geach (1916–2013), being free from internal as well as external compulsion, so that in some choices at least, after a full account of all the facts preceding an action, it would make equal sense to say either "And then, in full knowledge of what it meant for him, he

33. Dickinson, *Selected Poems and Letters*, 200.

34. Eliot, *Daniel Deronda*, 538.

did it" or "And then, in full knowledge of what it meant for him, he did not do it."[35]

I can illustrate what this might involve by quoting another of Christina Rossetti's poems.

Winter: My Secret

I tell my secret? No indeed, not I:
Perhaps some day, who knows?
But not today; it froze, and blows, and snows,
And you're too curious: fie!
You want to hear it? well:
Only, my secret's mine, and I won't tell.

Or, after all, perhaps there's none:
Suppose there is no secret after all,
But only just my fun.
Today's a nipping day, a biting day . . .
I wear my mask for warmth: whoever shows
His nose to Russian snows
To be pecked at by every wind that blows?
You would not peck? I thank you for good will,
Believe, but leave that truth untested still . . .

Perhaps some languid summer day,
When drowsy birds sing less and less,
And golden fruit is ripening to excess,
If there's not too much sun nor too much cloud,
And the warm wind is neither still nor loud,
Perhaps my secret I may say,
Or you may guess.[36]

This poem takes risks—the childish, stubborn "I won't tell," the *ose* rhymes, and the willful echoing of the nursery rhyme "Sing a Song of Sixpence." But there are darker tensions behind its witty defensiveness, fear of exposure, a sense of shame. For most of the poem, the speaker seems enclosed in herself, in the cold snows of winter. In

35. Quoted by Kenny, *Will, Freedom and Power*, 110.
36. Rossetti, *Works*, 87–88.

the last lines, however, the indolence of summer seems lazy, sensual, suggesting lack of vigilance, or effortless insight in the person addressed, who might, after all, be part of the secret, the object perhaps of undisclosed passion. All this feeds into the last two lines:

> Perhaps my secret I may say,
> Or you may guess.

At first there seems to be no problem here: *may* surely means "maybe I shall," "maybe you will." But "may" can also mean "will be allowed to"—in summer, the speaker will be permitted to tell her secret, and the person addressed will be permitted to see it. Nonacademic readers of poetry often protest that it is an evasion of responsibility on the part of poets not to say what they mean, or on the part of critics not to work out what was meant. Here, however, the problem does not arise, because it makes perfect sense to see the ambiguity as part of the permission granted by the poet: just as the person addressed may guess her secret as he or she chooses, so we may interpret the poem as *we* choose.

This openness to someone else's choices is as important a choice on Rossetti's part as it is in the personal poems of Milton. It is intelligent—the speaker knows, the poet knows, exactly what is being done—there is no loss of reason. But neither can calculate the consequences of her permissiveness. Rossetti is *not* like the voice in Blake's poem, carefully plotting an enemy's downfall, and so becoming a slave to his own plans. She is free, but also reasonable. She has genuine two-way choices, to keep her secret hidden as she does in winter or to risk its being guessed, to allow us to interpret her words as we choose, or to force a meaning on us. In granting us freedom, she is in the fullest sense exercising her own.

From this I conclude that it belongs to the very essence of what it is like to be a person to live freely in the presence of other persons and their freedom. And that only when we do so can we love them and glory in their glory.

That's it, really. I have completed my sketch of what it is like to be a person, beginning with the light and joy of infancy, moving on through glory to pride, secrecy, and deceit, and from there reaching tentatively toward reserve and freedom. There is one last image I want to offer. Being a person is generally complicated and full of stress, yet in the good-humored openness with which Rossetti ends her poem, there is a hint of possible peace, an easing of all the taut tensions of winter. For Jews and Christians, the only will in which we can fully find our peace is, of course, God, and the Psalmist offers us a wonderful insight into that relationship in the image of a baby when at last it gives up the breast:

> O Lord, my heart is not lifted up, my eyes are not raised too high;
> I do not occupy myself with things too great and too marvelous for me.
> But I have calmed and quieted my soul, like a weaned child with its
> mother;
> My soul within me is like a weaned child.
> O Israel, hope in the Lord from this time on and forever more.
> (NRSV, Psalm 131)[37]

This is a happier image than Blake's sulking baby. And if it is an image of slightly greater maturity than that of Wordsworth's suckling baby, it hardly overstates our independence as persons from the God who made us. It seems to me extraordinarily beautiful. At the same time, it is worth bearing in mind that these lines are attributed to the man who murdered Uriah the Hittite.

37. I have chosen the suggested alternative reading.

7

Five Suppositions

Supposition 1, Deconstructionism: Hillis Miller, Barthes, Derrida, and Volosinov

Language and other sign systems, Joseph Hillis Miller asserts, are "fundamentally constitutive . . . in human life."[1] The "notion of "lived experience," of the senses and emotions, as somehow primary is mistaken, reactionary, and oppressive. The world that makes people what they are consists entirely of signs (there is nothing outside the text), and signs are inherently unstable—always open to new interpretations, always at play. Signs are the site of freedom and oppression, of the struggle between those who would fix meaning and so control the world constituted by meaning, and those who would liberate the making and interpretation of signs, and the human life that they constitute, from the oppression of "presence" and "intention," the tyranny of a given world controlled by "the will."

This is "deconstructionism" in a nutshell, and it is antitheological. According to Roland Barthes, to treat meaning as "relative" liberates "an antitheological activity, an activity that is truly revolutionary since to refuse to fix meaning is, in the end, to refuse God and his hypostases—reason, science, law."[2] The word "hypostases" is in-

1. Miller, "But Are Things What We Really Think They Are?"

2. Barthes, *Image Music Text*, 147.

teresting. As well as signifying sediments and bases and substances, "hypostases" can signify persons. This last sense developed out of the Council of Chalcedon in 451 CE, which described the Christian doctrine of the Incarnation in terms of what came to be called the Hypostatic Union, the union of two natures—divine and human—in the one hypostasis or person of the Son of God. Without this definition, human beings generally would probably not have been perceived as *persons* too, and as such having, for example, "rights" that most other kinds of living thing do not have, or at any rate not self-evidently. Thinkers like Hillis Miller and Barthes aim in effect to obliterate this (apparently) fixed and imprisoning conception of the human individual. Thus, according to Jacques Derrida, the field of written language revealed "a stage or set on which the simplicity of the classical subject [i.e., of the rational adult human being] was not to be found."[3] If meaning is relativized as libertarian critics like Hillis Miller would like, not only is the world relativized but people are as well.

Writing, as scrutinized by Derrida, however, was not the first stage or set on which, in the twentieth century, the simplicity of human individuality was questioned. Valentin Nikolaevich Volosinov (1895–1936) held that the systems of meaning operating in society determine subjectively private systems of meaning operating on the mind of the individual. The concept of the person, for Volosinov, is ideological, socially constructed.[4] So, however much people may want to think of themselves as "persons" with "rights," it would *not* be irrational to suppose that Hillis Miller, Barthes, Derrida, and their colleagues are right.

3. Derrida, *Writing and Difference*, 277.

4. Volosinov, *Marxism and the Philosophy of Language*, 34.

Supposition 2, Transference and Countertransference: Sigmund Freud, Anna Freud, and Others

In 1895, Sigmund Freud noted of a patient that she was transferring onto her analyst the painful ideas that the analysis had brought to light. This insight was to develop significantly over the next ten years. In *Dora: An Analysis of a Case of Hysteria*, he describes transference as

> new editions or facsimiles of the tendencies and phantasies which are aroused and made conscious during the progress of the analysis; but they have this peculiarity, which is characteristic for their species, that they replace some earlier person by the person of the physician. To put it another way: a whole series of psychological experiences are revived, not as belonging to the past, but as belonging to the physician at the present moment. Some of these transferences have a content which differs from that of their model in no respect whatever except for the substitution ... Others are more ingeniously constructed; their content has been subjected to a moderating influence ... and they may even become conscious, by cleverly taking advantage of some real peculiarity in the physician's person or circumstances and attaching themselves to that.[5]

At this stage, Freud sees transference as a "creation of the disease," difficult to detect, but something that "cannot be evaded" because the patient uses it to conceal the problems that the analysis is addressing: "it is only after the transference has been resolved, that a patient arrives at a sense of conviction of the validity of the connections which have been constructed during the analysis."[6] Later, he thought transference ought to be encouraged in analysis so that it could be revealed for what it was and a cure effected.

In 1936, in *The Ego and the Mechanism of Defence*, Anna Freud (1895–1982) extended the concept to include the transference of defense. She suggested that during analysis the patient unconsciously

5. Freud, *Dora*, 138.
6. Freud, *Dora*, 138–39.

deploys against the analyst the same strategies for repression and defense acquired in the course of the original experiences that are now being transferred onto the analyst. Later, the concept was widened in another way. In 1967, Ralph R. Greenson (1911–79) described feelings, drives, attitudes, fantasies, and psychological defenses repeating and replacing reactions to important figures in early childhood. So, transference doesn't just happen during analysis—it can feature in everyday interactions. Unconsciously, I treat a woman colleague as if she were my mother and use against her the ways of behaving that I developed when I felt and concealed hostility toward my mother.

Let us suppose that all this is sound. How does it relate to our first supposition, that signs make us what we are and that signs are inherently unstable? Freud's patients seem to be functioning exactly according to Hillis Miller's formulae; the erotic and aggressive conflicts of childhood become for them a system of signs, and there seems to be no ground, no basis, no hypostasis for deconstructionists to question their being transferred onto other, later contexts, in analysis or in everyday life. Might we not challenge Freud's designation of such transference as a problem, and those who enact it as patients? After all, if transference is as common a feature of experience as Greenson suggests, if it characterizes relationships between spouses, colleagues, teachers and students, drivers and traffic cops, why should we not think of it as a normal kind of "play"?

But this would be inappropriate because Freud himself made this move in proposing the concept of countertransference, by which the analyst (functioning in psychoanalysis as the hypostatic union of "reason, science and law"!) also succumbs to transference in the course of the analysis. Freud saw countertransference as something to be overcome; you can't have clinicians being infected with the mental disorders of their patients. He therefore insisted that all psychoanalysts should first be analyzed. But should not the countertransference in the analyst also be analyzed? In which case, *quis custodiet ipsos custodes?* Who shall analyze the countertransference of the analyst's analyst? In the psychoanalytic tradition, this problem was resolved by Freud's asserting the legitimacy and validity of his own self-analysis: Freud is in effect the self-constituted hypostasis, foundation or ground, from which analysis derives its legitimacy and to which it must be related to make sense. This grounding deconstructionists, according to their own logic, should permit, at least provisionally, even though they would subsequently also have to challenge it if it appeared that all other moves were thereby be deemed illegitimate. This I take it is the basis for feminist critiques of Freud from within the psychoanalytical tradition.

It would be wrong, however, to assume that psychoanalytical practice can be so readily assimilated into deconstructionist premises. Psychoanalysis is nothing if it is not therapeutic: its business is to order the disordered in the name of "reason, science and law," ultimately in the name of the Father, that is, of Freud himself. Later, some analysts decided that the coexistence of transference and countertransference furthered this therapeutic goal by facilitating authentic interpersonal knowledge between analyst and analysand. Countertransference, recognized as such and as (in part) related to the patient's transference, became a field in which the patient and analyst could mutually know each other and work together. But doesn't this also suggest that analysis can get behind relevant signifiers to the primary level of experience that Hillis Miller and Volosinov believe cannot be encountered because it is not there?

It would seem that, after all, our first two suppositions are incompatible.

Supposition 3, Modern Christology: Schillebeeckx

Edward Schillebeeckx (1914–2009), a radical Catholic theologian, held (along with many other New Testament scholars) that the historical Jesus never applied the titles "Son of God" and "the Son" to himself. "These were Christian identifications of Jesus of Nazareth after his death."[7] Jesus was exclusively concerned with "the coming rule of God ... *metanoia* [radical mind-change] and the praxis of [or practical life in] God's kingdom."[8] But this coming rule, which required a total reorientation of Jewish life, was neither messianic nor apocalyptic. Jesus did not claim to be the Messiah or predict the end of the world. Unlike "the apocalyptical, Pharisaic, Essene and Zealotic conceptions upheld by ... movements which isolated themselves into remnant communities [in Jesus's day]," Schillebeeckx writes, "Jesus' message and praxis [were uniquely] for all Israel without exception, including all that was abandoned and lost,"[9] lepers, prostitutes, and profiteering tax collectors. In passing, we may note that this and similar reconstructions of the life and teaching of Jesus are not to be taken as facts, but as the result of reading late Jewish and early Christian texts in the light of Enlightenment assumptions, that is, "reason, science, law." Deconstructionists would insist on the provisional nature of this sort of scholarship, on the absolute equality between all acts of interpretation, and the inappropriateness of differentiating between them in terms of "truth" and "value."

With this caution, we may assume that there is no sound evidence of Jesus having ever made himself the subject of his preaching, the New Testament texts notwithstanding. Nevertheless, there are two ways, Schillebeeckx maintains, in which Jesus may be said to be inseparable from his message: he apparently practiced what he preached—his followers and opponents seem to have read the implications of *metanoia* from his way of life—and he addressed God not according to the Jewish formula as "Father, Lord of heaven and earth," but as "Abba," as if he himself were in a family relationship with God. In this he seems to have regarded himself as significantly different even from his closest followers.

7. Schillebeeckx, *Jesus*, 258.
8. Schillebeeckx, *Jesus*, 266.
9. Schillebeeckx, *Jesus*, 267.

But not as any kind of supernatural being. In Jewish wisdom literature, a son owes unconditional obedience to his father, by whom he is instructed, whom he obeys, and to whom he belongs. In calling God "Abba," Schillebeeckx's Jesus claims no more than to be obedient and instructed in a special sense. Even if we look at the "Q" texts—passages in the Gospels According to Matthew and Luke that may have been taken from a lost source document—Jesus, Schillebeeckx maintains, is not said to have claimed or enjoyed any kind of preexistence, as, say, the Divine Wisdom, still less as the co-equal Son of the Father. His manner of addressing God was nonetheless radical in its conception of God. For the God of Jesus (in "Q," in Schillebeeckx's hypothesis, and perhaps even in fact) seems not to have been the ineffable "Most High," the unsignifiable Transcendent One, the doing of whose will was "the kernel of Jewish spirituality," and who kept faith with his people by securing, historically—if necessary by miraculous intervention at the end of time—the vindication of the just. Rather, he was an accessible and nameable Father, "one who is against evil"[10] and unconditionally for all people, who offered "a hope not inferable from … history … To believe in this God is to put one's trust in Someone who takes his identity seriously (hence the Torah—the first five books of the Jewish Scriptures—as the revelation of God's will) and at the same time declines to disclose his identity in advance."[11] "I shall be who I shall be" is how, according to a possible translation of the Hebrew, he describes himself in the story of the Burning Bush (Ex 3:14).

The God of Schillebeeckx's Jesus, then, was known to him through a reading of the Torah, grounded in an experience of familial intimacy with him acquired, as the Gospel texts suggest, through prolonged, intense prayer. Schillebeeckx thus envisages Jesus locating himself within a deeply internalized worldview constitut-

10. Schillebeeckx, *Jesus*, 267.

11. Schillebeeckx, *Jesus*, 268.

ed by a culturally determined system of distinctively Jewish signs, his revolutionary use of the word "Abba" being a founding act of self-assessment. Would such a self-location be in any way comparable with Freud's self-analysis?

In some ways, apparently, yes. Psychoanalysis has its foundation in the self-analysis of Freud, his therapeutic work, his intimate communication with his immediate circle, his struggle with a cultural and scientific establishment, his sexual abstinence beginning in his early forties, even his passion and death in exile. More significantly, Freud's personal wholeness, like that of Jesus, is the foundation of his followers' search for it, and, insofar as that personal wholeness may be in doubt (Was Freud afraid of women? Did Jesus address the Syro-Phoenician woman in racially abusive terms?), excuses are sought for each in terms of their historical circumstances, Viennese or Palestinian culture.

There remains a problem, however. All this is now accessible only through the Scriptures, Judeo-Christian and psychoanalytical. Only by reading the canonical texts, the commentaries upon them, the developing tradition, the challenges on matters of fact (Did Freud deliberately falsify the record? Did Jesus call himself the Son of Man?) can we engage with the real claims of psychoanalysis or Christianity. The record in each case, apparently, is entirely constituted by signs. Neither Freud nor Jesus can be present, can they? Is there, then, anything *there*, anything primary, to be grasped? Can they be known and not just thought up?

Schillebeeckx is aware of the difficulties, though perhaps unwilling to bear the weight of deconstructionist negation:

> To go in search of the original and unique centre of someone's . . . experience [he writes] is a highly precarious undertaking. That is true (a) if the person gives direct expression to his private experiences . . . for then we have the problem of telling what may be the relation between the authentic element of experience and its clarifying interpretation, as the two are of course inextricably intertwined, without coinciding in a self-evident or transparent

> identity; and (b) when somebody does not articulate such experiences directly . . . This is . . . difficult . . . because we are . . . trying to penetrate to the very mystery of a personal being . . . what constitutes him as this particular person and provides ground for this being-as-a-person. Now the mystery of each person is only accessible to us in his behaviour, which on the other hand is just the inadequate sign of the person manifesting himself in it and at the same time conceals him. It is more than his several actions and yet is disclosed only *in* this activity. This does not stop us from acquiring through these acts a slant on the mystery of the person of another individual human being within the insuperable ambivalence of our history.[12]

But is even this limited optimism justified? Can signs make anything present but themselves? Is Schillebeeckx's distinction between the authentic element of experience and its interpretation allowable (except, of course, provisionally, playfully, without commitment)? Are the suppositions behind modern readings of who and what Jesus Christ was—is?—the suppositions of current "Christology," dissolved alongside those of psychoanalysis in a theoretically necessary deconstruction of hypostasis, of what it is to be a human being?

Supposition 4, A Subordinationist Christology: Milton

Milton was a subordinationist. He did not believe in the three equal and coeternal persons of the orthodox Christian Trinity. Consequently, when he discussed the divine essence in *De Doctrina Christiana,* he dismissed the distinction between person and nature as meaningless. But this made for difficulties when he tried to account for the unity of Jesus and his identity with the preincarnate Son, who he believed was "begotten" by the Father without fully sharing his Divine Nature. Here was a being whose essence or hypostasis placed him higher than the angels but who then assumed the essence or hypostasis of a man without losing his original identity or acquiring a second. Milton made a virtue of this difficulty by

12. Schillebeeckx, *Jesus,* 259.

declaring that "it is best for us to be ignorant of things which God wishes to remain secret."[13] Nevertheless, he believed that Jesus of Nazareth was the incarnation of a heavenly being and was represented to the people of Israel (initially by a voice from Heaven at his Baptism) as the Son of God. His subordinationism notwithstanding, his Christology would seem much more conservative and traditional than that of Schillebeeckx.

On closer examination, however, they turn out to be remarkably alike. Milton's is a modern Jesus. He has no memories or knowledge of his preincarnate life and must learn about himself and the world by reading. Like Schillebeeckx's Jesus, his self-knowledge is an act of introspective self-reading. Specifically, in *Paradise Regained,* which is about Jesus's temptation by Satan after his forty-day fast in the wilderness, Jesus and Satan have to work out what the title "son of God" means. "The Son" is a signifier on the slide in Milton, as are "God," "gods," and "godlike." "For Son of God to me is yet in doubt," Satan declares in *Paradise Regained* (IV, 501). It "bears no single sense / The Son of God I also am, or was" (IV, 517–18), and "All men are Sons of God" (IV, 520). He has therefore to determine "In what degree of meaning" Jesus is "called / The Son of God" (516–17).

In psychoanalysis, to question Sonship is to question not Mother but Father, who can be known only as the Mother chooses to reveal him. Having no mother but only the Creator/Father, Satan can therefore reduce the notion of Fatherhood itself to Nothing. At the early stage of his rebellion in *Paradise Lost,* the seraph Abdiel fiercely rebukes him, informing him that the creation of the angelic host was delegated to the Son. To this the outraged Satan replies:

> That we were formed then sayst thou? and the work
> Of secondary hands . . .
>
> who saw
>
> When this creation was? rememberest thou

13. Milton, *Complete Prose Works,* 6:424.

> Thy making, while the maker gave thee being?
> We know no time when we were not as now;
> Know none before us, self-begot, self-raised
> By our own quickening power, when fatal course
> Had circled his full orb, the birth mature
> Of this our native heaven, ethereal sons.
> (V, 853–54, 856–63)

Later philosophers, notably the German Romantic philosopher Friedrich Wilhelm Schelling (1775–1854) and Slavoj Žižek, would similarly assert that minds can beget and give birth to themselves from the vortex of Nothing.

In *Paradise Regained*, by contrast, Mary's motherhood of Jesus is a given for both Satan and Jesus, and therefore the identity of his Father can be authoritatively *narrated* by her. Jesus recalls how, as a young man, he engaged in intense self-exploration:

> These growing thoughts my mother soon perceiving
> … inly rejoiced
> And said to me, "…
> Thy Father is the Eternal King who rules
> All Heaven and Earth …"
> (I, 227–29; 238–39)

Jesus then knows the *name* of his Father, but not what he himself is. He remains without knowledge on this point even at the climax of the poem, as he stands on the pinnacle of the Temple and Satan is smitten with amazement and falls self-confounded, as the Sphinx does when Oedipus solves its riddle. Has Satan read the Jesus riddle? Possibly, for Satan knew the Son in his preincarnate state. But not even in this second fall does he admit to recognizing who Jesus is. The unique nature of the latter's Sonship is only made clear (or at any rate clearer) when Jesus hears angels singing about it before his quiet return to "his mother's house" (IV, 639).

Neither Jesus nor Satan, however, is an incompetent reader of the Jesus text. In Book IV, for example, Satan tells Jesus,

> soon thou shalt have cause
> To wish thou never hadst rejected thus
> Nicely or cautiously my offered aid.
> (IV, 375–77)

Being an expert reader of the signs of the times, he then predicts the kind of suffering Jesus will undergo. But he must also acknowledge that those same signs indicate that Jesus will inherit a Kingdom. Still, their ambiguity leaves him scope to frighten his antagonist:

> but what Kingdom
> Real or Allegoric, I discern not,
> Nor when, eternal sure, as without end,
> Without beginning; for no date prefixt
> Directs me in the Starry Rubric set.
> (IV, 389–83)

This compares well with Jesus's own prognostications in his opening speech in Book I. Both contain much that is "true," but "much" is not enough for Satan. He finds not knowing the when and how of Jesus's coming Kingdom intolerable. His assault on Jesus is based on the assumption that *anyone* would feel the same way.

For Satan, then, to quote Barthes, "plural is the Evil,"[14] yet he is stuck in a world entirely constituted by degrees of meaning, a world that constitutes him as "the world" constitutes Volosinov's human subjects. But for Milton this is only because in his damned condition Satan is doomed, as it were, to function as a neurotic whose analysis has failed. He transfers onto the person of Jesus the repressed fears and anxieties first aroused in him when the Messiah-Son was revealed to the angels before his fall, the Son's part in the great war in Heaven in Books V and VI of *Paradise Lost* being censored by Satan and his followers when, condemned eternally to Hell, they recall the war in Books I and II. Not even the Son's existence is acknowledged. Ironically, in this case, the transference lights on its original object,

14. Barthes, *Image Music Text*, 160.

though Satan fails to articulate his recognition of this in consciousness—hence his failure to benefit from his "analysis."

Jesus, however, aware of his own origins as related by his mother, of the promises of Scripture, and of the title conferred on him by the voice from Heaven, accepts in Barthes's words that the "plural of the Text depends … not on the ambiguity of its contents but on … the stereographic *plurality* of its weave of signifiers."[15] To fix a meaning, as Satan wants to do, is to eat up the sign: instead, Jesus accepts his self-reading as "play, activity, production, practice."[16] The difference between Satan and Jesus is in their responses to the multiplicity of all meanings, upon which Satan seeks to impose totalitarian closure, but in which Jesus discerns by faith his Father's will.

This is a far cry from Volosinov and Hillis Miller, for whom an unqualified relativization of all signifying arises from the nature of signs. For Milton and for his Jesus, accepting a relativized system of signs is prior to their being read, an act profoundly internal to the person, in consequence of which a world constituted by signs becomes the territory of personal autonomy and freedom. To say with Volosinov that the person is constituted by the world would be to deny that the individual can initiate a human reading of it, as Milton understands that activity, specifically the reading of the Scriptures. For, Milton writes in his pamphlet *Of Civil Power,*

> These not being possible to be understood without divine illumination, which no man can know at all times to be in himself, much less to be at any time for certain in any other, it follows clearly that no man or body of men … can be the infallible judges or determiners in matters of religion to any other men's consciences but their own.[17]

No one has guaranteed access to full meaning of signs, an automatic feed from the Spirit of Truth. Consequently, only the human in-

15. Barthes, *Image Music Text,* 159.

16. Barthes, *Image Music Text,* 162.

17. Milton, "Of Civil Power," in *Complete Prose Works,* 7:243 (spelling modernized).

dividual can judge when that feed is operating in his or her life. As readers, we are sole judges of *when* we are infallible. This, incidentally, is exactly what Newman means by "*Assent*" and "*Certitude*."[18]

To read authentically as a person, however, the Jesus of *Paradise Regained*, unlike the Christians who came after him, does not require the assistance of the Spirit of Truth (the Holy Spirit). According to *De Doctrina Christiana*, Jesus is a human being uniquely capable of thinking and acting without the aid of the Spirit because, as the Only Begotten Son, his generation by the Father antedates the creation of the Spirit. Both are subordinate to the Father: the New Testament refers to the Spirit randomly as the Spirit of the Father and the Spirit of Jesus. The self-constitution of Jesus in *Paradise Regained* is completed by Jesus alone and corresponds exactly to the self-legitimization of Freud's self-analysis in psychoanalytical theory. In his encounter with Satan, he has no need for the strategies of defense: there is no question of anything like countertransference on his part. Even by the end of the poem, he has not specified his own nature to himself—the world of signs in which he finds himself remains a plural text requiring unlimited collaboration. He accepts that he can never be fully in the presence of himself. But this does not cause him to panic. In his willingness to remain unresolved, he foregoes all need of transference or whatever might correspond to it. His acceptance of personal contingency is precisely the act that establishes his personal autonomy.

Moreover, having thus constituted himself as unconditionally open to his own plurality, the Jesus of *Paradise Regained* also becomes the Signifier of the Transcendental Signified, God. God is *entirely* absent from both *Paradise Lost* and *Paradise Regained*; he is *outside* the text. The absurd puppet, who is given a speaking part in the earlier poem, is a *sign* of the Father, but we are warned (by Milton in *De Doctrina Christiana* and by Raphael in *Paradise Lost*) that

18. See Newman, *Grammar of Assent*.

he is not a very good sign. There is only *one* adequate Similitude for the Father in the whole of creation, and that is the Son,

> In whose conspicuous countenance, without cloud
> Made visible, the Almighty Father shines.
> (III, 385–86)

But the central act of the Son's life is unconditional collaboration with the plurality of the signs, complete defenselessness. It follows that a similar act of self-effacement must be central to the unsignifiable life of Milton's God. Which brings us back to Schillebeeckx: "To believe in this God is to put one's trust in Someone who takes his identity seriously (hence the Torah as the revelation of God's will) and at the same time declines to disclose his identity in advance ('I shall be who I shall be,' Ex 3:14)."

Thus, granted the suppositions I have been attributing to Schillebeeckx and Milton, our first two suppositions no longer appear contradictory. The play of signifiers is limitless *only* when it is hypostatically constituted, that is, when persons are doing the playing.

Supposition 5, Games People Play: Wittgenstein

In *Tractatus Logico-Philosophicus,* Ludwig Wittgenstein argues that language has meaning only if it consists of propositions about facts. These have a precise, basically pictorial, sense. If two propositions are logically related to one another, one or both will reveal a logical complexity and can therefore be reduced to two or more further factual propositions that are not logically related. The *Tractatus* thus proposes a granular universe represented in language by logically discrete propositions. Propositions can never state the whole of what is the case, but language can say nothing about anything except the facts. The position adopted in his second great work, *Philosophical Investigations,* is different. "It is Wittgenstein's later doctrine that outside human thought and speech there are no independent, objective points of support, and meaning and necessity are preserved only in the linguistic practices which embody them."[19] So, does Wittgenstein suppose with Hillis Miller that the world is entirely constituted by signs and that there is nothing primitive underlying them? It seems so.

Consider his arguments against the hypothesis that you and I might have different sensations when our eyes encounter the same yellow object. Such a hypothesis implies that a specific sensation is something people can "have," as they can have butter in their fridges. But they can't. What, then, are the differences between these two kinds of having? Wittgenstein refuses to answer: that is his point. The feeling that there is a question to be asked and answered here is a case of the deceptive way language seems to point toward something. The only lesson to be learned is that it would be wiser not to talk of "having" a sensation at all.

Consider the propositions "I know that I have butter in the fridge" and "This sunflower is yellow." I may be honestly wrong about the butter. I might really have margarine in the fridge. But if I say, without any intention to deceive, "This sunflower is yellow" and I am holding a sunflower in my hand, I cannot be mistaken about the truth of what I am saying. That, however, is a fact about the *words* "I," "doubt," "sensations," and "yellow," which, in this particular conjunction, require me to play with them according to certain rules. Otherwise, I could never have learnt how to use them at all. There are sensation words like "yellow," which include in some of their meanings and uses the certainty that I cannot be mistaken about whether I am "having" them or not, and thing words like "butter," which include in their meanings and uses the conviction that I can be mistaken about whether I have them in the fridge. I can "have" the experience of seeing yellow and I can "have" butter in the fridge, but the having is as different as being "in touch" in football is from

19. Pears, *Wittgenstein*, 168.

being "in touch" on Facebook. Therefore, to be taught how to use the words "yellow" and "in touch," one must be able to play with them according to specific sensation rules, sporting rules, and social media rules in each case; consequently, if we understand each other, what is yellow for me is yellow for you, and what is in touch for you is in touch for me. What else could they be?

It equally makes no sense to say, "I know this sunflower is yellow." The "I know" is redundant. Wittgenstein writes:

> I can know what someone else is thinking, not what I am thinking.
>
> It is correct to say "I know what you are thinking," and wrong to say "I know what I am thinking."
>
> (A whole cloud of philosophy condensed into a drop of grammar.)[20]

And again:

> The kind of certainty is the kind of language game.
>
> We remain unconscious of the prodigious diversity of all the everyday language-games because the clothing of our language makes everything alike.
>
> Something new (spontaneous, "specific") is always a language-game.[21]

It does not follow, however, that the world is constituted by signs, as Hillis Miller et al. would have it. To say that would be to fall for another case of deceptive pointing. Only language as one plays with it is constituted by language. I say, "Look!" and you do. But if I then try to talk about the word "look," I have a problem. I may speak of "look" as an arbitrary signifier, but the word as used in my original command is subject to different rules from the word "Look" when it is presented for discussion as an arbitrary signifier. I cannot use them in the same game. Any attempt to do so will point me deceptively toward "universally valid" distinctions between "signifiers," "signifieds," and "referents." For if language cannot say whether the laws of logic and mathematics are "independently" or "objectively" valid,

20. Wittgenstein, *Philosophical Investigations*, 222.
21. Wittgenstein, *Philosophical Investigations*, 224.

it *can* distinguish between itself and the world, and it did so when I said, "Look!" as a command. If you want to find out more about "the world," therefore, you must identify the sets of rules governing the uses to which the words "world" and "signs" are put. I cannot think of the word "world" as Volosinov uses it without also thinking of people, and streets, and food, and laughter, and death as things and facts and realities that concern me. I don't think of them as signs *at all.* Such responses are internal to language. Who has the right to deny me my referents—that is, of the things to which my signs refer—when I say, "Catch!" as I throw a ball to my grandchild?

Like a rubber ball, then, the same word can be used in different language games played by divergent rules, but there can be no overall ball theory or game theory. Language can only be examined empirically, bit by bit, and the results must be expressed in language. But no language (even the most abstractly logical) can formulate the complete set of rules required to interpret it. Consequently, no general assertion about language such as deconstructionists make is ever "grammatical," that is, makes linguistic sense. Yet words are used in public; looking is something we can do together; we can be told to do it; we can go to the game and watch. Therefore it confirms the fullness of our presence to one another. We understand each other, not just our words. "If a lion could talk," observes Wittgenstein, "we could not understand him."[22] But we understand each other, and this full presence is surprisingly intimate. Curiously, Wittgenstein's comments partake of philosophy based on experience ("phenomenology") and its opposite, philosophy that ignores experience and analyzes what people do ("behaviorism"), without ever slipping from the particular case into the globally theoretical. This is his style.

The familiar physiognomy of a word, the feeling that it has taken up its meaning into itself, that it is an actual likeness of its meaning—there could be human beings to whom all this was alien. (They would not have an at-

22. Wittgenstein, *Philosophical Investigations*, 223.

tachment to their words.) And how are these feelings manifested among us?—By the way we choose and value words.[23]

Accepting Wittgenstein's suppositions, then, allows us to disabuse ourselves of the prejudices against presence in fashionable theory, and the author and meaning. For what does the word "teaching" teach? That teaching consists of a series of discrete teaching games played by teacher and pupil—in which they and their meanings are often truly present to each other. The presence is there in the language of teaching and the language of learning, the truth in what is taught. And that may be what we witness in *Paradise Regained*—not an essay in psychoanalysis, not a dramatization of the paradox of meaning and interpretation, just a lesson taught by a master, the subject of which is himself.

How is this different from "Q," the Gospels According to Matthew, Mark, and Luke, and even the Fourth Gospel? Who is present to us in those texts? And doesn't what Wittgenstein supposes suggest that my argument about the play of signifiers depending on personal essences was factitious? What Milton may have been on about, after all, was simply the presence of the truth and of persons that the *language* of passion, piety, or affection knows.

23. Wittgenstein, *Philosophical Investigations*, 218.

Part III

Freedom and God

The true vision and the true knowledge of what we seek consists precisely in not seeing, in an awareness that our goal transcends all knowledge and is everywhere cut off from us by the darkness of incomprehension.

—Gregory of Nyssa

8

"What Do You Want?"

NEWMAN'S "INTERMINABLE SCEPTICISM"

Newman's economical principle is an excellent and a dangerous idea—excellent because it makes at least some thinking possible, and dangerous because it threatens to destabilize thought. As Newman knew from the bitter experience that accounts for his great satirical essay "Who's to Blame?," this destabilization was not only theoretical, but also introduced a principle of corruption and self-serving guilt into the heart of the British polity. The dark logic and its redemptive resolution are worked out in his historical novel *Callista*.

The Economical Principle: Newman's *Discursive Enquiries*

"The principle of the Economy," according to *Apologia pro Vita Sua*, relates primarily to "religious conduct or statement" and "comes under the head of Prudence."[1] When we talk about religion, we can't say everything, and therefore have to select what we say and the order we say it in. In Athens, Paul did not begin his preaching with a full-blown statement of the doctrine of the Atonement. But New-

1. Newman, *Apologia pro Vita Sua*, 354.

man also refers to an argument in *The Arians of the Fourth Century* (1833) that human consciousness can only entertain "shadowy representations of realities," and that *everything* we feel, think, and say is modified and limited by how we feel, think, and say it. Nothing is as it seems, and the seemings themselves are always less than they might be. When the mind first masters this idea, he admits, it seems "to have cut all the ties which bind it to the universe, and to be floated off upon the ocean of interminable scepticism." God, of course, "cannot deceive," so the information supplied by the senses "must be practically certain." Nevertheless, *all* our thinking remains "philosophically inaccurate."[2]

This idea reemerges in the last of Newman's *University Sermons* (1843). The same mathematical fact, he points out, can be *represented* in a curve or algebraically. Different mathematical conventions can express the same "necessary truths," but we have no idea what those truths are "except in the terms of such economical representations."[3] But it is only in his notes for a book that he never got round to writing, provisionally titled *Discursive Enquiries on Metaphysical Subjects*—notes begun in 1859 and continued intermittently until the end of Newman's life—that he finally clarifies the implications of these ideas. The passage quoted from *The Arians of the Fourth Century* is copied back into these notes, which also return to the problems of mathematical truth.[4] Temporal and spatial data, Newman observes, can be *represented* in both differentials and fluxions. But while fluxions are minutely related to the idea of motion, differentials are wholly independent of space and time, from which it would appear that space and time are themselves economies.

This thinking is based on a remarkably modern understanding of *representational systems*. Let us take a modern example. The

2. Newman, *Arians of the Fourth Century*, 75–76.

3. Newman, *Grammar of Assent*, 345.

4. Newman, in Myers, *Thoughtful Heart*, 59.

soundtrack on an old film translates temporal relations between sounds into spatial relations between shapes on a surface, eliminating the temporal dimension and transferring a sequence of sounds onto a two-dimensional squiggle on a long strip of celluloid. *Discursive Enquiries* applies this principle to space as well as time. The phenomenal universe, Newman suggests, may be like the soundtrack on a film, the representation of a reality, not that reality itself, which in itself is otherwise unthinkable, as sound in itself is unseeable. Slavoj Žižek has argued that "the relativity of time and space" could not be formulated "prior to our age,"[5] but in November 1866, Newman suggested that as "space has three dimensions, perhaps also has time. Succession is length. Stand at right angles to a line and look down it and it is a point."[6] Time is not necessarily in a fixed relation to the three dimensions of space. Elsewhere in *Discursive Enquiries* he writes, "I don't believe in the existence of space as a reality . . . I don't believe in time."[7]

But the principle of economies surely has its limits. Music can be represented in digital blips, but isn't an actual performance what is really there? Perhaps, but no single performance of a piece of music *is* that music, if only because every performance works on memories or anticipations of other performances and other pieces. Nor is the score the music—a further reading might yield new insights even to the composer. Thus what Newman says of the content of mathematical expressions applies also to music: it cannot be accessed *as such*. And the same has to be said of anything we express in words, or in any other symbolic system.

Discursive Enquiries tries to identify exceptions to this in the "raw or pure effect of the senses" operating independently of "the power of combination." Newman recalls the story of a man who "laughed, when put on the rack a second time—and . . . said, when asked, 'As

5. Žižek, *Metastases of Enjoyment*, 200.
6. Newman, in Myers, *Thoughtful Heart*, 106.
7. Newman, in Myers, *Thoughtful Heart*, 54.

if one could undergo the pain twice.'" Newman himself had "the nerve of a tooth cauterised." He "never had such pain in [his] life." A subsequent, more protracted operation was less horrible. "I recollect at the time," he noted, "attributing the difference ... to the novelty and want of novelty."[8] He once saw "something as if on the floor near [him] and said 'What dirty piece of carpet is that?'" It was "the sleeve of [his] cotta [surplice], which was clean from the wash."[9] Another time, he found his tea "unpleasant" until he realized it was "very good coffee."[10] Newman accepts, however, that none of these examples registers the "raw or pure effect of the senses." They were all experiences of *difference* from established "combinations." As Žižek puts it, "the Real *qua* trauma is not the ultimate 'unspeakable' truth ... but that which makes every articulated truth forever 'not-all,'"[11] that which *compels* us to acknowledge the unknown unknown. The mind, Newman writes, interprets "the senses by its own ideas," while "the "information supplied by experience through the senses interprets the experience of mind."[12] Even experience of the body "may depend on *relation*."[13] Just as the changing shape of a reflected face in a moving spoon registers changes, not in the face but in its relation to the spoon, so "the changes in a man's body from birth to death" may be only spatiotemporal models of a non-spatiotemporal reality.[14] We do not know what our bodies *are*. Sir William Hamilton argued in 1830 that, since all phenomena depend on relation, on "difference," and even "mind and matter ... are known only in correlation and contrast ... [every] conception of self necessarily involves a conception of not-self."[15] But if I am always dimly

8. Newman, in Myers, *Thoughtful Heart*, 81.
9. Newman, in Myers, *Thoughtful Heart*, 83.
10. Newman, in Myers, *Thoughtful Heart*, 84.
11. Žižek, *Plague of Fantasies*, 216–17.
12. Newman, in Myers, *Thoughtful Heart*, 82–83.
13. Newman, in Myers, *Thoughtful Heart*, 97.
14. Newman, in Myers, *Thoughtful Heart*, 105.
15. Hamilton, "Philosophy of Perception," 165.

aware of something else when I focus on self, no account of "me" can be more than an economy, conditioned by the split between what is variously felt as not me, and whatever it is that does the feeling.

Ideas like these are still around. Newman's analysis of the "raw or pure effect of the senses" is precisely how Lacan would analyze "the Real," as the quotation from Žižek implies. Moreover, the idea that the self is known only in conjunction with a primitive sensation corresponds with Lacan's famous *l'objet petit a,* the little "something else" always present in self-awareness.[16] For Lacan, self-awareness "is bound up with that which determines it—namely, a privileged object—which has emerged from some primal separation."[17] This structural gap in self-awareness takes us to the epicenter of the economical principle.

Newman would not have been at all surprised to find he had thus anticipated later thinkers. On the day he clarified his *sentio, ergo sum,* he wrote in *Discursive Enquiries,* "if there is anything at once new and good" in a writer's thinking about subjects of this kind, "years must elapse, the writer must be long dead, before it is acknowledged and received."[18]

Nor would he have been surprised that the Catholic Church currently regards with suspicion these same ideas. The penultimate entry in the *Discursive Enquiries,* dated September 24, 1888, reads, "What I write, I do not state dogmatically, but categorically that is, in investigation, nor have I confidence enough in what I have advanced to warrant publication."[19] Nearly thirty years earlier, he had written that he only aimed "at what is . . . probable,"[20] and in 1866 that specific statements might not "approve themselves . . . fully to theologians."[21]

16. Lacan, *Écrits,* xi.
17. Lacan, *Four Fundamental Concepts of Psycho-analysis,* 83.
18. Newman, in Myers, *Thoughtful Heart,* 33.
19. Newman, in Myers, *Thoughtful Heart,* 31.
20. Newman, in Myers, *Thoughtful Heart,* 32.
21. Newman, in Myers, *Thoughtful Heart,* 31.

He was right to be cautious. To suggest that there is *no* secure point to which the mind is anchored—that time and space are illusory; that "the raw or pure effect of the senses" is known only negatively, as different from everyday experience; that self-knowledge is unstable because it is bound up with a variable nonself; and that there is a core of incompleteness in all experience—is to cast oneself adrift on an ocean of interminable skepticism indeed!

Constitutions and Symptoms: *Who's to Blame?*

The economical principle also has worrying implications at the level of society. I illustrate some of them through a series of articles about the Crimean War that Newman published pseudonymously in 1854 under the title *Who's to Blame?* and in which he relied on deliberately reductive journalistic categories ("the British Lion," "the Muscovite,"[22] "human nature"[23]) and a simplistic political fable in which a Man promises a Horse victory over its enemy, the Stag, "if he would let him mount him."[24] More subtly, however, Newman distinguishes between State, Nation, and Constitution. The *State* consists of the physical forces of control and defense, of law and order. The *Nation* is the communal activity of a people, its business, culture, social life. Uniting them is the *Constitution*, which is not just a body of law but also of ideas, "trivial . . . [and] superstitious," or "great and beautiful," yet functioning as "eternal truths, whether they be such or not," as "first principles . . . natural ties, a cause to fight for."[25] In all societies, Žižek writes, "there is a kind of 'trans-ideological' kernel . . . (notions and sentiments of solidarity, justice, belonging to a community etc.)" that the governing ideology "*has* to batten on and

22. Newman, *Who's to Blame?*, 309.

23. Newman, *Who's to Blame?*, 318.

24. Newman, *Who's to Blame?*, 314.

25. Newman, *Who's to Blame?*, 315.

manipulate."[26] The Constitution is the Horse, the temper of which the rider—the individual member of a society—must adjust to.

Who's to Blame? is primarily about the British Constitution in this sense. Newman's approach to it is forbearing and ambivalent. Take his description of the Army and the Church. The English, he writes, treat a soldier or a parson as a wild animal; they "tie him up . . . pare his claws . . . and . . . keep him low; then he will be both safe and useful;—the result is a National Church, and a Constitutional Army."[27] It is obvious that a Constitutional Army has to be restrained, but the National Church also? There is clearly some anger here, but it is combined with aloof, amused acceptance that merits further scrutiny.

It first appears in a discussion of juries, introduced with the bland observation that the "end of the Judicature is justice." Though jurymen were untrained and "chosen . . . as representatives of a class," they were under the direction, Newman tartly observes, of "a properly educated and experienced dignitary, called by courtesy the Judge." The irony is sharp but momentary, and the discussion continues with the proposition that juries are *politically* beneficial in associating those (then) liable to serve on them—lower-middle-class men—"with the established order of things"—the inheritors of privilege and great wealth, and that they prevent the courts from acting in ways unacceptable to the Nation. It is right, Newman suggests, striking a suspicious note of bland common sense, that public opinion should "give the law to Law" and decide matters "of national concern." Juries ensure that "the good of the country" takes "the lead of private interest; for better far is it"—and here he pounces—"that injustice should be done to a pack of individuals, than that the maxims of the Nation" should be set at naught by "its own paid officials,"[28] an appalling vista indeed.

26. Žižek, *Plague of Fantasies*, 21.

27. Newman, *Who's to Blame?*, 357.

28. Newman, *Who's to Blame?*, 348–50.

The explanation for this cutting, Caiaphas-inspired judgment is the Achilli affair, Newman's disgraceful conviction for criminal libel in 1852. Giacinto Achilli was a renegade ex-Dominican priest, banned by the Roman authorities from his priestly functions and ordered to undergo canonical penance for his sexual depredations. He managed to reach British territory and was granted political asylum when he announced his conversion to Evangelical Protestantism. Despite further sexual misconduct in Malta, he was supported in England by the chairman of the Evangelical Alliance. He married and engaged in sensationalized anti-Catholic propaganda. He returned to Rome during the brief period when the pope was in exile and the city was governed as the Roman Republic. He was arrested when the pope was restored by the troops of Napoleon III of France, at whose request, however, he was released. After his return to England, he was accused of raping and assaulting four of his servants. Newman gave a lecture outlining Achilli's personal history and was charged with criminal libel, for which the punishment was up to a year in prison. The prosecution was conducted by legal heavyweights, the Attorney General assisted by the Solicitor General, and Newman was defended in his turn by lawyers of great eminence. Documentary evidence in support of his case did not reach his lawyers in time, and the judge refused to allow important witnesses to give evidence. He was convicted. The resulting fine and costs came to about £150,000 in today's values but were paid for by public subscription, a large part of which was collected by poor Irish Catholics.

Nevertheless, *Who's to Blame?* remains wonderfully detached from the situation it depicts. By describing the victims of miscarriages of justice as a "pack," Newman conceals the fact that he is one of them, and there is a Swiftian relish in the way he ties up, pares down, and keeps low the animals in his metaphor. The corruptions in the Constitution are left in place, almost sanctioned: "It is not a high system, but no human system is such"; the Russian knout and the American tar-barrel "are less pleasant"; under the British system, the individual is at least generally consulted. "Injustice is the exception; a free and easy mode of living is the rule. It is a venal *régime; que voulez-vous?*"[29]

Social processes like these, Žižek explains, exemplify what he calls the sadistic superego that comes into play when the "Law . . . is compelled to search for support in an *illegal* enjoyment."[30] Public law, he argues, is always founded on an illegal seizure of power that it never admits to. Thomas Cromwell's Reformation, Dutch William's "Glorious Revolution," and the genocide and ethnic cleansing in the Americas and Australia are obvious examples. There is a gap at the heart of every legal system, structurally comparable with the gap at the heart of self-consciousness. But whereas the discontinuity of self-awareness generates anxiety, the extralegal basis of law generates a sense of guilt. In Newman's remarkable words, "Men call themselves the *nation* when they sin in a body."[31] The "primordial lie that founds a community," Žižek writes, "is ultimately always based upon some shared guilt or, more precisely, upon the *fetishistic disavowal of this guilt*,"[32] or, as Newman puts it, "the nation, being a name, has nothing to answer for." So, what Newman calls "the anti-Catholic virulence of the present race of Englishmen"[33] could represent the "spirit of community"[34] for his fellow countrymen. By violating "the explicit rules of community life,"[35] anti-Catholic virulence enabled the Lord Chief Justice and Sir John Taylor Coleridge to run in spirit alongside the patriotic Birmingham street urchins who pursued Newman with the gleeful cry "six months in quod!"[36]

29. Newman, *Who's to Blame?*, 352.
30. Žižek, *Metastases of Enjoyment*, 54.
31. Newman, *Parochial and Plain Sermons*, 4:97.
32. Žižek, *Metastases of Enjoyment*, 57.
33. Newman, *Who's to Blame?*, 322.
34. Žižek, *Metastases of Enjoyment*, 55.
35. Žižek, *Metastases of Enjoyment*, 54.
36. Ker, *John Henry Newman*, 374.

All Newman will say of these practices, however, is *Que voulez-vous?* Lacan would have approved. He regarded the symptoms of a mental disorder as "particular" to the life of the person under analysis,[37] and in his psychoanalytic practice, he made no attempt to eliminate them by uncovering their hidden causes. When the analysand asks the Lacanian analyst, "As the expert here, what do *you* want me to want?" the only appropriate reply, Lacan writes, is "'Che vuoi?'—'What do *you* want?'": this alone leads the analysand "to the path of his own desire."[38] The analysand in *Who's to Blame?* is the reader, eager to know what Newman wants, as diagnostician in this case. But the only answer one gets is his Lacanian question: *Que voulez-vous? Che vuoi?*

This is why *Who's to Blame?* is so disturbing. Newman confronts us with the gaps and fissures at the heart of all our thinking, feeling, and relationships, but he refuses to fill them in. He leaves *us* to decide what we want, to make our *own* choices about the fissures in minds, society, and the world—all symbolized, perhaps, by the locked jury room in which, on June 24, 1852, twelve of his fellow countrymen gave the law to Law, and convicted Newman of criminally libeling Giacinto Achilli—false, fleeting, perjured Giacinto.

"What Do You Want?": Callista

We can now make some preliminary judgments about the economical principle. Lacan identifies two levels of mental life: the Imaginary, arising out of sense experience, especially seeing, and the Symbolic, constituted in language and other cultural economies; he calls these "the Big Other," the Big Other for him being "France" and "Psychoanalysis." Cultural economies unite in endlessly fruitful combination: think of opera, liturgy, sport. But their incompleteness is also evident, especially at the personal level, where the question "What do you want?" breaks down into two parts—"What is *really*

37. Lacan, *Écrits*, 81.

38. Lacan, *Écrits*, 312.

to be desired?" and "What or who does the desiring?"—questions I shall now consider by examining the desires of the heroine of Newman's historical novel *Callista* (1855), and those of her brother Aristo.

Callista is a proto-feminist character. Exiled from Greece with Aristo, in the middle years of the second century CE to Sicca in North Africa, she is a gifted artist, painting sculptures of the pagan gods for a prosperous dealer in idols, Jucundus. But she is intellectually and emotionally restless and disinclined to be governed by her worldly brother. Jucundus encourages his nephew and potential heir, Agellius, in his wooing of Callista, hoping that, as his wife, she will draw him away from Christianity. (Agellius has a brother, Juba, a deeply disturbed young man who rejects religion of any kind. Their mother, Gutta, is a witch.) But Callista contrasts Agellius's tepid Christianity with the exultant devotion of a young Christian female slave, now dead. Agellius is drawn more deeply into his Christian faith by a priest, Caecilius, a character based on St. Cyprian, Bishop of Carthage, who was martyred in 258 CE under Emperor Valerian. Caecilius entrusts Callista with a copy of the Gospel According to Luke. Two factors bring catastrophe on the Christian community: a plague of locusts for which the Christians are scapegoated, and a decree by Valerian's predecessor, Decius, that all Roman citizens must offer sacrifice "for the safety of the Empire." In the resulting mob violence and persecution, the as yet unbaptized Callista refuses to call herself a Christian but refuses also to sacrifice to gods in which she no longer believes. She reads the Gospel in prison and is visited by Caecilius, who baptizes, confirms, and gives her the Eucharist. She is then subjected to brutal treatment by the authorities and is finally executed. I think Lacan would have found *Callista* of great interest, especially in the light of what he identifies as "the Real." Žižek should read it—he would be especially interested in Juba and Gutta.

The ego, Lacan maintains, is "formed of a verbal nucleus"[39]—be-

39. Lacan, *Écrits*, 89.

ginning with a word, "I," "me." The unconscious likewise has "the structure of language,"[40] that is, of metaphor and metonymy. The parables in Matthew 13 illustrate what this means. As parables, they are all metaphors, but they are not *just* parables; each is a little story in its own right, and to call them parables is to identify the whole by a part common to them all. They form a chain of connected metonymies. But there is a gappiness in metaphor and metonymy, as there is in consciousness and society: what mustard seed, leaven, and buried treasure have in common can only be amplified in another image, say, of a pearl. So, as well as giving us *something* to think about, metaphor and metonymy give us *nothing* to think about. They are haunted by the Real, that which falls outside their "power of combination."

But the Real is to be avoided. That is why in psychoanalysis, Lacan suggests, the ego is "the centre of all the *resistances* to . . . treatment."[41] Rather than face *everything* that desire entails, the analysand clings like a limpet to its mere signifiers. For, though each partial object finally disappoints, we can always move to the next, from a pearl that has lost its luster to a net bulging with still-glittering fish: we would rather choose another signifier than enter the unknowable kingdom. "What sort of subject," Lacan asks, "can we conceive" for desire thus compulsively on the move?[42] His answer? Someone whose instincts are "eternally stretching forth towards the *desire for something else*."[43]

As well as being linguistic, Lacan suggests, desire is also socially determined. It is *always* "*qua* Other" that we desire,[44] what will be the next link in the metonymic chain that we will fondle like a bead on a rosary. This is certainly how the mind of Callista's brother is constituted. An accommodating conformist, his desire becomes

40. Lacan, *Écrits*, 298.
41. Lacan, *Écrits*, 23.
42. Lacan, *Écrits*, 298.
43. Lacan, *Écrits*, 167.
44. Lacan, *Écrits*, 312.

"lost in a will that is will of the other."[45] He wants to know what the world expects young men to want so that he can want it too. His goal is what Lacan derides as the "American" project of "obtaining 'success' ... [by] demanding 'happiness,'"[46] as defined by others. Aristo thinks Callista mad because her desire isn't "defined" at all. So, he takes his restless heart into the postmodern disorders of Carthage, leaving her to a terrible fate.

His flight is from the Real, which makes its first appearance in *Callista* in a tour de force of virtuoso prose, the description of the swarm of locusts. This prompts a crisis in the social economy of North Africa and a second eruption of the Real, when the mob sets about the Christians. Their violence leads to Callista's martyrdom, and a final encounter with the Real, first, when she is thrust into the *barathrum*, "the public cesspool"[47]—another secret, enclosed space, more unspeakable than an English jury room, around which a great empire revolves—then put on the rack, to feel a pain that can only be felt once. Faced with this nightmare and asked, "What do you want?" Aristo could only have cried, "Not *that*!" The implications of Callista's desire are for a mind such as his unthinkable.

So, what *does* Callista want? Like Aristo, she at first tries to base her desires on those of others, specifically of Agellius. But he wants her. This undermines, she thinks, the seriousness of his belief in a spiritual world, and her own "yearning after some object that may possess [her]." But she refuses to fall back on what "philosophers call wisdom, and moralists call virtue," on "the Big Other." She wants "something to love."[48] What is she repudiating here, and what does this tell us about her desire?

First, she is repudiating sex—she finds "noble Grecian forms" and "manly" voices attractive, but they cannot give her what she is

45. Lacan, *Écrits*, 105.

46. Lacan, *Écrits*, 127.

47. Newman, *Callista*, 365.

48. Newman, *Callista*, 132.

looking for. But she is also repudiating the Big Other itself. Symbols, Lacan writes, "envelop" human life,[49] and the foundational symbol is a name, "Father." Motherhood, after all, is a physically given fact, but "no one would ever know" (until very recently) about fatherhood "without a signifier."[50] Yet on this arbitrary sign, kinship systems, laws against incest, "the never-failing cycle" of "wives and goods," and therefore civilization itself were precariously founded.[51] Callista's chastity is not, therefore, a private matter. It challenges the patriarchal Big Other—Rome, Sicca, "the movement of the 'Great Debt.'"[52]

This is why she must be compelled to sacrifice to the gods. Such sacrifices, of course, are mere formalities—that is their point. Human beings need wholeness, and must pretend that the Big Other supplies it, even though the Big Other is based on illegality—in Rome's case the imperial system that subverted the ancient republic—though the pretense is kept up that it is still in existence. Sacrificing to nothing while pretending it is something expresses the truth while covering it up. Such cynical charades constitute a social bond—just like the deference paid in Victorian England to "twelve good men and true," or the Articles of Religion. What gives *Callista* "so much of its interest is the largely unexpressed analogy between [the Roman world and] ... nineteenth-century Protestant England"[53]—the world, that is, of *Who's to Blame?* Except, of course, that Rome had a more extreme way with nonconformists than six months in quod, or even exposing them to ridicule on a station platform.

So much for what Rome wants her citizens to want, but what does Callista want? Further consideration of Lacan's imaginary order will help to elucidate this question, specifically his account of a still-uncoordinated baby recognizing its image in a mirror, *seeing* it-

49. Lacan, *Écrits*, 68.
50. Lacan, *Écrits*, 199.
51. Lacan, *Écrits*, 68.
52. Lacan, *Écrits*, 67.
53. Ker, *John Henry Newman*, 420.

self as whole but *feeling* its immature body as disordered. Its sense of self is thus, yet again, split—"that there," the ideal self in the mirror, is better than "this here," the felt self that is physically out of control. This produces a "narcissistic fear of damage to [the] body," "a neurosis of self-punishment,"[54] and images "of . . . mutilation, dismemberment, dislocation, evisceration"[55]—just what Callista can expect from Roman justice.

Callista therefore chooses our oldest, worst nightmare. Why? Does she allow her felt self to be dismembered merely to protect the infantile fantasy of an ideal self? Does she choose an "attitude of radical self-instrumentalization, of turning [herself] into the pure instrument-object of the Other's *jouissance*,"[56] of the Christian God's and/or the mob's delight? This is the position Lacan identifies not as neurotic but as *perverted*, and Newman's less sympathetic readers might interpret Callista's behavior in just such terms.

But we are still only at the level of motives, of the partial objects of desire in the metonymic chain. According to Lacan, however, there is another, unspecifiable energy, into which desire resolves itself, once it is freed from attachment to partial objects, whether they are "healthy" like harvest and pearl, or "perverted" like *barathrum* and rack. This he calls blind drive. Blind drive emerges in a third moment in our psychic formation. In addition to seeing its reflected image, and learning the word "father," the child discovers how to play with death in the game called in German *fort-da*—"All gone! Back again!" In making mother symbolically disappear and return, the child learns about extinction as an experience of power. Desire "becomes human" when it is spoken.[57] The words "All gone! Back again!" make *what* comes and goes unimportant. The action be-

54. Lacan, *Écrits*, 28.

55. Lacan, *Écrits*, 11.

56. Žižek, *Plague of Fantasies*, 232.

57. Lacan, *Écrits*, 103.

comes "its own object," and this eliminates compulsive attachment to partial objects. This is blind drive, and it is linked to a disclosure that everyone is inclined to suppress: the path of desire is always absent and is never me. Ultimately, there is nothing to desire, just drive without content, indistinguishable from death, from nothing.

The Lacanian answer to the question "What is to be desired?" is, then, "Nothing." But who or what does this blind desiring? What is this me from which the path of desire is always absent? Žižek summarizes the Lacanian answer. I am constituted when my infant self first says, "Me!" when "I posit my unity . . . in a signifier which represents me." But this "positing" is "blind" because "Me!" is a word I have learned from others. It is "outside myself." Moreover, it does not signify anything that can be observed; it is the assumption that makes observation possible, another instance of the gap, or fissure on which all signifying depends. "Me!," Žižek declares, is "*a signifier . . . which stands for 'nothing,'*"[58] another "fundamental, constitutive, primordial *lie*."[59]

In Lacanian logic, therefore, the answer to both our questions is the same—Nothing. Callista must stop "yearning after some object that may possess [her]," and surrender to "the purity of Non-Being."[60] This is not a counsel of despair, however; something comes of the Lacanian nothing, or if not "something," at any rate, *Jouissance*. I cannot begin to summarize what *Jouissance* entails, but it is at once close to the vision driving Callista and Newman, and profoundly *heretical*. Christians can accept Lacan's assertion that so long as people function in a signifying process, they "cannot aim at being whole"[61]—their socially constructed identities must fall upon the ground and die. They might also agree that an absence of *Jouissance* "makes the universe vain."[62] What is intolerable from the

58. Žižek, *Indivisible Remainder*, 43.

59. Žižek, *Indivisible Remainder*, 1.

60. Lacan, *Écrits*, 317.

61. Lacan, *Écrits*, 287.

62. Lacan, *Écrits*, 317.

Christian perspective is the conclusion that *Jouissance* entails "the purity of Non-Being," an enthusiastic denial that the self and the other *exist.*

It is of some importance, therefore, to be able to demonstrate that Callista's martyrdom does not imply a comparably nihilistic logic. This is difficult to accomplish, however, because Newman treats her inner life with reserve. For "the novelist," Lacan writes, "situations . . . [make] possible the emergence of 'depth psychology,'"[63] but Callista is never *situated,* her psyche never penetrated. From the start, she has lost interest in tangible objects of desire—no young Greeks compete with Agellius for her attention, nor does she observe them like the heroine of a novel by Jane Austen. Her "depths" are invisible: as a heroine, she is uninteresting compared, say, with Charlotte Brontë's Lucy Snowe or Henry James's Isabel Archer. She is simply driven and consumed with anxiety in case what drives her is without value. The narration does not follow her into the *barathrum*—who would wish to?—but it also remains aloof from the path of her desire, from any explanation for her behavior. The question *Que voulez-vous?*—"What do *you* want from the story of Callista?"—is returned to Newman's readers with exemplary reticence.

"Ergo sum": *Discursive Enquiries* Again

Callista, then, presents us with a problem. I used the word "heretical" of Lacan's *Jouissance* because the Lacanian tradition explicitly subverts the doctrine of the Word in the Fourth Gospel. According to Žižek, Lacanianism goes back at least to Schelling, for whom the "Word" is not a Person, but merely the act by which "God," understood not as a Personal Being but as the "Absolute," posits itself "as Reason."[64] Although this positing takes place "in the beginning," there is a phase of mental or spiritual self-formation that somehow

63. Lacan, *Écrits,* 217.

64. Žižek, *Indivisible Remainder,* 16.

precedes it, "when God ... was ... at the mercy of the antagonism of matter, without any guarantee that ... Light ... would eventually prevail over ... Ground."[65] This mysterious state of "divine" helplessness, however, is no less mysteriously *preontological*[66]—always already. Žižek's updated version of what he calls this "basic insight" is that it is not the absolute as Schelling envisaged it but the human subject that begins as the pure "night of the Self" and then generates "the symbolic order, the universe of the Word, *logos*."[67]

Either way, of course, the prologue to the Fourth Gospel is being turned on its head. Schelling and Žižek both represent the Flesh or matter becoming Word, not the Word becoming Flesh. Their version of the *logos* is multiple and contingent, and so, finally, nothing. They agree, in effect, with St. Athanasius that "Men have many words, and after those many, not any one ... for the speaker has ceased and ... his word fails." "But," St. Athanasius continues, "God's Word is one and the same, and ... *remaineth forever*,"[68] and "flesh" is something this Divine Word could *become*. From the first Epistle to the Thessalonians, therefore, to the condemnation of the Monothelites (who held that Christ did not will as a human being but only as God) over six hundred years later, the mind of the Church, though principally concerned with the mystery of the Word, had necessarily to think about the flesh, and in finally affirming that the human being has a "natural will," she completed her understanding of what being "made flesh" amounts to. The result was a new conception of what it is to be a thinking and acting being, a conception to which, in the West, we have given the name "person," a hypostasis or person that *wills*. There was no such term in the ancient world. In both Greek and Latin, the word coming nearest to "person" was "head."[69] And it is this

65. Žižek, *Indivisible Remainder*, 32.

66. Žižek and Schelling, *Abyss of Freedom/Ages of the Word*, 6.

67. Žižek and Schelling, *Abyss of Freedom/Ages of the Word*, 8–9.

68. Newman, *Select Treatises of St. Athanasius*, 2:339.

69. Frankel, *Early Greek Poetry and Philosophy*, 77.

conception that the Lacanian tradition in general, and the economical principle in particular, apparently subvert.

Therefore the question that Newman needs above all to address is how creatures of flesh, circumscribed as they are by the economical principle, can nevertheless enjoy the "unity ... individuality ... and ... independent existence" explicitly and authoritatively attributed to human beings by the Church Fathers and the early Councils. His answer is to be found in his impatient and repeated rejection in *Discursive Enquiries* of the suggestion that reasoning is founded on "an act of foi aveugle," of blind faith[70]—in effect Žižek's blind positing. It is meaningless, he argues, to speak of "faith in [the] reasoning process."[71] My unity, individuality, and independent existence may not be immediately obvious, but the *ergo* with which I infer them is self-evidently mine. *I take intellectually responsible possession of the gap between me and any minimally felt object.* The soul only gains "the notion of [its] unity ... individuality ... and ... independent existence" when it is roused by "some external stimulus ... [and] reflects upon itself."[72] "Sentio, *ergo sum*" ("*I feel*, therefore I am") ... from what I have experience of I argue the certainty of that of which I have not experience, viz. my existence."[73] Self is not known immediately; it is inferred. The word "therefore" signifies not a self-constituting moment—I am always already a person—but a moment of self-discovery. Obviously, no baby ever *said* "therefore" before saying "me." But even in Lacan's account, the infant makes an inference about its own image before it says anything at all. The *word* "me" is "outside myself," the recognition of self in the power to make inferences is not, and such a power may fittingly be predicated of the emergent human consciousness of the Eternal Word made flesh.

The speculations in *Discursive Enquiries* have, therefore, incalcula-

70. Newman, in Myers, *Thoughtful Heart*, 49.

71. Newman, in Myers, *Thoughtful Heart*, 50.

72. Newman, in Myers, *Thoughtful Heart*, 45.

73. Newman, in Myers, *Thoughtful Heart*, 86.

ble philosophical importance. The "phenomena to which [the metaphysician] appeals," Newman observes, "and the principles which he assumes [are] within his own breasts … His hermit spirit dwells in his own sphere."[74] Two great intellectual traditions converged in his own hermit spirit, the theology of the Fathers, and the great achievement of modern self-analysis, the relativist understanding of the human condition, inscribed in the economical principle. Newman's crucial contribution was to bring these two apparently incompatible streams of thought into fruitful union.

Two consequences of his *ergo* indicate how fruitful. The first concerns his ability to hold back from complete explanation. When he read an account of the German philosophers, he was pleased to find that they too had practiced his introspective method. He was particularly impressed by Schelling's view that conclusions "can never be *demonstrated*"; one can only find "corroboration" by self-attention.[75] But he was not otherwise impressed with Schelling because there were, apparently, "no less than three or four, and even five modifications of his system."[76] This, Newman thought, showed the folly of trying to be systematic. "Of course truth is always consistent with itself," he writes in *Discursive Enquiries*, "but that does not prove that we can always show that consistency."[77] He accordingly indulges in intellectual "negative capability," accepting the Church's teaching on the Incarnation and defending economy, without feeling any requirement to "refer everything to *one* principle."[78]

Philosophers like Schelling, Lacan, and Žižek, however, are denied this freedom. For them, *everything* must arise within a single field—"matter" or "ground" or the "night of the Self." Schelling has

74. Newman, in Myers, *Thoughtful Heart*, 32.

75. Chalybäus, *Historical Development of Speculative Philosophy*, 250; Sillem, *Philosophical Notebook of John Henry Newman*, 1:321.

76. Chalybäus, *Historical Development of Speculative Philosophy*, 262.

77. Newman, in Myers, *Thoughtful Heart*, 113.

78. Sillem, *Philosophical Notebook of John Henry Newman*, 232.

to describe "the causal chains of Reason"[79] arising from the random irrationality of material ground, according to Lacan how desire gets to be boxed in by language. They are both locked into the arbitrary and self-defeating task of describing the prehistory of description, of putting into words the generation of word—hence Schelling's endless revisiting of the same problem. Žižek sees this revisiting as a strength: the "great works of *materialist* thought, from Lucretius . . . to . . . Lacan," he writes, "tackle the same nodal problem again and again . . . [but] although they ultimately fail . . . their very failure is theoretically extremely productive."[80] An alternative description of these endless reconsiderations might be what Lacan calls "the vanity of repetition," "the ever avoided encounter . . . the missed opportunity."[81] Newman certainly would have thought so. Secure in his *ergo*, he knew that the foundation of being is not ground, or matter, or spirit, but person. He had no need to construct a single, systematic view of the world outside his hermit spirit; as a person, he could live with disparate economies. And so, therefore, can we.

Finally, there is the argument for the existence of God from conscience. Newman copied back into *Discursive Enquiries* Callista's assertion that conscience is no "mere law of my nature . . . [but] the echo of a person speaking to me."[82] In itself, this is hardly an argument. But, Newman points out, "if one external unexperienced fact"—my personal existence—"may be known by *reasoning upon* experience, perhaps another may. Therefore the idea is not absurd that . . . from *conscientiam habeo* ["I have a conscience"], I infer the existence of God, and again from the phenomena of sense . . . the existence of matter."[83] This is not, strictly, a "proof." It only suggests that, provided the experience of moral accountability in my hermit

79. Žižek and Schelling, *Abyss of Freedom/Ages of the Word*, 16.

80. Žižek and Schelling, *Abyss of Freedom/Ages of the Word*, 6–7.

81. Lacan, *Four Fundamental Concepts of Psycho-analysis*, 128.

82. Newman, in Myers, *Thoughtful Heart*, 57; idem, *Callista*, 244.

83. Newman, in Myers, *Thoughtful Heart*, 88.

spirit really is as closely "bound up with the idea and the fact of my being"[84] as the *sentio* itself, then my *ergo*—a "Divine Person" is as rational as my "*ergo* me" or my "*ergo* the world." Certitude of God's existence, therefore, is not in principle *ir*rational, nor is Callista by definition mad, perverted, to live and die *as if* in the presence of the Divine Person that her intelligence infers from her conscience and then corroborates by self-attention. It follows that even a skeptical reader is under an obligation to take her choice seriously.

It is a choice that puts her into a different universe from that envisaged by Schelling and Lacan. There can be no distinction of persons in Schelling's understanding of "God," only distinction of moments—the Word is merely an *event* in the history of the Absolute. And there is no distinction of persons either when Schelling's Romantic, quasi-theological metaphysic is revisited by tough-minded materialists like Lacan and Žižek. In their account, the self struggles to define itself in and against the nonself, and can only gain release from its compulsions by relinquishing all claim to Being. Unlike the Lacanian "analysand," however, Callista can ask God, "What do *you* want?" and expect an answer.

By the same token, we too can say what *we* want from her story. We want Callista, in extremis, to have her question returned without conditions and with unqualified love. We want her to hear the *Que voulez-vous?* of the Eternal Word, one and the same and abiding forever, welcoming her into the joy of her Lord (*la Jouissance de son Seigneur*?). "Our hearts," wrote St. Augustine, "are ever restless until they rest in you."

84. Newman, in Myers, *Thoughtful Heart*, 59.

9

Good, Happy, and Free

Consider (again) Wordsworth's description of a baby being nursed by his mother. The baby gathers "passion from his mother's eye," which, "like an awakening breeze," stimulates him to engage in "the first trial of his powers"

to combine
In one appearance, all the elements
And parts of the same object, else detached
And loth to coalesce.

In bodily intimacy with his mother, the baby's "mind spreads / Tenacious of the forms which it receives." It is certainly true—I have seen it—that immediately after birth, if left with the cord uncut and lying on its mother's breast, in a warm, quiet environment, a newborn baby can exchange peaceful little grunts with its mother, and it is a fair guess that even then it is beginning "to combine / In one appearance, all the elements" of its new world, that it makes a leap of mind, profound possibly, mysterious certainly. It might even be *thinking*.

Wordsworth first writes of feelings passing into the baby's "torpid life / Like an awakening breeze," a simple, unchallenging *simile*. Later, he declares that the baby's "filial bond" is with "nature" as well, that, like the mother, the "*active* universe" is interacting with the baby. This is not a simile or metaphor. The world is not just there to be grasped but like the mother is *involving* itself with the baby. You may think this exaggerated, that the material world of molecules, gravity, and light cannot as it were *exchange* grunts with a baby, that for the baby the universe is only active *in a sense*. But if you choose to go along with Wordsworth's grammar, you will find yourself entertaining a radical idea indeed. So, we have two possible leaps of mind here—the baby's and the reader's.

T. J. Clark, in an essay on "Frank Auerbach's London" in the *London Review of Books*, describes seeing a painting in the apartment of the art historian Michael Podro. The painting is apparently abstract, in roughly two halves, a splashy blue section at the top, a larger, less splashy, but roughly applied yellow section at the bottom, and in between, running from left to right, where it rises into the blue area, a thickish series of brown, dark blue, green, and yellow squiggles. One double yellow-and-dark-blue squiggle plunges down from the top left-hand corner; the yellow streak separates from the blue, swings over to the right, and rises, sloping back up to the left and stops. The dark blue streak continues downward over two pale blue, crudely parallel lines running slantwise across the top of the yellow half, turns brownish, and comes to a halt at a blue squiggle. The latter starts off on the left-hand side near the top of the yellow section, describes a large, left-slanting, broken "W," and then rises to the top of the "middle" section, runs straight toward the right, and halts about three-quarters of the way across. Above it, in the blue area, "echoing" the "W" below on the left but slanting to the right, is another "W" in yellow, below which, in the middle of the series of squiggles, is a combined "W" and "M" figure in deep blue. At first, Clark thought the painting "a crazy inconsequential daub." Eventually, however, it "took hold" of him, and he began to see it "but slowly, and not as a result of an act of judgment (or not one [he] was aware of) ... that it was bloody marvelous." The picture has a title, *Primrose Hill, Autumn Morning*. This experience, Clark writes, is as close as he has

> ever come to what is supposed to be the primal scene of modern art: the experience of making (or if you're a viewer, seeing) something that is truly senseless and preposterous as it comes into being, unknown and unidentifiable, and *therefore*, if you're lucky, a glimpse of freedom, a unique particular, a way to slip off the mind-forged manacles.[1]

What happened to Clark is, I suggest, analogous with what happened to Wordsworth's baby, and what happens to the reader confronted with Wordsworth's "irrational" insistence on mutuality and interaction between mind and nature. The painting, or at any rate Auerbach's mind, is not just there to be grasped but, like Nature for Wordsworth's baby, *interacts* with the viewer's mind. I think Clark's italicized "therefore" particularly significant. I will return to it.

In another essay in the *London Review of Books*, "Against Self-Criticism," Adam Phillips takes a strong line on conscience. His piece begins:

> Lacan said that there was surely something ironic about Christ's injunction to love thy neighbour as thyself—because actually of course, people hate themselves. Or perhaps you could say that, given the way people treat one another, perhaps they had always loved their neighbours in the way that they loved themselves: that is, with a good deal of cruelty and disregard.[2]

According to Freud's *The Interpretation of Dreams* (1899), Phillips notes, conscience "was there to protect and prohibit the individual from desires that endangered him, or were presumed to ... we have conscience so that we may not perish of the truth—the truth, that is, of our desire."[3] But this, Phillips suggests, *buries* the self—that indeed may be the "primary function" of conscience, or that of its modified version in *The Ego and the Id* (1923), the superego, since to know the self is to know one's desire. Conscience may therefore be "a form of cowardice," a possibility that raises a number of ques-

1. Clark, "Frank Auerbach's London," 5.
2. Phillips, "Against Self-Criticism," 13.
3. Phillips, "Against Self-Criticism," 13.

tions. What "would a morality be like that was inspired by desire?"[4] What "is this appetite for confinement, for unrelenting, unforgiving self-criticism?" How have we become enslaved to this part of ourselves, and how and why have we consented? Freud's answer, Phillips writes, is "beguilingly simple: we fear loss of love."[5]

He asks another question: "in what sense is the super-ego Freud's implied critique of the Judeo-Christian religions and their god?"[6] This too seems easy to answer. Consider Psalm 38:

> O Lord, rebuke me not in thy anger,
> nor chasten me in thy wrath!
> For thy arrows have sunk into me,
> And thy hand has come down on me.
> There is no soundness in my flesh
> because of thy indignation;
> there is no health in my bones
> because of my sin.
> For my iniquities have gone over my head,
> they weigh like a burden too heavy to bear.
> My wounds grow foul and fester
> because of my foolishness,
> I am utterly bowed down and prostrate;
> and all day I go about mourning. (Ps 38:1–8)

Or, in the Christian tradition the self-loathing of the founder of the Carthusians, St. Bruno: "I rejoice, indeed, as is right, for the growth of the fruits of your virtues," he writes to his brothers, "but I lament and am ashamed that I lie inert and torpid in the filth of my sins."[7] Bruno's brothers would not have welcomed being loved by the saint in the same way as he loved himself.

There is, however, a difference between conscience, as formed within the Judeo-Christian tradition, and the superego, which in the

4. Phillips, "Against Self-Criticism," 14.
5. Phillips, "Against Self-Criticism," 16.
6. Phillips, "Against Self-Criticism," 15.
7. St. Bruno, "Letter to His Sons the Carthusians," in *Divine Office*, 3:381.

postreligious culture of late nineteenth-century Vienna was its "secular heir."[8] The Psalmist and St. Bruno *articulated* their self-loathing, if its specifics were thrust into the unconscious, but self-loathing as such has had to be suppressed in the culture of rationally scientific modernity. The superego must now insist on its own niceness, liberality, tolerance, and rationality, even though its morality is *not* "inspired by desire," however modernity may insist that it is. If Freud, Lacan, and Phillips are right, it conceals (entombs) more, not less, of the self, and is thus crueler and more self-abasing than its Judeo-Christian ancestor.

Ricoeur thinks that "Freud can encounter morality only as a wounding of desire, as interdiction and not as aspiration."[9] Certainly, conscience and morality generally focus on wrongdoing, not rightdoing, and moralists accordingly think sadistically. People seem only to become aware of themselves, and especially of others, as moral beings when the question of the immoral arises. "Man has free-will," writes St. Thomas Aquinas, "otherwise counsels, exhortations, commands, prohibitions, rewards and punishments would be in vain."[10] For Aquinas, a good conscience consists in systematically subordinating "the sensitive appetite" to the dictates of reason: "the goodness of the will depends on reason."[11] And for the saved, one of the rewards of rational control over the sensitive appetite will be to "rejoice in the punishment of the wicked, by considering therein the order of Divine justice and their own deliverance which will fill them with joy."[12]

Since the Enlightenment, such thinking has become unacceptable. Since the Romantic Movement, "the sensitive appetite" has become precisely where freedom is believed to flourish. Neverthe-

8. Phillips, "Against Self-Criticism," 15.

9. Ricoeur, *Rule of Metaphor*, 186.

10. St. Thomas Aquinas, *Summa theologiae* (*ST*), I, q. 83, a. 1.

11. *ST* I-II, q. 19, a. 3.

12. *ST* I-II, q. 94, a 3.

less, if intolerance of one's own impulses and those of like-minded others is currently taboo, the punishment of outsiders is not. John Stuart Mill thought it right to punish children for their own good, as well as adult populations (he probably had the peoples of the Indian subcontinent in mind) whom he judged to be still in an infantine state; and arguments have been advanced for justice based on "a shift from the past tense of 'could have done otherwise' to the future tense 'could do otherwise.'" People may be "blamed" for actions, provided it "would not have required much more knowledge, thought, carefulness or whatever" for them to have acted differently. Granted that the way the perpetrator was and the way the world was were such that the necessary "knowledge, thought, carefulness or whatever" were inaccessible at the time, a near-miss justifies blaming the perpetrator because blame "for past events" has a good effect "on the present and the future."[13] Brains need to be "rewired" "to stop people doing it again." Thus "criminal justice rests on the need to change behaviour," on coercion or measured sadism.

Is it possible, in the teeth of this punishing and self-punishing tradition, to suggest what a good conscience might be like? We have a telling example, I suggest, in Jane Austen's *Northanger Abbey*. The seventeen-year-old Catherine Morland, staying in Bath with the stupid Mrs. Allen, is befriended by the worldly and unreliable Isabella Thorpe, who has her eye on Catherine's brother James. James joins them in Bath, proposes to Isabella, she accepts, and he departs to get his father's leave to marry. In his absence, Isabella attracts the attention of Captain Tilney, the swaggering elder brother of Henry Tilney. Catherine is, obviously, in love with Henry, a clever, slightly sardonic, well-read young clergyman who has been flattered by Catherine's feelings and has pleasantly but condescendingly patronized her. At the beginning of the second volume of the novel, Catherine and Isabella are together at a dance. On behalf of his brother,

13. Baggini, *Freedom Regained*, 145.

Henry asks Catherine if she thinks Isabella would agree to dance. Naively, Catherine tells Henry that she is "very sure Miss Thorpe [does] not mean to dance at all." The narration continues:

> "Your brother will not mind it I know," said she, "because I heard him say before, that he hated dancing; but it was very good-natured in him to think of it. I suppose he saw Isabella sitting down, and fancied she might wish for a partner; but he is quite mistaken, for she would not dance upon any account in the world."
>
> Henry smiled, and said, "How very little trouble it can give you to understand the motive of other people's actions."
>
> "Why?—What do you mean?"
>
> "With you, it is not, How is such a one likely to be influenced? What is the inducement most likely to act upon such a person's feelings, age, situation, and probable habits of life considered?—but, how should *I* be influenced, what would be *my* inducement in acting so and so?"
>
> "Me?—yes; I cannot speak well enough to be unintelligible."
>
> "Bravo!—an excellent satire on modern language.... I only meant that your attributing my brother's wish of dancing with Miss Thorpe to good-nature alone, convinced me of your being superior in good-nature yourself to all the rest of the world."
>
> Catherine blushed.[14]

Briefly, Henry maintains his patronizing attitude ("Bravo!—an excellent satire on modern language")—he's right, of course—but then, taking thought, he suddenly falls in love, partly because Catherine finds him "irresistible," but decisively because of his sudden recognition, not wholly unlike Phillips's more drawn-out acceptance of Auerbach's painting, that not only in her good nature, her consciousness, and her conscience, is she superior "*to all the rest of the world*," but also that, within herself, she is happy, and therefore secure, for him as well as for herself. He, his brother, and his sister have internalized the tyrannical conscience driven into them, with cruelty and disregard, by their father, General Tilney—Henry's sardonic

14. Austen, *Novels*, 5:132–33.

humor is surely a defense against the concealed fear and loathing of himself induced by his father's power—but Catherine comes from a happy home and has wise, loving, trusting parents of a steadiness with which Freud and Lacan were apparently unfamiliar. Henry might die of his desire, but whatever else might happen to her, Catherine would not die of hers. That at least is how I came to see the novel the last time I read it.

But what significance attaches to Catherine Morland, who is, after all, only a fiction? As much or as little, perhaps, as attaches to anyone. Ever since Hume invented the "bundle theory" of mind (the mind is *nothing but* the stream of its experiences), "the self" has been a problem for philosophers. Is there such a thing? Indeed, is there such a thing as a thing? Spinoza held that only "God or Nature" (he didn't distinguish between them) can properly be called a thing. John Stuart Mill, on the other hand, thought that material things were just "permanent possibilities of sensation" and that there was no self, just events in consciousness. For other philosophers, however, consciousness is just a by-product of neural processes. Wittgenstein pointed out that it didn't make sense to point yourself out to yourself. Dennett has compared the mind to a newspaper office with lots of deputy editors processing and publishing a continual flow of stories that are under constant revision and may be deleted at any time. People are nothing, apparently, but the ever-changing "narratives" they tell themselves and each other about themselves and each other and the world. This goes too far for Galen Strawson, who holds that "each distinct experience [does have] its own experiencer." But he thinks Descartes's "view that selves last a very long time" is "ruled out by materialism."[15] I think that all this comes perilously close to nonsense, but if any of it is true, Phillips's argument that conscience is designed to bury the self must be abandoned—there is no self to bury—or to love.

Newman, who admired and detested the writings of Hume,

15. Strawson, *Selves*, 401.

attempted to meet these difficulties with an argument based on Descartes's *cogito*. Descartes's argument for his own existence on the strength of his supposed immediate awareness of himself in thought—"a pearly Cartesian ego," Dennett calls it[16]—has few current supporters, but recent readings of Descartes[17] do him an injustice, and in any case the arguments used against him do not apply to Newman. Newman explicitly denies the possibility of *direct* awareness of the self. In his "Philosophical Notebook," he writes:

> I have an intuition of three things prior to my knowledge of the fact of myself:
>
> 1. in consciousness;
> 2. in thought;
> 3. in a certain analysis, which afterwards becomes the principle of reasoning.
>
> These are involved in the words "*Cogito ergo sum*." (Certain philosophers say that the first act of thought is not a simple apprehension but a judgment ...)
>
> ... The "*ergo*" in Descartes's proposition, "*Cogito ergo sum*" denotes my power of apprehending the *aspects* of an idea.[18]

First there is the experience of a simple sensation, the taste of mother's milk, say, or an emotion such as fear; then the recognition, how-

16. Dennett, *Freedom Evolves*, 285.

17. Most readings of Descartes accept that the Cartesian self "is fully revealed to introspection" (Nagel, *View from Nowhere*, 34), that it is "an island of certainty, clarity, and spirit in a storm of transience and illusion" (Maleuvre, *Religion of Reality*, 8). Maleuvre's reading of Descartes is the antithesis of my own. He claims that Descartes's *Cogito* "means in essence 'There is existence because I can think clearly'" (25), and that Descartes thereby subordinates "the whole of being to a mental act" (31). In my view, Descartes claims only that he *knows* there is existence because he can think. This is an epistemological, not an ontological, argument. In any case, it is primarily on Newman's version of the self as an inferrer that I base my notion of a process of continuous self-unfolding in a succession of "therefores" in time and even in eternity, so that the *whole* self is and will remain a known unknown, and will *never* be "fully revealed to introspection." I agree with Nagel (though not perhaps in the sense he has in mind) that "the concept of the self does not tell us fully what we are" (39)—or what it is.

18. Newman, in Myers, *Thoughtful Heart*, 61.

ever basic, that the sensation *is* something, the emotion *about* something; and finally the recognition that this recognition—this "ergo," this "therefore"—points to ... *me.* I am a conclusion *entailed but not directly known* in the experience of a conclusion being reached about something else. In Newman's words,

> it is *true* that I *am*—or that my consciousness that I am represents the fact external to my consciousness, *viz.* of my existence. Now see what is involved in this one assumption, *viz*: My consciousness that I am not *immediate* but indirect—"sentio, *ergo sum.*"[19]

This *sentio* discloses the richness in Newman's "therefore" compared with the "therefore" of Descartes's *cogito* (as it is commonly understood), and consequently the richness of Newman's sense of the self. Of its very nature, "therefore" is not based on time. A theorem declares the permanence of what it demonstrates, and *therefore* the permanence of the one grasping that permanence. But for Newman, the public, rational, or notional "therefores" characteristic of (say) Euclidean geometry were relatively uninteresting. He would have relished the implied "therefore" in the mind of Wordsworth's baby, however, and, though he would have been puzzled by Clark's "*therefore*"—his was a conservative aesthetic sense—Clark's *assent* would have interested him intensely. But above all he was interested in moral "therefores," in conscience.

> There is a moral feeling ... which does not attend on a mere intellectual assent as a consciousness, "I am beautiful, or clever, *etc.*"[20]

> ... the feeling of conscience is one of a specific kind, but which we could not describe except from the example and analogy of sensible experiences. We could but say "It is peculiar special—it is not like a taste, not like a feeling of propriety, of honour, of mathematical truth *etc.* It is one which he who feels knows and bears witness about to those others who feel it, but it is indescribable."[21]

19. Newman, in Myers, *Thoughtful Heart*, 87.
20. Newman, in Myers, *Thoughtful Heart*, 70.
21. Newman, in Myers, *Thoughtful Heart*, 83.

> The feeling is one analogous or similar to that which we feel in human matters towards a *person* whom we have offended; there is a tenderness almost tearful on going wrong, and a grateful cheerfulness when we go right, which is just what we feel in pleasing or displeasing a father or revered superior.[22]

One has only to compare Catherine Morland's having such thoughts and feelings with Henry Tilney's, or Clark's, or St. Bruno's having them, to see how rich, varied, real, and sometimes happy human "therefores" and therefore human selves can be. It is even possible that Catherine Morland's "therefore" suggests what "a morality [would] be like that was inspired by desire."

Inspired but not determined by it, as Catherine Morland would have taken for granted. Though it is impossible to imagine her knowing anything about what the Scholastic philosophers called the *actus humanus,* Henry Tilney, as an intellectual young clergyman, might have been familiar with it.

Acting "humanly," according to this tradition, involves the use of will and reason, each being "free" in its own way. If a conscious agent is offered an object that is not good from every point of view, or if there is more than one desirable object on offer, a choice must be made, and for the choice to be "human," it must be based on reason, and if it is to be moral, on reasoning about values as well as desire. In this situation, the will is free to "nudge" reason one way or the other; equally, reason's guidance of the will can be more or less honest. An act of the will can thus precede or follow a process of reasoning. But what determines the reason to (mis)direct the will, or the will to "nudge" the reason this way or that, and what "motivates" or "moves" each of these powers to act with or without "integrity"? In this account of human freedom, therefore, there seems to be a concealed vicious regress that is ultimately deterministic.[23]

There are two arbitrary ways out of this logical difficulty. Deter-

22. Newman, in Myers, *Thoughtful Heart,* 58.

23. See O'Connor, *Aquinas and Natural Law,* 55–56.

minism can be taken as a basic truth. But this problematizes notions of justice and morality. Alternatively, with Newman, one can assert, as a matter of experience, that the will is self-evidently free. Newman writes:

> Is not *human volition,* in its action upon mechanical processes, a *miracle*? I put out my hand and stop the pendulum of a clock. The clock stops.[24]

> The very idea of a person is a being who is beyond law ... what belongs to God belongs in a true sense to man, who is created after the image of God, and is what Bacon calls "*deaster quidem.*"[25]

For Newman, in other words, the self is "a sort-of god"—"a first cause," not subject to material law. Many modern philosophers find this view of freedom nonsensical.

But is there another way out of the difficulty? Recall Clark's "glimpse of freedom, a unique particular, a way to slip off the mind-forged manacles" whenever one accommodates oneself to the "madness" of modern art. Set beside it a suggestion of Phillips that Freud began to worry "that psychoanalysis, at its worst, could be a method of under-interpretation."[26] Under-interpretation (Freud's word) would fix psychoanalysis into dogmas and rule-governed procedures. But over-interpretation, Phillips suggests, "means not settling for a single interpretation, however apparently compelling. The ... more persuasive, the more authoritative the interpretation the less credible it is, or should be." Reading this, I was reminded (again) of the struggle between Jesus and Satan in Milton's *Paradise Regained.*

Jesus in *Paradise Regained* is the incarnate Son who in *Paradise Lost* drove Satan and his rebel angels out of Heaven, and undertook to redeem human kind. As a human being, however, he has no memory of this and is as uncertain about his selfhood, about who or what he *really* is, as any other human being, but with more reason. At his

24. Newman, in Myers, *Thoughtful Heart,* 107.
25. Newman, in Myers, *Thoughtful Heart,* 112.
26. Phillips, "Against Self-Criticism," 14.

Baptism he hears, and Satan overhears, a voice from Heaven addressing him as "beloved son" (I, 285). Satan is terrified. Is he up against his old enemy? He cannot bear *not* knowing. Jesus, by contrast, soliloquizes as follows:

> And now by some strong motion I am led
> Into this wilderness, to what intent
> I learn not yet, perhaps I need not know;
> For what concerns my knowledge God reveals.
> (I, 290–93)

He fasts for forty days and is then tempted by Satan. Before the third and final temptation—Milton follows the sequence in the Gospel According to Luke—Satan, who is an acute if feverish reader of Scripture and the stars, and accordingly foresees what awaits Jesus when he reaches Jerusalem, warns Jesus of the consequences of his rejection of what Satan has offered him—dominion over the whole world. Soon, says Satan,

> thou shalt have cause
> To wish not never hadst rejected thus
> Nicely or cautiously my offered aid.
> Which would have seen thee in short time with ease
> On David's throne; or throne of all the World ...
> Now contrary, if I read aught in heaven,
> Or heaven write aught of fate ...
> Sorrows, and labours, opposition, hate,
> Attends thee, scorns, reproaches, injuries,
> Violence and stripes, and lastly cruel death,
> A kingdom they portend thee, but what kingdom,
> Real or allegoric, I discern not.
> (IV, 375–79, 381–82, 385–89)

In a last, desperate effort to find out who Jesus is, to determine the one and only meaning of what the Voice from Heaven has said—that is, to "over-interpret" the text of Scripture and the stars—Satan takes Jesus to the pinnacle of the Temple and urges him to cast himself down,

safely if Son of God:
For it is written, He will give command
Concerning thee to his angels, in their hands
They shall uplift thee, lest at any time
Thou chance to dash thy foot against a stone
(IV, 655–59)

Satan is taking a huge risk here. If Jesus *were* to cast himself down and was then uplifted by angels, his "divine" stature would be revealed and Satan would face defeat and horror. And if Jesus were not uplifted, Satan's reading of Scripture and the stars would be obscured and he would not know where he was. But the prospect of an underdetermined text is too much for him. But it is not too much for Jesus, whose reply is wholly outside Satan's compass:

To whom thus Jesus: Also it is written,
Tempt not the Lord thy God, he said and stood.
But Satan smitten with amazement fell.
(IV, 660–62)

By leaving himself open to *whatever* the Divine Text might signify, by under-interpreting it, Jesus opens himself unconditionally to the Divine Will in an act that is fully human, deliberate, rational, and free. At this point of *Paradise Regained*, we are confronted by a remarkable "glimpse of freedom, a unique particular, a way to slip off the mind-forged manacles," that transcends all lesser "therefores" yet points to something universal in human potentiality in the here and now. Aquinas, unlike St. Augustine, holds that it is possible to be blessed, to achieve real if only partial beatitude in this life:

those things which are set down as merits in the beatitudes, are a kind of preparation for, or disposition to happiness, either perfect or inchoate: while those that are assigned as rewards, may be either perfect happiness, so as to refer to the future life, or some beginning of happiness, such as is found in those who have attained perfection, in which case they refer to the present life.[27]

27. *ST* I-II, q. 69, a. 2.

The Jesus of *Paradise Regained* is of course a fictional character, like Catherine Morland. Nevertheless, like her, he is *exemplary.*

Christians believe something more is promised. For Aquinas, freedom is *redundant* in the face of Divine Glory. In *Paradise Lost,* however, the angel Raphael takes a different view:

> My self and all the angelic host that stand
> In sight of God enthroned, our happy state
> Hold, as you yours, while our obedience holds;
> On other surety none; freely we serve,
> Because we freely love, as in our will
> To love or not; in this we *stand or fall*:
> And some are fallen.
> (IV, 535–40, my emphasis)

The vision of God, for Milton, is a text that can *never* be finally interpreted, not even in Heaven. It is the knowledge of inexhaustible desire and its unceasing gratification. If he is right, the Blessed shall for all eternity be good and happy—and free. It is (at least) a pleasing prospect.

10

Transcendental Relativism; or, The Death of God and the Jesus Thought Experiment

Human beings experience only a narrow range of radiant energy, some as light, some as heat; what they know as color is just a function of the relation between their central nervous system and a part of the spectrum. All knowledge seems to be similarly based on the way in which, in experience, a limited set of things relates to a limited set of other things, and not on the way they "really" are. All knowledge, in short, is "economical"; everything is relative, and relativism makes many people, and perhaps religious people especially, unsettled and insecure.

The riskiness is felt particularly in language. Many people believe (or at any rate hope) that words have fixed meanings, and sentences can express true propositions. But how does a word get its meaning? The sound "bat" is just a sound. It can stand on its own, or it can be part of a word—"battle" or "batten." On its own, you can't know what it signifies until it is used. In one sentence it is a noun—"The bat was hibernating"—in another a verb—"Bat for England!"—in another a metaphor. A journalist asks a politician a tricky question, "Bat that one, Minister," murmurs a civil servant. "Oh, *well* played!" To grasp fully what the civil servant means, you need to know the question asked and its context; the answer given; the characters of the questioner, the minister, and the civil servant; the tone adopted by each; and their relationship—the civil servant might be showing off to a superior, or patronizing a dunce, or whispering ironically to a colleague. The exact, particular sense of the civil servant's "bat" is uniquely related to a vast, mostly invisible set of mainly linguistic circumstances, each of which is what it is by virtue of *its* context. And once its moment has passed, the civil servant's "batted" will never be fully recoverable—it was lost the moment it was found. Language, then, is just a system of relations in language and nothing else. Meaning is unfixed and unstable.

According to Leibniz,[1] that is also the nature of the universe, but he thought there was a way of pinning everything down. He envisaged a world constructed of what he called "monads." Any material thing—a leaf, a snowflake, or Leibniz's own body—consisted of an infinity of monads in unique combination, each of which contained a register of *all* its relations past, present, and future, with *all* the other monad making up that body. In Leibniz's own case, however, there was also a Leibniz-soul-monad containing a complete register of its relations with *all* the material monads forming the Leibniz body as they did with it. The Leibniz body monads and the Leibniz soul monad also contained information about their relations with *all* the other monads in the universe. In much the same way, Newton held that every material object is gravitationally in relation with every other material object in a vast, mathematically exact system of attraction and counterattraction. Soul monads, happily, had only a limited consciousness of these relationships—Leibniz believed in the unconscious if only to keep his soul monads from going mad from data overload. There was thus an infinite set of relations between monads that were by definition consistent with one another

1. My summary of Leibniz's philosophy is based largely on Bertrand Russell, *Philosophy of Leibniz*.

in an infinitely complex system of intermonadic "harmony." Because each was its own past, present, and future by being a record of its relations with the past, present, and future of every other monad in the universe, there was no need for actual interaction between them, and no need for absolute time or space. A monad didn't have to be anywhere at any time. Despite its oddity, the principles underlying this system exerted a powerful influence, since the beginning of the twentieth century, on philosophers like Bertrand Russell and physicists like Lee Smolin. They see it as a model of what a theory of everything *ought* to be, comprehensive and self-consistent. However, there seems to be no way of proving or disproving it. But then there is no way of proving or disproving a lot of current theory—that brains are computers, for example. (Could a computer prove that it was only a computer?)

In addition, as Leibniz's younger contemporary Berkeley realized, soul monads make material monads redundant. If you accept the principle of "parsimony"—that is, that philosophers should rely on as few entities as possible—material monads *ought* to be eliminated. Thus if the soul monad of Leibniz contained the record of a journey from England to visit Spinoza in Holland, and the soul monad of Spinoza a corresponding record of Leibniz coming on such a visit, there would have been no need for the separate existence of the infinity of body monads in each philosopher, never mind those forming their clothes, the ship Leibniz sailed in, or the chairs the two men sat on as they exchanged their views of the universe. In principle, you could go further than this. All you would *really* need, after all, would be a single monad, since it would contain a comprehensive register of the whole of reality. Spinoza made something much like this proposal. But Berkeley couldn't go that far since such extreme parsimony would have undermined the notion of human beings as unique, potentially immortal facts. So, soul monads had to be posited. But since they could never know the infinity of their own body monads, never mind the infinities of all the other monads in the universe, soul monads could never know themselves. Leibniz and Berkeley were therefore lost to themselves, just as the sense of the civil servant's "Bat that one" comes into being and is at once lost within the world it has entered and changed.

Both Leibniz and Berkeley resolved this difficulty by positing God. To people in today's world, this may look like a solution that is more convenient than convincing. In any case, both conceded that from within the system of intermonadic relations—that is, from where we are—God as he is and the world and every monad within it, whether imaginary or real, are necessarily ungraspable. So even if we are revolving round a Divine Something, we can never know what it is that we are revolving round, and consequently we can never know our own essence—or indeed if we have an essence at all. Perhaps we may be revolving around Nothing after all?

There is another difficulty. If Leibniz's monadology checkmates relativism, it does so at a price. If I am the sum total of my relations with the rest of the universe, past, present, and future, does it make sense to praise or blame me for what I do? Isn't everything simply there, not so much determined as given? Leibniz meets this difficulty by distinguishing between the necessary and the contingent. A sentence is necessarily true if its subject contains its predicate. The propositions "Leibniz is a human being" and "Human beings are rational animals" are necessarily true because humanness is implied by the name "Leibniz," and rationality and animality are implied by the expression "human beings." Necessarily true propositions are therefore about words rather than facts, though facts may be what they express. Propositions that assert something to *be* the case, however, are only *contingently* true. The sentence "Leibniz was a philosopher" is true only if Leibniz existed and he was a philosopher, but the noun "Leibniz" does not assert the existence of Leibniz, the philosopher, any more than the noun "Utopia" asserts the existence of Utopia or "the King of France" the existence of the King of France.

But not all contingent propositions are the same. There is an important difference between the contingent propositions "Leibniz was sea-sick on the voyage to Holland" and "Leibniz went to Holland to discuss philosophy with Spinoza." "Leibniz was sea-sick" says nothing about Leibniz as a rationally motivated being, but "Leibniz went to Holland to discuss philosophy with Spinoza" does, and, in Leibniz's account, the combination of contingency and rational motive makes it possible to say that an action is praiseworthy or blameworthy. If we speak of an action that didn't have to happen, but did and was rationally determined, may we not also say that it is something a rational being was responsible for? But to say I am responsible for an action *because* it is determined (albeit rationally) seems like a verbal trick. This is why some philosophers hold that I am only properly deemed to be responsible for actions that *I*—not my reasoning, nor my emotions, nor my impulses, but *I*—originate. *I* must be a kind of First Cause as God is supposed to be. Newman accordingly called the human being "a little god"[2]—we need to think of ourselves as making something out of nothing. Others, however, think that to describe as responsible the actions of a rational being that are *not* rationally determined makes no sense, as if what makes me responsible is an ability to act for no reason at all. Wouldn't this suggest that my personal being is centered on—nothing?

But suppose that Spinoza heard Leibniz was coming to Holland and strongly desired a visit from him, that he also believed that philosophers communicated best when they do not try to pressure each other, and that he therefore did nothing to encourage or discourage Leibniz's visit, even though this might result in Leibniz going straight home to Germany. Wouldn't I be justified in describing Spinoza's forbearance and humility as praiseworthy and responsible in a way that goes beyond mere contingency combined with rationality?

Such a notion of personal responsibility seems especially important in science, which is why my example focused on two scien-

2. Newman, in Myers, *Thoughtful Heart*, 112.

tifically minded philosophers. What it takes to become a scientist has been well described by Michael Polanyi (1891–1976). Science, Polanyi holds, involves "a passionate pouring of oneself into untried forms of existence":

> even though intellectual standards are acquired by education while our appetitive tasks are predominantly innate, both may deviate from current custom; and even when they conform to it they must both be ultimately accredited by ourselves.[3]

But something else is needed as well:

> the learner ... must believe before he can know. But ... the intimations followed by the learner are based predominantly on ... confidence in others ... The continued transmission of articulate systems, which lends public and enduring quality to our intellectual gratifications, depends throughout on these acts of submission.[4]

Confidence in the openness of others to a shared acceptance of a postulate of objectivity seems inseparable from the self-belief required for science to flourish. In the delicate and complex relations of submission, mutual interdependence of equals, and private speculation and understanding that Polanyi's picture of science requires the kind of relation that I am imagining between Leibniz and Spinoza would be invaluable. Trust and being trusted would emancipate philosophers and scientists from the need to base decisions about communicating with their fellows exclusively on calculations on the probable effects of doing so. There is no reason to envisage, of course, such unqualified trust operating universally in the intellectual community. But there is every reason to suppose that philosophers and scientists have in fact felt the interpersonal character of their work and the responsibilities arising from it—to respect the autonomy of their fellow intellectuals and to tell them the truth, the whole truth, and nothing but the truth. Respect for such principles

3. Polanyi, *Personal Knowledge*, 174.
4. Polanyi, *Personal Knowledge*, 208.

could, admittedly, be pragmatically or ideologically determined, conditional, and utilitarian, but it could also be based on a recognition and acceptance of mutual autonomy as the most human way of engaging in intellectual activity.

There could be no guarantee that this mutual recognition of a common value, objectivity, and acceptance of mutual responsibility would always prevail in scientific or any other human endeavors. One person's respect of the autonomy of another could be exploited from time to time by brutal self-interest. It could be abandoned by those attempting it. The emergence of responsibility opens up the prospect of its opposite. But then many human traits—promiscuity and sexual fidelity, aggression and cooperation—remain in play in the human mix; in terms of reproductive effectiveness, one has not succeeded in eliminating the other.

The fact of mutual autonomy might therefore give rise to an ideal of (say) justice ("I *owe* it to my colleagues to disclose this!" "Her contribution to this discovery *ought* to be acknowledged!"). The ideal of justice might also give rise to a strong, possibly discomfiting form of conscience. An experience of conscience or self-blame is possible in the context of utilitarian or prudential values—hence the notion of moral stupidity. But if relations based on mutual autonomy and justice operated in the manner I have been suggesting, conscience might become more than this—one could even find oneself feeling guilty about actions that presented themselves as entirely justifiable on rational grounds ("I did the sensible thing in the circumstance—but it wasn't right!") Some nuclear scientists have felt this way.

This ideal of justice has wider application than in the field of science and intellectual endeavor. Moral anguish arising not just from perceived injustice but also from guilt may extend across the whole of human life, sexual, social, economic, military, and intellectual. To these the cosmic structures of chance and necessity, to which science is equally committed, would, of course, be as indifferent as they are to the color of an insect's wings or the survival of a species. Nevertheless, once notions of justice and guilt, of right and of wrong, of good and evil enter into experience, "ought" may refuse to submit to "is."

The strength of moral feeling in the work of John Stuart Mill illustrates this passionate intensity. In *An Examination of Sir William Hamilton's Philosophy*, Mill accused the Christian God of outright wickedness. While we "cannot know God as he is in himself," he declared, we can judge actions attributed to him by his followers. After all, we judge human actions without knowing human beings as they really are but rather as we see them, and why should God be different? Mill accepts that, in human beings, attributes such as "goodness, knowledge, power, are relative" and that God is supposed to be Absolute, but to argue that "the Relative attributes of an Absolute Being are unknowable" and that divine goodness "is not the goodness which we know and love in our fellow-creatures" is, he maintains, an abuse of language. He accepts that Christians believe that their God is all-knowing, all- powerful, "infinite," and "absolute." He also accepts that knowledge and power in finite beings are relative. But he insists that we may only use one kind of moral language for God and for ourselves. The only morality *we* have, after all, is embedded in the moral language we use of ourselves, and we are betraying our own values if we use it of our "God" in a way that makes nonsense of it. The wickedness is in the verbal dishonesties of Christians themselves. So, if God's actions are described in ways that are incompatible with "the best human attributes," Mill will not worship him. "I will call no being good," he declares, "who is not what I mean when I apply that epithet to my fellow-creatures; and if such a being can sentence me to hell for not so calling him, to hell will I go."[5] In effect, "the goodness which we know and love in our fellow-creatures" really matters in some ultimate sense: whatever nihilist philosophy may say, in knockdown arguments, the morality

5. Mill, *Examination of Sir William Hamilton's Philosophy*, 100–103.

suit *is* trumps, even though "goodness" has no objective standing in the scheme of things.

How well does Mill's argument stand up? Mill understands the word "God" to signify a Creator-God—one, all-knowing, infinite, absolute, and eternal—who initiates creation and keeps it in being. But creation would be utterly other than such a God, who would be *transcendent* with respect to it, outside the text of the world. Creation would be a closed system, and its deterministic or random operations could not in principle contain evidence as such of God's "design." Equally, if God "as he is in himself" is unknowable because we can *only* think in terms of relations, and God is absolute, out of all relation, it makes no sense for us to call God "just," or "merciful," or "good," unless we somehow indicate that we are not using these words in their ordinary sense at all. As Absolute, God is One and Indivisible, without distinguishable "attributes." We would need (as it were) to asterisk any adjective we use of God—"loving*," for example, or "long-suffering*," or "jealous*," or "violent*,"or indeed as "One*," to indicate that we are *not* using such words as we use them about our fellow creatures.

Should we, however, asterisk the word "responsible" when we use it of God? Let us suppose that the laws of chance and necessity in the closed system of creation gave rise to communities of mutually responsible "little gods"—of which I have chosen Spinoza and Leibniz and the world community of scientists as examples. By definition, the Creator would know the consequences of this in every detail, how community and individualism, conscience and guilt, creative mutuality and radical injustice, could arise among finite intelligences. In other words, insofar as God allowed not only the settled and determined order of the world to operate according to its own laws, but also human beings to exercise their own capacity for autonomy and mutuality, or not, as they chose, we could think of God, as it were, as an "infinite Spinoza," just as we think of Spinoza as a "little god." The network of co-responsibility would encompass

"God" as well as "science"—and "Law" and "Duty" and so forth. Thus the absence of God from Creation and from human affairs, the Divinity's abstention from all control over what is "not God," the very existence of vast injustice to which human history bears terrible witness, would be, logically, the full realization of Divine Responsibility in Creation and therefore of the Divine Presence at its heart. By allowing us our autonomy, God would be most fully present as Divine Inaction or Sabbath Rest. This is what would make people *the image of* their Creator. The evolution of their capacity to act as responsible beings toward one another, a capacity that gives rise to unassuageable longings for justice and limitless opportunities for unmanageable injustice, would, paradoxically, be a sign of God's hidden but Real Presence, a Presence, however, that felt like, that *was* an inexorable Absence. Divine *immanence* would be indistinguishable from the death of God, and the existence of such a God would be, as the Jesuit poet Gerard Manley Hopkins put it, "a comfort serves in a whirlwind."[6]

For two millennia, Christians have pondered a thought experiment that involves a different relation between God and creation, and that infuses the relativism many people fear with transcendental power. They have tried to think through what might be involved if God—one, infinite, absolute, immutable, simple, timeless, and out of all relation with our contingent, mutable, multiple, violent and unstable world—chose, somehow, to become a contingent, mutable, unstable, potentially violent human being. Without overwhelming the humanness to which the Divine Nature united itself, or allowing that humanness to compromise the "God-ness" united to it, they have supposed the Creator becoming manifest in a particular human life, to have been born of a Jewish woman in the reign of Emperor Augustus, to have been circumcised on the eighth day, to have grown from babyhood to boyhood, from adolescence to adulthood, to have

6. Hopkins, *Poems and Prose*, 61: "No worst there is none."

learned to work, to defend himself, to love as children and adults do, to have read the Scriptures, to have gone to Synagogue and to the Temple, and to have been crucified.

But this would have meant his praying—and how could this Jewish man, how could Jesus, pray to the Jewish God if he *was* that God? The Christian thought experiment meets this difficulty as follows. The principle of Divinity incarnated in Jesus is supposed to be *in relation with*, and so in some sense *distinct from*, yet *within*, the "God" to whom Jesus prayed. This distinct principle of Divinity made manifest in Jesus is identified in the thought experiment as "the Word," and the principle with which the Word is in relation as "the Father."

But because its roots are in Judaism, the Christian thought experiment presupposes that God is *absolutely* One. So how does this duality not compromise the Divine Unity? The notion of mutual autonomy between persons provides a possible answer. It enables us to suppose an unqualified, absolute, and eternal openness in the Father to the autonomy of the Word, and an unqualified, absolute, and eternal openness in the Word to the autonomy of the Father, Divine Unity (the unqualified One-ness of Father and Word) being thus indistinguishable from Divine Freedom. If freedom presupposes mutuality, how else could God be both free and one? We may also suppose that Jesus, despite the limitations of his humanity, discovered in himself (however inchoately) exactly this infinite and absolute principle of surrender, so that he could approach God as "Abba," Father, to a degree that no other human being could conceivably match. And that no other human being would want to, since it led to the Cross—that is, to yet another Divine Absence—to Divine Light as Absolute Darkness.

But this leaves out the Spirit. In the Christian thought experiment, the Godhead is not "Duality" but "Trinity." If the Word is the image of the Father, the total self-abnegation of the Father may be understood as having a twofold aspect in the Word, as the Word's personal act certainly, and perhaps primarily—if "primarily" makes any sense in such a context—as a result of the Word's imaging of the Father. But God being God, the Father's self-abnegation (matched without qualification or diminution by that of the Word), though total, could not, self-evidently, un-God God. The Spirit accordingly proceeds from the free implosion of the mutuality between Father and Word.

In the Christian thought experiment, "the Coming of the Spirit" is thus Presence, Light, and Penitude, just as the Divine Absence from Creation and the death of the Word in Jesus are Absence, Darkness, and Nothing. But the "Spirit" or "Breath" or "Wind" discloses another kind of Absence, elusiveness, invisibility, so that, in grasping the Spirit as being, without qualification, Divine, one is confronted with another intolerable mystery—the *utter* emptiness effected in the Father's self-abnegation before the Word, and in the Word's imitation of the Father. If this were not total, if it did not render *everything* null and surd from our point of view, indeed from every point of view, the Presence, Light, and Plenitude of the Spirit that fills that emptiness would be less than "God"—the Spirit would be a mere god of the gaps. But the Spirit *is* God, and therefore the sign for us of how Divine Freedom both is and is not Divine Nothingness, and of how *completely* we, locked into fear and trembling and creaturely need of Something, are precluded from participating in it. Except, of course, or so the thought experimenters tell us, one human being did manage to do just that, and thereby opened it up for the rest of us.

11

Beginnings and Endings

PASSOVER AND PASSION

> No retrospect will take us to the true beginning; and whether our prologue be in heaven or on earth, it is but a fraction of that all-presupposing fact with which our story sets out.
>
> —*George Eliot*

Beginnings

The Bible begins with the words "In the beginning," and thereby makes history possible. If George Eliot is right, however, that beginnings exist only as ways of fixing narrative—in effect as convenient lies—the human condition is founded on Nothing. Can a beginning be found? Consider first a special beginning, the beginning of "Judaism."

There is a terrible scene in the Book of Ezra (10:1–17) in which, trembling, in fear and on account of pouring rain, the Jews "make a covenant with [their] God to put away all these [foreign] wives and their children according to the counsel of my lord [Ezra] and of those who tremble at the commandment of our God . . . accord-

Epigraph. George Eliot, *Daniel Deronda*, book 1, chap. 1 (epigraph).

ing to the law." During the long years of the Exile in Babylon, Jewish men had married non-Jewish women. Now, under the terms of the Covenant with Moses, these wives and children are to be put away. Ezra himself is weeping, though probably because the Law has been violated, not because families are to be torn apart. The scene is carefully constructed as a historical event—the rain apparently clinches it. The same occasion, with an even greater emphasis on covenant, seems to be described in Nehemiah, chapter 9. In Ezra, the defining commitment is to the principle of Jewishness being passed from mother to child. "Judaism" has begun.

The consequences of this collective decision, rain soaked but apparently free, were immense. Without the "Judaism" that developed in the years after the Exile and that Ezra may be said to have initiated, the pre-captivity documents of the Jewish Scriptures would never have been collected and edited in the form they have come down to us, nor would the Jews have had any reason to resist being "Hellenized" by the dynastic tyrannies that arose in the wake of the conquests of Alexander the Great. There would have been no need for them to reject the Samaritans, the Herodians, and the Romans, or to reconstitute themselves as the People of the Covenant after the fall of the Temple in 70 CE. There might have been "Sadducees" of a sort, but there would have been no Pharisees or Essenes—and no Shoah. Nor would the world of John the Baptist and Jesus of Nazareth have come about. So, the "real father of Judaism is Ezra with his three dominant conceptions: the chosen race, the Temple, the Law."[1]

We cannot, however, date this momentous day. Perhaps it is a fiction, realistic, even novelistic (like much later Jewish writing), true in essence, but not fact. In any case, whether it happened or not, it would *not* have seemed a beginning to those taking part, but rather the renewal of an existing covenant. A covenant as such is never a beginning; it is always based on earlier events, embodying (1) a claim

1. *New Jerusalem Bible*, 510.

about the past by one contracting party; (2) an acknowledgment of that claim by the other; (3) demands and promises for the future in consequence by the first party; and (4) submission to those demands and expectation of the fulfilment of those promises by the second.

This is how the covenant at Sinai is structured. God makes a covenantal claim: "I am the Lord your God who brought you out of the land of Egypt, out of the house of bondage" (Ex 20:2). Israel is declared to be in the Lord's debt, and this is the legal justification for the Lord's requiring Israel to "have no other gods" but himself (Ex 20:3). In acknowledgment of this debt and duty, Israel accepts circumcision (Lv 12:3), the Sabbath, and the duty to observe the laws of purity, to perform the sacrifices, and to observe the feasts ordained by the Lord. A key word in Exodus 19–24 is *bĕrît* ("obey"). "In the first divine speech in 19:4–6, the word has a central function: 'Now, therefore, if you will obey my voice and keep my covenant . . .'" (v. 5). "Here . . . the human side [of the covenantal relationship] is particularly emphasized."[2] In return, the Lord promises to establish the children of Israel in the Land of Canaan according to his promise to their father, Abraham. The covenant is codified and read to the people and confirmed when the people are sprinkled with "the blood of the covenant which the Lord has made with you, in accordance with all these words" (Ex 24:8b). Foundational as Exodus is, it must construct the backstory on which it is itself based.

This leads to the real beginning in Genesis (or so it seems), and its two main voices, "E," who uses the generic word "God," and "J," who uses the Holy Name, which is conventionally translated as "the Lord." Their accounts do not always tally. I note briefly first the main features of the creation of the world by "God" (Gn 1:1–2:1), and then the story of its creation by "the Lord" (Gn 2:2–3:24).

The "E" creation story is about imposing order on the earth,

2. Rendtdorff, *Canon and Theology*, 129.

which "was without form and void" (Gn 1:2a). Order means division—of "the light from the darkness" (1:4b), of "the waters which were under the firmament from the waters which were above the firmament" (1:7b), of the waters from the dry land, of days and years, the festive and the common, and above all of humankind from all the rest of creation, made, "God" says, "in our image, after our likeness . . . [to] have dominion" over all the other living things (1:26). His final act is to separate the Sabbath from the other days in the week and to hallow it (2:3b). "Creation is fundamentally a work of separation and organization, the maintenance of clear boundaries, is essential to the notions of election and Covenant."[3]

The same principle operates in the "J" creation story. The breath of life separates Adam from the earth, the tree of life and the tree of the knowledge of good and evil are separated from the rest of the trees, and Eden itself from the rest of the world. This is the foundation for the first covenant in Scripture:

> The Lord God took the man and put him in the garden of Eden to till it and keep it. And the Lord God commanded the man, saying, "You may freely eat of every tree of the garden; but of the tree of the knowledge of good and evil you shall not eat, for in the day that you eat of it you shall die." (Gn 2:15–17)

Adam, as the firstborn, witnesses the creation of the animals and names them, and finally he himself is divided and Eve is created. At this point an exception to the process of division is made—Adam and Eve become "one flesh," their union having as its foundation another covenant:

> Then the man said,
> "This at last is bone of my bones
> and flesh of my flesh;
> she shall be called Woman,
> because she was taken from Man."

3. Nodet and Taylor, *Origins of Christianity*, 36.

> Therefore a man leaves his father and his mother and cleaves to his wife, and they become one flesh. (Gn 2:23–24)

But covenants, of course, can be broken, and the "fall" is precisely that. The divinely ordered division of the world is shattered when the serpent persuades the Woman that the division between the human and the divine can be breached. She and Adam in consequence must live in a condition of uncleanness, in which division is horribly obliterated. Though their now shameful, unclean nakedness can be covered, the animal skins in which they are clothed are contaminated by the uncleanness of death, and breach the division between the human and the animal that marked Adam's original sovereignty. Cut off from the purity of Eden, Adam and Eve will enter fully into the two defining but unavoidable states of impurity: death and childbirth. Characteristically, however, the Lord at once begins the process of establishing a new covenant on the basis of a defining *opposition* between the serpent and the woman's offspring (3:15). And it is this pattern that persists—the establishment of covenants based on division and their repeated violation, even in the history of Israel after the Exodus. Witness the establishment of the Kingdom against the wishes of the Lord, the covenant with David leading to the exile in Babylon, and the terrible misfortunes of the Jewish people after the renewal of the covenant under Ezra.

The Exodus in effect recapitulates the creation, from formlessness to division. "Out of a situation where there is no identity … no names, only the anonymity of slavery or the powerlessness of the ghetto, God makes a human community, calls it by name … gives it or restores it to a territory … from human chaos God makes human community."[4] The drama and intimacy of Moses's encounters with the Lord are unmatched in biblical literature. The vast assemblage of law, ritual, Levitical, and priestly consecrations and duties around the Ark of the Covenant, culminating in the mo-

4. Williams, *On Christian Theology*, 57.

ment when the "cloud covered the tent of meeting, and the glory of the Lord filled the tabernacle" (Ex 40:34), is circumstantial and all-encompassing—reconstituting, apparently *for all time,* effective boundaries between the clean and the unclean, the holy and the profane, so disastrously breached in Eden. Reinforced by Leviticus—I am of course concerned only with the Pentateuch in its final form—the Book of Numbers shows that this reconstitution of saving division can withstand terrible pressures. The separate tribes surround the Ark of the Covenant in order and move majestically through the desert, but there is again infidelity, again scandalous failures to respect divinely ordained separateness; nevertheless, after forty years, Israel is at last poised to advance into Canaan, the division of the land between the tribes being established in advance, down to the last detail. The divinely ordered, cosmic division of purity from uncleanness, of the holy from the common, which it is the role of Israel, separated by circumcision and the Sabbath from the rest of mankind, to restore and sustain, has been definitively established.

> You have seen what I did to the Egyptians, and how I bore you on eagle's wings and brought you to myself. Now therefore, if you will obey my voice and keep my covenant, you shall be my own possession among all peoples, for all the earth is mine, and you shall be to me a kingdom of priests and a holy nation. (Ex. 19:4–6a)

The covenant with Moses, then, is the decisive act of divine ordering and is different from all the others, even the Creation. In the first place, we only have the story of the beginning because, according to ancient Jewish tradition, "Moses received the Torah [i.e., both the first five books of the Scriptures and the unwritten or oral Law] from Sinai, then transmitted it." Thus Sinai appears as an absolute beginning, both for the written and for the oral instruction."[5] Moses is doubly vindicated, first as recipient of the covenant with Israel, three months and two days after the Exodus from Egypt (Ex 19:16–

5. Nodet and Taylor, *Origins of Christianity,* 25.

25, 17:1–21), and then as negotiator of the second covenant, after the people have turned to worshipping a golden calf in his absence (Ex 32–34). From within the Scriptures, in effect, we only know of the earlier beginnings, the Creation, the covenant with Noah, the promise to Abraham, the Exodus, on the strength of this legitimization of Moses at Sinai. According to their own internal logic, therefore, the Jewish Scriptures really do begin here with covenant.

We cannot date the days of Ezra's covenant renewal, but we can date some prior events that it presupposes, the edict of Cyrus, perhaps sixty years earlier in 538 BCE, ordering the return of the exiles and the rebuilding of the Temple, the first return from Babylon, under Sheshbazzar the prince of Judah (Ezr 1:9b), the resumption of sacrifices and the celebration of the feast of Succoth or Tabernacles under Jeshua and Zerubbabel on the site of the old Temple (Ezr 3:1–6), and finally, in 515 BCE, the joyful, seven-day celebration of the Passover and the days of unleavened bread (Ezr 6:22). This suggests a different kind of beginning, not a formal renewal of covenant, but with the reestablishment of a ritual, the Passover, commemorating Israel's beginning as a nation, the annual reenactment of the night of the Exodus, when the children of Israel in Egypt killed a lamb for each household, sprinkled blood on their doorposts with hyssop as a sign to the destroyer that their firstborn should not be slaughtered like the firstborn of the Egyptians, and ate the lamb standing, together with bitter herbs and unleavened bread (Ex 12).

Passover was a feast that could not be abrogated: "you shall observe it as an ordinance for ever" (Ex 12:14b). It was also a definitive sign of membership of the community of Israel, through its solemn association with circumcision: "no foreigner shall eat of it, but every slave that is bought for money may eat of it, after you have circumcised him" (Ex 12:43b–44). Accordingly, the first Passover in the Promised Land (an event commemorated in later Judaism at Passover in addition to the principal commemoration, the Exodus itself) was preceded by a mass circumcision at Gilgal (Jos 5:2–12)—

the practice of circumcision had been abandoned during the forty years the Children of Israel had spent in the wilderness after they had been miraculously rescued from Egypt and God had parted the waters of the Red Sea so that they could escape from the armies of Pharaoh. Passover has another layer of meaning also: in the Book of Isaiah, the return of the exiles from Babylon is proclaimed as a second Exodus:

> Thus says the Lord,
> who makes a way in the sea,
> a path in the mighty waters,
> who brings forth chariot and horse,
> army and warrior;
> they lie down, they cannot rise,
> they are extinguished, quenched like a wick:
> "Remember not the former things,
> nor consider the things of old.
> Behold, I am doing a new thing;
> now it springs forth, do you not perceive it?
> I will make a way in the wilderness
> and rivers in the desert." (Isa 43:15–19)

Since 135 CE, and possibly since 70 CE, the Jewish people have celebrated Passover in a domestic setting. In the Scriptures, however, it is tied to Jerusalem and the Temple, where in their thousands the lambs were slaughtered on Preparation Day. It was a public celebration underlining the political and religious significance of the Temple and the priesthood, and of Jerusalem as the Holy City: the Paschal meal had to be eaten there, and participants had to spend the night in its precincts. The Feast of the Unleavened Bread (matzoh) overlapped with Passover and was fused with it. On the first Passover night, the Children of Israel were said to have eaten unleavened bread and bitter herbs with the Paschal Lamb as a sign of their imminent hasty departure from slavery, and when they entered the Promised Land, they "had manna no more" (Jos 5:12b), and had again to eat unleavened bread as at the original Passover.[6] Unlike Passover, however, the feast of matzoh lasted seven days and was associated with the ritual offering in the Temple of the first fruits—a loaf made from newly harvested barley—on the first day of the week after the Passover.[7] (A more important offering of the first fruits—this time of a loaf made from the newly harvested wheat—took place at Pentecost, the Feast of Weeks.) This suggests an altogether different kind of beginning for all three festivals.

Matzoh is said to belong "to a series of agricultural feasts which derive from the pre-Israelite tradition of the cultivated parts of Palestine," and the combination of the two feasts was a consequence of their falling at the same time of the year; "there may also have been special impetus towards it from the fact that at . . . Passover . . . it was usual to eat 'unleavened bread and bitter herbs' [Ex 12:8]." But elements of Passover itself, notably the killing of the lamb and the ritual of protecting the firstborn with its blood, may also have their "own special cultic prehistory," belonging "almost certainly" to an even earlier period, "the milieu of nomadic shepherds" before the tribes of Israel "settled in a cultivated region."[8] It is possible that the family nature of the festival that was to become so prominent when the Temple rituals ceased has its origins in this nomadic prehistory.[9]

This widely accepted suggestion illustrates a fundamental principle of religious and cultural studies, that ritual depends on, and therefore generates, both story and law, assumed always already given though often and necessarily the products of later invention. Beginnings define themselves precisely as not beginnings at all, but rather as commemorations or restorations. Thus even the instructions of Moses at the original Passover as recorded in Exodus are validated by his having been sent by "the Lord, the God of your

6. Nodet and Taylor, *Origins of Christianity*, 111.
7. Nodet and Taylor, *Origins of Christianity*, 53.
8. Noth, *Exodus*, 89–90.
9. See Noth, *Exodus*, 95.

fathers, the God of Abraham, the God of Isaac, the God of Jacob" (Ex 3:15c)—though we have to rely on Moses's word for this.

A New Beginning? The Last Supper

Rowan Williams has suggested that the "Last Supper ... is ... the event that finally sets Jesus and his followers apart from the continuities of Israel."[10] This can only mean, from a Jewish perspective, a blasphemous violation of all that Israel held sacred, an attack not just on the identity of Israel, but, since the "Unity of the Torah finds expression only in the oneness of the God who gave it,"[11] on the holiness of God himself. Is this the price that must be paid for a new beginning? There must be "Nothing" before there can be "Something"?

The Fourth Gospel and the Synoptic Gospels (Matthew, Mark, and Luke) disagree about whether the Last Supper took place before Passover (John) or was a proper Passover meal (the Synoptics). I am inclined to follow the latter, partly because there are signs that John has cut out Passover references from his account of the Last Supper, but that the editing has not been entirely consistent. Thus, while Mark has Jesus and Judas simultaneously dipping their hands into the same dish, as was customary at Passover (14:20), in John, Jesus dips bread into a dish and hands it to Judas, suggesting an ordinary meal.[12] But there is (admittedly not entirely conclusive) evidence that the only meal at which Jews "reclined" (like their political masters, first the Greeks, then the Romans) was the Paschal meal, signaling their divinely ordered freedom. Again, if the Last Supper was not a Passover meal (or if it were an anticipated Paschal meal), there would have been no reason for it to be eaten at a late hour—"It was night" (Jn 13:30b)—or for Jesus to remain in the precincts of the city afterward, as he does in John as well as in the Synoptics. More

10. Williams, *On Christian Theology*, 203.

11. Nodet and Taylor, *Origins of Christianity*, 256.

12. See Fenton, *St Matthew*, 416.

important, however, than any apparent discrepancy about timing is the fact that in their accounts of this Passover meal, the Synoptics apparently *suppress* the traditional Passover rituals.

In Mark, the meal is described three times as "the passover" (14:12, 14:14, 14:16). The lateness of the meal, the wine replacing the water usual at ordinary meals, the way the participants recline at table support this. "On the other hand, central features of the Passover meal—the Passover lamb, the bitter herbs, the explanation of the ritual as a re-enactment of the Exodus—are missing."[13] The words "This is my body" may indeed be "reminiscent of those used at the Passover meal to describe the bread: 'this (is) the bread of affliction,'"[14] but if there is a *change* in the ritual here, it would, from a Jewish point of view, be unprecedented and unjustifiable. The "hymn-singing" at the end of the meal (Mk 14:26) is suggestive of the Passover, but the prescribed psalms (the psalms of the Hallel, 113–18) are not specifically mentioned. Could this be deliberate, and if so, why?

In Matthew's account, Jesus breaks the bread, says the blessing, and distributes the bread, but this "was the . . . way of saying grace among Jews" at all meals.[15] Moreover, as in Mark, the words "this is my body" are completely out of place at a Passover meal, which is not the setting for innovative parable, but for ritualized *remembering*. Later, in a manner that is more specific to Passover, Jesus hands round the cup and gives thanks. But he commands them to drink it *because* it is his "blood of the covenant, which is poured out for many for the forgiveness of sins," and, following Mark, he concludes with a solemn declaration: "I tell you, I will not drink again of the fruit of the vine until that day when I drink it new with you in my Father's kingdom" (Mt 26:26–29; Mk 14:25b). This may refer us to the great-

13. Hooker, *Gospel According to Saint Mark*, 333.
14. Hooker, *Gospel According to Saint Mark*, 340.
15. Fenton, *St Matthew*, 417–18.

of-the-age banquet of described in the Book of Isaiah (25:6–8), but, again, it is hardly appropriate at the Passover.

In Luke, Jesus says specifically that *he will not eat the Passover again* "until it is fulfilled in the kingdom of God"; he then hands round a cup, and again announces that he will "never again drink wine until the kingdom of God comes." Only then does he give thanks, break the bread, and give it to the disciples, saying, "This is my body given for you; do this in remembrance of me." The cup is handed round again after the supper with the words "This cup is the new covenant in my blood poured out for you" (Lk 22:14–20). The possibility arises, therefore, that at the Last Supper Jesus is to be understood as formally *abolishing* the feast. This might explain John's decision (if that is what it was) to break the connection between the meal and the feast altogether. He would be saying, in effect, that the new, the *real*, Passover occurred, *once and for all*, at Golgotha. It would also explain why in Paul's account of the Last Supper there is no reference to the Passover. He simply describes Jesus giving thanks, breaking the bread, and saying, "This is my body, which is for you," and in the same way, with the cup after supper, saying, "This cup is the new covenant in my blood. Whenever you drink it, do this as a memorial of me" (1 Cor 11:24b–26). It is clear, from his letters and the Acts of the Apostles, that the Eucharist was celebrated by Paul's converts far too frequently to have retained a connection with the strictly annual feast of Passover. Thus, while "the primitive community cannot have invented the paschal setting of the Last Supper which does not correspond to its practice,"[16] they no longer commemorated it in conjunction with Passover itself. But to propose suspending or abolishing Passover—which seems to be implied in all this—would have been deeply shocking to Jews.

No less appalling would have been Jesus's references to his blood. Wine is called "the blood of grapes" in the Jewish Scriptures (Gn

16. Fenton, *St Matthew*, 104.

49:11c; cf. Dt 32:14c), but this is far from calling it the blood of a man, with the command that it should be drunk as such. The prohibition on drinking blood was basic, dating back in the tradition to the covenant with Noah[17] and persisting in the Apostolic Church (Acts 15:29b): even as a metaphor, the idea would have been crudely distasteful. That is not all: Jesus calls the wine that his followers are to drink not the blood of the Paschal Lamb, but the blood of the covenant, which has nothing to do with the Passover or with lambs, but with the events at Sinai, of which Pentecost, celebrated fifty days after Passover, was the memorial feast. This would make the Last Supper a covenantal event relating to Sinai as well as a cultic event relating to the Exodus, and so to Pentecost as well as to Passover.

Jesus also speaks of his blood being that of a new and everlasting covenant. In principle, there would be nothing improper in the notion of covenant renewal. The covenant with Moses, after all, had had to be renewed even before the children of Israel had moved away from Sinai, and a "new" covenant is promised in the Book of Jeremiah (31:31)—this is clearly evoked in the Synoptic accounts of the Last Supper. But in addition to abolishing Passover, at least implicitly, at the Last Supper, Jesus comes near to usurping the Temple Cult itself by taking on himself the roles of victim and priest. The expression in Matthew, "poured out for many for the forgiveness of sins" (literally, "that which for many is being shed for the forgiveness of sins"), is especially reminiscent of passages from Exodus 24 mentioned above—"And Moses took half the blood and put it in basins, and half of the blood he threw against the altar . . . And Moses took the blood and threw it upon the people, and said, 'Behold the blood of the covenant which the Lord has made with you'" (24:6, 24:8). With these actions, Moses is modeling the practice of the Levitical priesthood, which is about to be established. But as the Letter to the Hebrews reminds us, Jesus "came from Judah, a tribe which Moses

17. See Fenton, *St Matthew*, 226.

did not mention at all when dealing with priests" (7:14b). So Jesus's actions would have seemed insolently subversive of the Torah itself, as they probably still do to observant Jews. The usurpation of priestly functions was punishable with instant death (Nm 16) even by members of the priestly family (Lv 10:1), their bodies being buried "out of the camp" (Lv 10:4b, 5b).

There is another subversive element in Luke's account that has a bearing on John's. Luke's Jesus tells the disciples: "I am among you as one who serves" (Lk 22:27b). But at Passover in Jesus's day, the role of servant was customarily assigned to gentiles. This may explain why the expression "to serve tables" is used in Acts 6:2b for the role of the seven men of good reputation who are given responsibility for the support of widows—they all have Greek names. Is Jesus, then, assuming a *gentile* role in Luke's Gospel?—a shocking possibility, bearing in mind that for "the rabbinic tradition there is an impurity inherent in Gentiles,"[18] and that gentiles were prohibited from eating Passover. And what are the implications of his actually doing the work of a servant in John? The answer would be much clearer if we could be certain that his account draws on earlier material representing the Last Supper as an actual Passover meal. Even so, the subversive extravagance of Jesus's gesture in John is palpable.

In any case, there is little doubt about the other role that Jesus assumes in the opening phase of his long farewell discourse in John: "I give you a new commandment" (13:34a). That the commandment to love, vastly significant as it is, is not new is beside the point. What is striking is both the "covenant theme . . . implicit" in the reference to a commandment[19] and the fact that one who has just enacted the role of servant should take it upon himself to issue it. That the one who has just washed the feet of his disciples should make such a claim is a further instance of the scandalous elimination, in the Last Supper

18. Fenton, *St Matthew*, 45.

19. Brown, *Gospel According to John*, 557.

and Passion narratives, of "lines" that traditionally were thought to have fallen "in pleasant places" (Ps 16:6).

The Crucifixion and Resurrection

The First Letter of Peter describes the blood of Jesus as that of "a lamb without blemish or spot" (1:19b), but it would be hard to find a condition more *impure* than that of Jesus on the cross. In the place of the skull, "outside the gate" (Hb 13:12a; cf. Lv 16:27–28), scourged, naked, bleeding, incontinent, hanging on a tree, "a curse of God," so that "your land which the Lord your God gives you for an inheritance" is in danger of pollution (Dt 21:23b), Jesus on the cross is as degraded as a Jew could be. Golgotha is the absolute obverse of Eden. This is a "fall" more unqualified than Adam's. Consequently, to think of it as a Temple sacrifice, not to mention the purifying, redeeming blood of the covenant itself, would be, should be, an abomination to an observant Jew. But (taking account of the Gospels only) such a thought would have occurred to no one but for the Synoptics' accounts of the Last Supper. The scandal of the words said over the cup in Matthew and Mark, and over the bread as well in Luke, only becomes evident in the light of Golgotha, just as the crucifixion (however horrible) is only *scandalous* in relation to the words pronounced over the bread and the cup. Each event interprets the other, and it is in this sense especially that in the Eucharist Christians "proclaim the Lord's death until he comes" (1 Cor 11:26b).

The horror would be all the stronger if John's account, as scholars suggest, intentionally aligns the crucifixion and death of Jesus with the ritual slaughter in the Temple of lambs for the Passover feast to be eaten on the Friday evening itself.[20] This possibility is reinforced by 1 Corinthians 5:7b: "Christ is called 'our Passover which has been immolated.'"[21] There is evidence that the lamb was roasted with the

20. See Brown, *Gospel According to John*, 62, 883.

21. Nodet and Taylor, *Origins of Christianity*, 106.

forequarters outstretched in the form of a cross,[22] but even if this suggestion is not well founded, John's Passion Narrative unquestionably returns to John the Baptist's identification of Jesus with "the lamb of God that takes away the sin of the world" (Jn 1: 29b), notably when the narrative recalls Exodus 12:46b ("nor may you break any of its bones"). But to Jewish eyes, a *flogged man*, nailed to a cross and exposed in a most unholy place, the place of the skull, would be an obscene parody of the Paschal Lamb, which had to be "*an animal without blemish*" (Ex 12:5a).

This is the scandal of which Paul writes (1 Cor 1:23), and it is not to be underestimated by Christians cut off from Jewish traditions of reverence for the holy both by their own ancient reverence for the cross and by the evangelists' moving, if implicit, evocation of Isaiah's Suffering Servant, "despised," "stricken," "bruised," dumb, "like a lamb that is led to the slaughter, like a sheep ... before its shearers" (Isa 53:3c, 53:4c, 53:7c). The relevance of these celebrated passages to the theology of the New Testament is so obvious and powerful that one can easily forget that the Servant was not understood as a messianic figure by Jews, and that the lamb in the prophecy is not a sacrificial lamb.

The theme of the lamb in the tradition associated with the Fourth Gospel is full of tensions. It has been suggested that "the Lamb of God is a reference to the lamb (*amnos*, Ex 24:38–46) offered twice a day in the Temple," or (more doubtfully) to the lamb (*probaton*, Lv 4:32) offered as a sin offering.[23] But like the Paschal Lamb, sacrificial animals had to be without blemish, as indeed we must assume the lamb (*probaton*) was that God provided as a substitute for Isaac when his father Abraham was about to slay him as a sacrificial victim (Gn 22:8, 22:13), and with which Jesus may also be readily identified, especially as "a relation was established between the Passover Lamb

22. Nodet and Taylor, *Origins of Christianity*, 35.

23. Brown, *Gospel According to John*, 63.

... and the sacrifice of Isaac, since that sacrifice was dated to the 15th of Nissan,"[24] the day after Passover. In some Jewish traditions, Isaac was understood to have actually died and been restored to life. Again, Moses was compared to a lamb in a Targum (a paraphrase in Aramaic of the Hebrew Scriptures) in Exodus 15.[25] If any of this was in the evangelist's mind, however, he must surely have been aware also how offensive to Jews such comparisons would have seemed.

Then there is the detail that the sponge soaked in vinegar or sour wine that Jesus is offered before his death is held up to his mouth "on hyssop" (Jn 19:29b). A bunch of hyssop soaked in the blood of the Paschal Lamb was used to smear "the lintel and the two door posts" of the house in which the lamb was being eaten, as a sign that the Lord should "pass over the door and ... not allow the destroyer to enter your houses to slay you" (Ex 12:22b, 12:23b). If the liquid in the sponge is (sour) *wine*, this would seem to be both a Passover and "Last Supper" moment: the Crucifixion is a Passover meal at which wine is drunk, while wine on a hyssop stick symbolizes saving blood, thus implicitly endorsing the words spoken by Jesus over the cup in the Synoptic accounts, and also perhaps signifying that, however it may appear, the destroyer will not finally overcome *this* appallingly unprotected firstborn son, or alternatively that blood on hyssop no longer protects.

A further detail relates to John's account of the Resurrection. On the first day of the week after Passover, the first fruits were offered in the Temple in the form of a loaf of barley. The coincidence is not remarked on in the Gospels any more than the coincidence between the crucifixion and the slaying of the Paschal Lamb is spelled out in John. St. Paul, however, tells the Corinthians:

24. Brown, *Gospel According to John*, 917.

25. Nodet and Taylor, *Origins of Christianity*, 376.

> Christ has been raised from the dead, the first-fruits of those who have fallen asleep. For as by a man came death, by a man has come also the resurrection of the dead. For as in Adam all die, so also in Christ shall all be made alive. But each in his own order: Christ the first-fruits, then at his coming, those who belong to Christ. (1 Cor 15:22–23)

So the early Church made a connection between the Resurrection and the offering of the first fruits on the "Sunday" after Passover and later at Pentecost. Relevant also is the fact that in John's account of the feeding of the five thousand, the original five loaves are barley loaves. Here we have a clear connection between the bread of the Last Supper, the *body* of the risen Christ, and the offering of the first fruits of the barley harvest after Passover: "in the early church *barley* bread was used for the Eucharist."[26]

It is the Resurrection story, of course, that changes everything. It "amounts to a very serious tampering with boundaries, since the necessary separation of life and death ... the pure and the impure, is thus compromised."[27] But by "descending into Hell" (Sheol) and then rising, Jesus has surely conquered uncleanness itself, and so has done away with the *need* for division. This core insight lies at the heart of Paul's theology and Jewish opposition to it. Thus, though Jesus has risen from a tomb, the place of absolute uncleanness, there is no question of his being "unclean" till sundown, according to the law. That is emphatically *not* why Mary of Magdala must not cling to him (Jn 20:17a). Impurity as such, the death that all die in Adam, has now been *cleansed*. This is one massively important reason why the Resurrection is integral to the Christian understanding of redemption. All Christ's followers become *fit* offerings, *without blemish*, to be presented to God. And for this reason, the massive, disgusting perversion of the law and subversion of Israel, which are implicit in the New Testament accounts of the Last Supper and the Passion,

26. Brown, *Gospel According to John*, 248.
27. Nodet and Taylor, *Gospel According to John*, 45.

become instead their fulfillment. The whole point of Israel, from a New Testament perspective, is that *this* Son of David should secure *this* quintessentially Jewish but also cosmic victory over uncleanness and therefore over division.

Another way of looking at it, however, is that the Passion and Resurrection Narratives simply cancel the Jewish Scriptures and return the universe to its original condition, "without form and void" (Gn 1:2a)

Conclusion

The crucifixion narrative in John is twenty verses (about five hundred words in the original Greek), and the Last Supper narratives in the Synoptics about thirty verses. From one point of view, the Jewish Scriptures force themselves on our attention as we read the Passion Narratives, but most of the meanings that scholars find in these brief and bare bits of narrative are not obvious. So perhaps we have read altogether too much into them. It is also worth registering how minor the incidents in the New Testament really were, compared even with Ezra's rainy day (which in the context of Cyrus's great empire would itself have seemed a trivial event indeed), never mind with the majestic roar of Sinai. If the Last Supper *was* a Passover Meal, it was one of thousands taking place in Jerusalem at that time. Otherwise it was just a minor private occasion, as the Fourth Gospel suggests. Nor is there reason to suppose that the Temple authorities would have been chiefly preoccupied with Jesus that day, whatever the impression the Evangelists leave us with. He was a potentially dangerous problem intruding on their main concern: celebrating Passover. As for the Romans, whether the Jews were celebrating their strange festival on Thursday or Friday, the Friday would have been just another day for routine floggings and executions. What were three more crucifixions among so many? Also, we need to keep in mind how marginal the people were by whom and for whom these stories were told, a tiny scattered, yet irritatingly obtrusive set of social nobodies in the great Roman scheme of things. How could such roughly written literary scraps (a.k.a. *pericopae*) into which the Jewish Scriptures, and pastoral and agrarian traditions more ancient than Israel herself, have apparently poured their improvised meanings, be accorded lasting human importance? But they certainly started something.

12

Freedom in the Gospel According to Mark

The Gospel According to Mark gives important if only partial support to the commonly held opinion among New Testament scholars that, historically, Jesus never applied the titles "son of God" and "the Son" to himself.

Considered on its own, "son of God" could simply mean "a man," or "the King of Israel" or even "Israel,"[1] but the Gospel seems to suggest that it has a special sense unique to Jesus. The opening sentence speaks of "the gospel of Jesus Christ, Son of God" (1:1), and at the very beginning of the Gospel, Jesus is baptized in the Jordan and a voice from heaven declares, "You are my beloved Son" (1:11). "Christ," the other title given to Jesus, means "Messiah." "Son of God" may have meant "Messiah" also,[2] though this is strongly contested. In Mark's account, however, Jesus never uses either title of himself;[3] *only* Jesus sees the heavens being ripped open and "the Spirit descending on him like a dove" (1:10c), and *only* Jesus hears the heavenly voice. Mark subsequently recounts how the spirits exorcised by Jesus are fiercely rebuked when they address him as "the

1. Vermes, *The Passion*, 47.

2. Wright, *New Testament and the People of God*, 395; *Jesus and the Victory of God*, 227–28.

3. Kermode, *Genesis of Secrecy*, 43; O'Hanlon, *Mark My Words*, 239.

Holy One of God" (1:24), or know who he is (1:34), or call him specifically "the son of God" (3:11). Admittedly, Jesus does not rebuke a demoniac, who calls him "son of the Most High God" (5:7). But only the disciples are present, they and Jesus are on foreign territory, and Jesus in Mark's account is much more open with his immediate followers than with the crowd. The next time he is identified as "son" is by the voice from heaven at the Transfiguration (9:7); this time only three disciples—Peter, James, and John—are present, and Jesus makes no allusion to what they have heard.

The nearest he comes to publicly indicating that he is in some sense the Son of God is when he recounts the parable of the vineyard at the end of his ministry (12:1–11).[4] Having leased a vineyard to tenants, its owner sends numerous servants to collect his share of the crop, but they are all mistreated and even killed. Last of all, he sends his beloved son, but the tenants kill him too and deny him honorable burial. The owner then destroys the tenants and leases the vineyard to others. We can take it that the owner is God, the vineyard the Temple, and the son Jesus himself. As with all the parables, however, Jesus refuses to explain in public and has not made any *explicit* claim about himself, even though his meaning is clear to the Temple authorities, and they start looking for ways to get rid of him.

Finally, there is a mysterious reference to "the Son" in the address to four of the disciples about the end of the age at the very end of his ministry: "of that day or that hour," Jesus tells them, "no one knows, not even the angels in heaven, nor the Son, but only the Father" (13:32). Sons were thought to know less than Fathers; however, this "son" is apparently greater than the angels.[5] But if Jesus *is* talking about himself, he doesn't say so. In the light of the evidence of the demons, of the voice from Heaven, as well as the parable of the vineyard, the natural interpretation of Jesus's words is that he is

4. Kümmel, *Theology of the New Testament*, 120.

5. Witherington, *Many Faces of Christ*, 64.

talking about himself, but again this is only by implication, and Jesus is speaking in private.

As well as "the Son of God" and (possibly) "the Son," another title frequently associated with Jesus in the Gospel is "son of man." Many scholars think that Jesus actually used this expression, which sounds odd in Greek but not in the Aramaic that Jesus spoke. The first time he speaks of "the Son of man" in Mark's account is striking. A paralyzed man is unceremoniously lowered from the roof in front of Jesus, and he scandalizes some scribes by telling the man that his sins "are forgiven." "Why," they ask in their hearts, "does this man speak thus. It is blasphemy. Who can forgive sins but God alone?" (2:4–7). But Jesus has *not* said that he is the one who has done the forgiving. On the contrary, by using the passive—"are forgiven"—he has attributed the forgiving to God,[6] this being a conventional way of describing an action of God's while avoiding the use of his Holy Name—it is often used in the Septuagint, the Greek translation of the Jewish Scriptures.[7] But as Jesus then heals the paralyzed man, he apparently makes the scribes' case for them, in his own words, so that they "may know that the Son of man has authority on earth to forgive sins" (2:10). Admittedly, he has not explicitly identified himself as "son of man," but the implication that he is referring to himself seems clear enough.

Jesus's second use of the expression, however, makes this conclusion rather less certain. He is challenged by some Pharisees for allowing his disciples to do some trivial "work" on the Sabbath, and his reply to them is provocative: "The sabbath was made for man, not man of the sabbath; so the Son of man is lord even of the sabbath" (2:28). Like RSV, most modern translations give the word "son" an initial capital letter, but there is no distinction between upper- and lowercase letters in the early manuscripts, and without

6. Vermes, *Authentic Gospel of Jesus Christ*, 41; Sanders, *Jesus and Judaism*, 273.

7. O'Hanlon, *Mark My Words*, 79.

the capital letter, the expression "son of man" in Aramaic could indicate a modest reference to oneself, [8] but it could also mean *any* male human being, *any* son of Adam ("Adam" meaning "man")[9]—this is how it is most frequently used in the Jewish Scriptures—or in some circumstances it could signify specifically the People of Israel (as in the Book of Daniel 7:13–14). Some scholars have therefore argued that Jesus could be saying that human beings, or at any rate God's People, must decide for themselves what is or is not permitted on the Sabbath,[10] an interpretation strengthened by the preceding sentence, "The sabbath was made for man, not man for the sabbath." Before the earlier healing of the paralytic, therefore, Jesus *may* be saying that the forgiveness of sins is also a human or at any rate a Jewish prerogative. This would be radical stuff and shocking to his hearers, but not a claim specifically about himself. Nor would Jesus necessarily be talking about the way things currently are; he could be talking about how things soon will be in the coming kingdom.

Subsequently, Jesus refers to the son of man in two distinct ways. In private, talking to his disciples, he speaks about the coming suffering of the Son of man, and they have no doubt that he is referring to himself (8:31). All Jesus's predictions about himself as the suffering Son of man are confirmed in his words to the disciples immediately before his arrest: "It is enough; the hour has come; the Son of man is betrayed into the hands of sinners" (14:41). His second way of referring to the Son of man, once in public (8:38) and once to four of his disciples (13:26), links this mysterious figure not with suffering but with the great saving-judging event at the end of time. This end-of-time Son of man recalls a prophetic vision in the Book of Daniel:

8. Hooker, *Gospel According to Saint Mark*, 92; Vermes, *Authentic Gospel of Jesus Christ*, 237.

9. Vermes, *Authentic Gospel of Jesus Christ*, 234 and 235.

10. Hooker, *Gospel According to Saint Mark*, 105.

> I saw in the night visions,
> And behold, with the clouds of heaven
> there came one like a son of man.
> and he came to the Ancient of Days
> and was presented before him.
> And to him was given dominion
> and glory and kingdom,
> and all peoples, nations, and languages
> should serve him;
> his dominion is an everlasting dominion,
> which shall not pass away,
> and his kingdom one
> that shall never be destroyed. (Dn 7:13–14)

The standard Jewish understanding of this passage was and is that the "one like a son of man" (i.e., the one like a human being, rather than an angel in the heavenly court) is a personification of Israel, the Holy People of God, and this could well be how the ordinary people in the Gospel would have understood Jesus, when at Caesarea Philippi he spells out to the crowds that they are obliged to follow him, even though the cost of their doing so would be extreme indeed.

> And he called to him the multitude with his disciples, and said to them, "If any man would come after me, let him deny himself and take up his cross and follow me. For whoever would save his life will lose it; and whoever loses his life for my sake and the gospel's will save it. For what does it profit a man to gain the whole world and forfeit his life. For what can a man give in return for his life? For whoever is ashamed of me and of my words in this adulterous and sinful generation, of him will the Son of man also be ashamed when he comes in the glory of his Father with the holy angels." (8:34–37)

Like all subjects of the Roman Empire, the multitude would have been familiar with the common spectacle of scourged, naked slaves and rebels being forced to carry their crosses to a place of execution prior to their being crucified. Having previously seen Jesus as a great healer, exorcist, and homely preacher, this terrible warning about what it might cost them to be his followers would have come as a shock to them—and to his disciples also. But it is necessary, Jesus tells them, if they are to avoid being objects of shame when, at the end of the present age, "the Son of man comes in the glory of his Father with the holy angels." In Mark's account, however, the multitude have not heard Jesus's earlier reference to *himself* as the son of man who "must suffer many things," so they would have had no reason to identify "the Son of man" figure in his prophecy with Jesus. They would naturally understand him to be talking of Daniel's one like a son of man, and therefore Israel or the Messiah who was yet to come. The disciples, on the other hand, *would* have realized that Jesus was talking about himself coming in the glory of his Father, and they would therefore have been thoroughly confused, especially as they could have had no idea what his earlier words about his rising again after three days might mean. In the Jewish Scriptures, a general rising from the (finally) dead was only to be expected at the end of the age; no one envisaged the resurrection of an individual before then (see Dn 12:1–2).

None of this is inconsistent with, and indeed tends to support, the judgment that the Jesus of history did not think or speak of himself as the Son of God or even "the Son" in the strong sense of the opening words of the Gospel. All of Jesus's references to himself in these terms could be "editorial," reflecting the views about him developed in early Church communities. It *is* possible, however, that in life Jesus used the word "Abba" or "Father" when he addressed God in prayer, as he does in Mark's account, before his arrest in Gethsemane (14:36), and this could have been the seed out of which the "son of God" tradition developed. In the same way, he *could* have used the idiomatic Aramaic expression "the son of man," possibly in reference to himself, and this too might have been deployed in new ways when his story was told in the light of stories about his resurrection. At the very least, then, there is nothing in Mark's account that challenges current, mainstream New Testament scholarship. The fact that the theme of Jesus's Sonship is much more fully developed in the later Gospel accounts—I assume with most scholars that the Gospel According to Mark was the first to be completed—might be taken as evidence in favor of the scholarly consensus.

But I have a problem with this sort of reading. It places a necessarily hypothetical "historical Jesus" between us and what Mark makes of Jesus and what in the Gospel Jesus says about himself, which is perhaps the most fundamental issue in Mark's story and around which he skillfully organizes his narrative. This emphasis is obscured if our reading of the Gospel is overlaid with historical speculation. Moreover, it is the issue around which the drama of freedom in the Gospel is constructed, a drama that has four principal aspects—the relations of Jesus with the disciples, his interaction with the Temple authorities and Pilate, his relations with his Father culminating in the horror of the cross, and the mystery of his resurrection.

Until the departure of Peter after he denies knowing Jesus in the courtyard of the high priest after Jesus's arrest (14:72), Jesus is never presented in any detail except from the point of view of his disciples.[11] We do not see him through the eyes of the paralytic; of Jairus, whose daughter he brings back to life (4:22–23, 4:35–43); of Bartimaeus, the blind man whose sight he restores (10:46–52); or of the multitude. Readers are allowed just two ways of looking at him—the one proclaimed not only by the evangelist but also by the demons and the voice from Heaven, as Son of God and the Jesus whom the disciples both see and do not see, the person whom Jesus reveals and relentlessly conceals. In the light of this, the fidelity of the disciples to Jesus amid their confusion and weakness seems to me to be heroic.

Consider their reaction to Jesus's first "nature" miracle.

11. Baukham, *Jesus and the Eyewitnesses*, 168.

On that day, when evening had come, he said to them, "Let us go across to the other side." And leaving the crowd, they took him with them in the boat, just as he was. And other boats were with him. And a great storm of wind arose, and the waves beat into the boat, so that the boat was already filling. But he was in the stern asleep on the cushion; and they woke him and said to him, "Teacher, do you not care if we perish?" And he awoke and rebuked the wind, and said to the sea, "Peace! Be still!" And the wind ceased, and there was a great calm. He said to them, "Why are you afraid? Have you no faith?" And they were filled with awe, and said to one another. "Who then is this, that even the wind and sea obey him?" (4:35–41)

They might well ask. The sea is entirely under God's control in the Jewish Scriptures:[12]

> You rule the raging of the sea;
> when its waves rise, you still them. (Ps 89:9)

> Then they cried to the Lord in their trouble,
> and he delivered them from their distress;
> he made the storm be still,
> and the waves of the sea were hushed.
> Then they were glad because they had quiet,
> and he brought them to their desired haven. (Ps 107:28–30)

Psalm 104:6b–7a reads: "the waters stood above the mountains. / At thy rebuke they fled" (see also Ps 93:3–4, 106:8–9, 107:28–30, and Isa 51:10). The disciples, in other words, might well be saying in their hearts, "Who can calm the sea, but God alone?," and the fear they feel might be the holy fear that takes possession of everyone in the Jewish Scriptures who comes into intimate contact with the Divine. Their confusion would be all the greater since they had spoken roughly to the sleeping Jesus moments before,[13] especially if they are recalling the reaction of Manoah, the father of Samson in the Book of Judges. An "angel of the Lord" has appeared first to his wife, then to Manoah himself. Manoah has offered a kid and a cereal

12. Hengel, *Studies in the Gospel of Mark*, 45.

13. Hooker, *Gospel According to Saint Mark*, 139; Nineham, *Gospel of Mark*, 148.

offering, and the angel has ascended to heaven in "the flame of the altar"; Manoah and his wife then fall "on their faces to the ground and Manoah [says] to his wife 'We shall surely die, for we have seen God'" (Jgs 13:19–22). Is Jesus, then, a messenger as close to God as the angel who appeared to Samson's parents? The latter, however, ascended to Heaven. Jesus remains with the disciples, and eats and argues with them. Who or what Jesus really is, then, is a question that everybody in the Gospel asks,[14] sometimes in fear and trembling, and that, except on one occasion and then doubtfully, Jesus refuses to answer.

There is another crucial moment at Caesarea Philippi.

> And Jesus went on with his disciples, to the villages of Caesarea Philippi; and on the way he asked his disciples, "Who do men say that I am?" And they told him, "John the Baptist and others say, Elijah; and others one of the prophets." And he asked them, "But who do you say that I am?" Peter answered him, "You are the Christ." And he charged them to tell no one about him. (Mk 8:27–30)

"The Christ"—that is, "the anointed one" or "Messiah"—is the important title attached to Jesus's name in the opening words of the Gospel. It is implicit in the later address of the blind man, Bartimaeus to Jesus as "son of David" (10:48), that is, the legitimate anointed King of Israel. The appearance of a Messiah figure as herald of God's final intervention on the part of his People was widely anticipated at the time of Jesus,[15] even if what the term might mean in detail was uncertain. (In some quarters, two "anointed ones" were envisaged—a kingly messiah and a priestly messiah—anointing being required for kings and priests alike.[16]) At Caesarea Philippi, however, Jesus once again falls just short of confirming what is said about him. He does not explicitly confirm or contradict it. In the corresponding

14. *The New Testament* (trans. King), 99; Myers, *Binding the Strong Man*, 106.

15. Witherington, *Many Faces of Christ*, 15.

16. Levenson, "Messianic Movements," 540.

passage in Matthew, Peter calls Jesus "the Christ, the son of the living God," and Jesus endorses what Peter has said in the strongest possible terms: "Blessed are you. Simon Bar-Jona! For flesh and blood has not revealed this to you, but my Father who is in heaven" (Mt 16:16–17). Mark's Jesus simply tells the disciples not to talk to people about him without explicitly endorsing Peter's declaration.

He then promptly foretells his own death, Peter objects, and a furious row develops between him and Jesus, ending with a terrible insult to Peter—Jesus calls him Satan (8:31–33). Yet a week later, as if nothing had happened, Jesus takes Peter with James and John to the top of a mountain, where Jesus is seen dressed miraculously in brilliant white, talking with Moses and Elijah until he is enveloped in a cloud (always in the Jewish Scriptures a sign of God's presence) and a voice proclaims, "This is my beloved Son; listen to him." As Jesus and the disciples come down from the mountain, however, he says *nothing* to them about what they have seen, except that they are not to tell anyone about it "until the Son of man should have risen from the dead. So they [keep] the matter to themselves, questioning what rising from the dead meant" (9:11). They ask him a related question, however, about the prophesied return of Elijah before the end-time, to which Jesus again does not give a straight answer. Moreover, to increase their confusion, he adds: "it is written of the Son of man, that he should suffer many things, and be treated with contempt" (9:1–13). But the son of man is *not* referred to in these terms in Jewish Scriptures. Rather (in the Book of Daniel), he is described being "given dominion and glory and kingdom." By Jesus's own choice, therefore, the question of who and what he is hangs over his ministry from his first appearing at the Jordan until his arrest and is never answered. He clearly *knows* that the disciples do not, cannot, understand him. That he never explains *and* that they continue to follow him dramatizes the mutual freedom that unites them and him without explaining it.

The crucial question of Jesus's identity is also the central point at issue in his nighttime inquisition before "the high priest . . . and all the chief priests and the elders and the scribes" (14:53) after his arrest in Gethsemane. The most serious allegation against him, apparently, is the curious claim of false witnesses that they had "heard him say, 'I will destroy this temple that is made with hands, and in three days I will build another, not made with hands.'" "Yet not even so," Mark continues, "did their testimony agree" (14:57–59). The expression "even so" is important. It implies that if this particular accusation had stood up, Jesus could have been convicted. So, what exactly is the blasphemy in the words attributed to him? It is not the declaration that he would destroy the temple as such, but his alleged use of the expression "made with human hands," which in the Jewish Scriptures is a dismissive way of describing idols (Dt 4:28, 27:15; 2 Kgs 19:18; 2 Chr 32:19). Though built by men, the Temple was constructed according by God's specific command (1 Chr 28:6). If Jesus had used this expression when speaking of the Temple, therefore, he would indeed have uttered blasphemy. But the evidence of witnesses at a Jewish trial had to be consistent—see the story of the trial of Susannah in the Deutero-canonical version of the Book of Daniel (chap. 13)—and it is apparently on this technicality that the accusation is about to fail. The high priest therefore tries to get Jesus to defend himself in a way that would have amounted to his admitting that the words were his, but he remains silent. So, exasperated, the high priest asks him directly, "Are you the Christ, the Son of the Blessed?" (14:61), and Jesus is apparently no less direct in his answer: "I am; and you will see the Son of man seated at the right hand of Power, and coming with the clouds of heaven" (14:62).

At the Last Supper (14:21) and before his arrest (14:41), Jesus openly refers to himself as "son of man" but these are both private occasions, and he speaks of himself as passive and betrayed. In his earlier prophecies at Caesarea Philippi and to the four disciples about the end of the age, "the son of man," by contrast, is a gloriously powerful figure, and it is of the latter that Jesus speaks to the high priest. The exchange between them is tense and subtle. Both avoid the blasphemy of using the Holy Name. Because there is no punctuation, the high priest's words could be as much a sarcastic exclamation as a question—"*You* are the Christ, the Son of the Blessed!" In any case, Jesus, for the first and only time, declares that this is indeed so. But what has he said? Since the Kings of Israel—and David in particular—were repeatedly identified as the adopted Sons of God,[17] he might simply be claiming to be David's successor, and therefore the Messiah. Wicked as such a claim would be if it were untrue, it would not be blasphemous.

He then describes "the Son of man" as "seated at the right hand of Power, and coming with the clouds of heaven." This is significantly different from the one like a son of man in Daniel's prophecy, who is clearly an earthly figure (he is *like* a son of man) invested by God with supreme authority over an earthly kingdom. By contrast, Jesus's Son of man is seated beside God, possibly or almost as an equal. Insofar as he is invested "with clouds of glory," he is enclosed within Divinity Itself.[18] Technically, of course, Jesus has not identified himself with this figure, but the inference is not difficult to make. This would account for the high priest's tearing his garments and saying, "You have heard his blasphemy." Again, this could be translated as "You have heard his blasphemy, haven't you?," meaning "You know what he is *really* saying, yes?" It would account also for the other judges declaring that he *deserves* death (14:61–64) instead of simply passing sentence upon him, which they would have been able to do if he had been more explicit. Conveniently, however, there is no further need of witnesses because, by agreeing that he is the Son of God, Jesus has in effect committed treason under Roman law by giving himself a title claimed by the Emperor Tiberius.

17. Vermes, *The Passion*, 47.

18. Hooker, *Gospel According to Saint Mark*, 217.

The important point is that throughout Jesus remains in control. By one forthright answer, he has made it possible for the Jewish authorities to release him or to hand him over to Pilate if they want to. In enabling the rulers of the people to act freely as they choose, he has exercised his own sovereign freedom as a person. They hear, they understand, and therefore they could acknowledge the freedom he has granted to them by freely granting him his freedom in return. They refuse to do so. The contrast with the behavior of the disciples at least before their flight when Jesus is arrested is marked.

Before Pilate, Jesus reverts to his usual stance of imperturbable ambiguity: "And Pilate asked him, 'Are you the King of the Jews?' [or, "*You* are king of the Jews?!"] And he answered him, 'You have said so'" (15:2). He then refuses to answer any more questions. Pilate, however, sees that he is innocent—"For he perceived that it was out of envy that the chief priests had delivered him up" (15:10)—yet, like Herod ordering the beheading of John the Baptist (6:26–27),[19] he orders Jesus's execution. They both act against what they know to be the just course of action, without being under serious pressure to do so. Had Jesus replied to Pilate as he replied to the high priest, Pilate would have had to condemn him on the spot, but by leaving him without a clear answer, Jesus makes it possible for Pilate to acquit him, as Pilate knows he could and should. Once again, in his own sovereign freedom, Jesus allows others either to honor that freedom in return, or to surrender to impulse or calculation. If responsibility for his execution falls equally and with perfect symmetry on both Jewish and Roman authorities, it is because Jesus himself has freely allowed it to do so.

But what about Pilate's offer to release Jesus if the crowd asks for it? The chief priests stir up the crowd to demand the release of Barabbas instead, so Pilate asks them, "Then what shall I do with the man whom you call the King of the Jews?" (15:12), and the crowd re-

19. Hooker, *Gospel According to Saint Mark*, 161.

peats its demand for Jesus's crucifixion. Pilate asks them what evil Jesus has done, but they again repeat their call for Jesus to be crucified, so Pilate ostentatiously accedes to their wishes and orders Barabbas's release. But this apparent accession to the wishes of the crowd hardly counts as an instance of Pilate's acting freely, since the people are not given real choice. Mark's readers would have known that Pilate was notorious for the arbitrary and tyrannical exercise of power. They would have recognized the trap in the alternatives presented to the crowd—whether to ask for the release of a genuine rebel, Barabbas, or a man labeled a rebel by Pilate himself. Outrageously, Pilate then insists that it is they not he who called Jesus their King. Mark thus shows Pilate successfully transferring responsibility for the death of Jesus from himself onto the crowd—and manipulation of others is the opposite of freedom.

For his part, having made no attempt to lead either the chief priests or Pilate in the decisions they make, Jesus remains the only fully free agent in the whole Passion narrative and paradoxically the one who, though bound, flogged, and nailed to a cross, remains in control of events, at least until his final moment. And this without his ever giving a clear answer to the great question "Who, then, is this?," though so many people seem to know the answer, and tremble.

There are two ways in which Jesus is seen in relation to God in the Gospel. The first is declaratory. He is named the Son of God by the evangelist, addressed by the Voice from Heaven as Son at the Baptism, and identified to the three disciples in the same terms at the Transfiguration. The second is personal. Early in the morning of his second day in Capernaum, he goes out to a lonely place to pray (1:35), and after the feeding of the five thousand, he sends the disciples away by boat and goes up a mountain and prays alone until the fourth watch of the night (6:46, 6:48). Prayer is thus the only thing in the Gospel that he does on his own and in the dark. It is utterly private.

This changes in Gethsemane. Jesus announces to the disciples that he is going to pray, and, moving off with Peter, James, and John, he confesses his extreme distress, begs them to "remain here, and watch," and, at a short distance from them, prays in their hearing: "Abba, Father, all things are possible to you; remove this cup from me; yet not what I will, but what you wilt." He returns to them three times and finds them sleeping. On the third occasion, Judas and an armed crowd advance on them, and he asks, "Are you still sleeping and at rest? It is enough; the hour has come; the Son of man is betrayed into the hands of sinners. Rise, let us be going; see, my betrayer is at hand" (14:32–42). Thus, for the first time in the Gospel, Jesus as Son of God (the one who calls God "Abba") and Jesus as Son of man (the way he speaks of himself) are brought together. This is also the only time that Jesus reveals something of his "private life." "Abba" is an intimate (but not a childish) form of address to a father.[20] In his use of it in prayer, Jesus acknowledges his sonship not in terms of a formal title, like the "sonship" with which a king of Israel was invested, but in an idiom that expresses his intimate sense of who and what he is. It is as a Jewish son that he places his future in the hands of the Jewish God.

Jesus's final, public prayer is on the cross: "And at the ninth hour Jesus cried with a loud voice, 'Eloi, Eloi, lama sabachthani' which means, 'My God, my God, why have you forsaken me?'" (15:34). This is the only occasion in the Gospel where he uses a set form of prayer—he is quoting the opening words of Psalm 22. For its first twenty-one verses, Psalm 22 consists of a series of changes of direction. The psalmist begins by crying out in agony about his abandonment by God; but God is enthroned in power and the prayers of the psalmist's fathers were heard and *they* were saved; but the psalmist is now less than human, despised and ridiculed; but God took him from his mother's womb and he still looks to God to be near him; he is surrounded by enemies as savage as beasts; but he is poured

20. Vermes, *The Passion*, 220.

out like water, wretched, racked, exhausted, thirsty, surrounded by dogs, pierced, ridiculed, his clothes divided by lot; but he begs God to remain nearby to rescue him from the mouth of the lion and the horns of the wild oxen. The last ten verses triumphantly praise God before the People of Israel for not despising the afflicted, but feeding and satisfying them; the whole earth will worship him; dominion belongs to him; the proud will bow down before him; and his deliverance will be recounted to the coming generation.

On the face of it, therefore, Jesus could be proclaiming his faith in God despite the horrors to which he has been subjected. A darker reading is possible, however, and is generally considered sounder. In the first place, the words *Eloi, Eloi, lama sabachthani* are an odd mix of Hebrew and Aramaic[21] and are not in the form that the psalm would have been recited liturgically; they may even have been a proverbial and bitter adaptation of the words of the psalm to express bewilderment at God's failure in practice to help the afflicted.[22] Second, the actual death of Jesus runs counter to the Psalmist's triumphant faith. Finally, the events surrounding his death are troublingly ambiguous. A bystander speculates that Elijah might rescue and vindicate Jesus (15:36). Instead, Jesus dies and the darkness that has covered the earth since the sixth hour is lifted. The curtain of the Temple is ripped apart (15:38), degrading the Holy of Holies, where once a year the high priest came into solitary contact with the Almighty—this could be interpreted as God's withdrawal from his People as well as from his Son. And the words of the gentile centurion, "Truly this man was the Son of God!" (15:39), *can* be read in the unpunctuated Greek as a jeering reference to Jesus's use of an expression that put him on equal terms with the emperor himself. In any case, Jesus's death prevents him from expressing any faith in God—he dies before he can be consoled, abandoned and in utter

21. Brown, *Death of the Messiah*, 1046, 1052.

22. Vermes, *The Passion*, 75.

uncleanness. If his freedom consists in his complete surrender to the freedom of his Father, in the manner of his dying, it may be said to pass all human measure. How can the human mind begin to grasp that this is the kind of freedom operating between "God" and his "son"?

The cry of dereliction needs also to be understood in the context of another strongly emphasized feature of Mark's account of the crucifixion. The events from the arrival at Golgotha to the death of Jesus are recounted in 208 words in Greek. Of these, 65, or nearly a third, recall the mockery of the chief priests, the bystanders, and the criminals:

> And those who passed by derided him, wagging their heads, and saying, "Aha! You who would destroy the temple and build it in three days, save yourself, and come down from the cross!" So also the chief priests mocked him to one another with the scribes, saying, "He saved others; he cannot save himself. Let him come down from the cross, that we may see and believe." Those who were crucified with him also reviled him. (15:29–32)

Clearly, those reviling Jesus have seen his healings and exorcisms—"He saved others"—but these could be of diabolic origin. When the Pharisees asked him for "a sign from heaven, to test him" (8:11), they wanted the kind of spectacular nature miracle repeatedly granted to Moses in Exodus and Numbers, and to Elijah in his contest with the priests of Baal on Carmel, when water-drenched burnt offerings were consumed by fire sent from heaven (1 Kgs 19:36–39). Jesus coming down from the cross would be just such a sign. The chief priests, the bystanders, and the criminals have not of course seen the actual signs that Jesus has performed—calming the sea (4:37–41, 6:51), walking on the water (6:48–50), and feeding the multitudes (6:34–44, 8:1–8). But Mark's readers have been told about them, so for them there are two questions that need to be answered: Why was Jesus forsaken, yes, but also why did he not save himself? At the heart of the crucifixion story is a great mystery—the vast emptiness of two unanswered questions.

I have been suggesting that the consistent ambiguity in the sayings and actions of Jesus in the Gospel maximize the capacity for freedom in those who see and hear him and are for that very reason a manifestation of his own freedom as a person acting in the presence of God and his fellow human beings. This freedom culminates in his unexplained passivity on the cross and the extreme desolation of his encounter with abandonment and death. I would also suggest that a matching ambiguity is mirrored in Mark's relations with his readers. He never explains either Jesus's behavior or that of his followers. If Mark's Jesus consistently resists offering his listeners explanations, so does Mark.

It is generally agreed that it is difficult if not impossible to distinguish between the women who watch the crucifixion from afar, the women who watch the burial, and the women who come to the tomb hoping to anoint the body after sunrise on the first day of the week. But the account of what happens when "Mary Magdalene, and Mary the mother of James, and Salome go to the tomb very early on the first day of the week" (15:40, 15:47, 16:1–2) is ambiguous in a much more challenging way. They speculate about who might roll away the stone that was laid against the door of the tomb (15:46) but find that it has already been rolled back.

> And entering the tomb, they saw a young man sitting on the right side, dressed in a white robe; and they were amazed. And he said to them, "Do not be amazed; you seek Jesus of Nazareth, who was crucified. He has risen, he is not here; see the place where they laid him. But go, tell his disciples and Peter that he is going before you to Galilee; there you will see him." And they went out and fled from the tomb; for trembling and astonishment had come upon them; and they said nothing to anyone, for they were afraid. (16:3–8)

Mark has nothing more to tell us. It is possible that a longer ending has been lost. Standard editions of the Gospel, including RSV, add eleven additional verses, but they are absent from the best early manuscripts and are evidently not the work of Mark.

The ending as we find it in the earliest manuscripts, which many scholars think is down to Mark, has other remarkable features. The Greek word meaning "because" or "for" never introduces the clause in which it appears, as it always does in English ("for they were afraid"); it usually comes second and is very rarely the last word of a sentence. The Gospel According to Mark, however, is the *only* extant Greek text to actually *end* with "because." Even an English version in which the last sentence read "They were afraid, that's why" or "They were afraid, you see" would fail to reproduce the abrupt raggedness of Mark's final sentence. Grammatically, it leaves the mind reaching forward—toward nothing.

This bewildering grammar, however, is only one aspect of an ending that refuses to conclude, and that specifically fails to disclose what the key words "He has risen" actually mean. Yet the validity about every claim made about Jesus in the Gospel, by the evangelist, by Jesus himself, and even by the Voice from Heaven, depends on these words being true.

Jesus speaks of his resurrection for the first time at Caesarea Philippi, and again as he comes down from the mountain of the Transfiguration with Peter, James, and John. In what is known as the Second Passion Prediction, as he and his followers are traveling through Galilee on the first stage of their journey to Jerusalem, he repeats what he had said at Caesarea Philippi: "The Son of man will be delivered into the hands of men, and they will kill him; and when he is killed, after three days he will rise. But they did not understand the saying, and they were afraid to ask him" (9:31). Later, he predicts what is going to happen to him in more detail:

> Behold, we are going up to Jerusalem; and the Son of man will be delivered up to the chief priests and the scribes, and they will condemn him to death, and deliver him to the Gentiles; and they will mock him, and spit upon him, and scourge him, and kill him; and after three days he will rise. (10:33–34)

The disciples evidently understand the prophecy about Jesus's death—that is obvious from Peter's reaction at Caesarea Philippi.

The second Passion Prediction repeats the first, and the third makes clear that Jesus will be put to death according to the savage practice of the Romans. But as the conversation between Peter, James, and John after the Transfiguration makes clear, they had no idea "what the rising from the dead meant" (9:10). It is impossible that they should.

At the Mount of Olives, Jesus says, "You will all fall away; for it is written, 'I will strike the shepherd, and the sheep will be scattered.' But after I am raised up, I will go before you to Galilee." What sense can the reader, never mind the disciples in Mark's narrative, make of this slightly inaccurate quotation from the Prophet Zechariah? The passage from which it is taken reads:

> "Awake, O sword, against my shepherd,
> against the man who stands next to me,"
> says the Lord of hosts.
> "Strike the shepherd, that the sheep may be scattered;
> I will turn my hand against the little ones.
> In the whole land, says the Lord, two thirds shall be cut off and perish,
> and one third shall be left alive.
> And I will put this third into the fire,
> and refine them as one refines silver,
> and test them as gold is tested.
> They will call on my name,
> and I will answer them.
> I will say, 'They are my people';
> and they will say, 'The Lord is my God.'"
> (Zec 13:7–9)

Presumably (at the time or later), the disciples are meant to recall this prophecy—and, presumably, Mark expected his readers to do so—but Zechariah will have provided little comfort to the disciples. Even if they grasped that they would be among the third left alive, this would still mean that they could expect to be put into the fire and refined like silver and tested like gold.

Nor is it clear *when* this mysterious and terrible drama would happen, since Zechariah's prophecy is about the tumultuous end of the age, and the meaning of the three days Jesus has been talking about was not at all obvious. Throughout the Jewish Scriptures, three days is a symbolic or ritualistic period, as it certainly is in the unsatisfactory evidence given by the false witnesses at Jesus's interrogation: "We have heard him say, 'in three days I will build another, not made with hands'" (14:58). If Jesus had said these words, or something like them, he could not have been talking about a physical rebuilding of the temple in a three-day period.

The most important three-day interval in the Jewish Scriptures, however, occurs before God gives Moses the Ten Commandments on Mt. Sinai:

> And the Lord said to Moses, "Go to the people and consecrate them today and tomorrow, and let them wash their garments, and be ready by the third day; for on the third day the Lord will come down upon Mount Sinai in the sight of all the people. And you shall set bounds for the people round about, saying, 'Take heed that you do not go up into the maintain or touch the border of it; whoever touches the mountain shall be put to death; no hand shall touch him, but he shall be stoned or shot, whether beast or man, he shall not live.' When the trumpet sounds a long blast, they shall come up to the mountain." (Ex 19:10–13)

One obvious meaning of Jesus's five utterances to his disciples concerning his resurrection on the third day, as well as of the Temple's being rebuilt after the third day (assuming he said this or something like it) would be that his rising and/or the Temple's restoration would match the drama and spectacle of God's coming to Moses on Mt. Sinai in the presence of the whole people. In accordance with the teachings about resurrection in the Book of Daniel (12:2–3), the Deutero-canonical Book of Wisdom (3:1–9), and the Deutero-canonical Second Book of Maccabees (12:44), he would be in a mysterious and spectacular way at the center of a mass resurrection three days after his death. But what Mark tells us about the events on the first day of the week after the crucifixion is the *opposite* of an end-of-the-age cosmic drama. All that happens is that three women, who in Jewish law do not qualify as witnesses, meet a striking young man in an empty tomb; he speaks to them and they run away in terror.

The tomb narrative thus imitates Jesus's own method of teaching in a manner that is extreme. When Jesus publicly refers to the Son of man, he implies that he is speaking of himself but never explicitly does so. He declares himself the Christ only once before the high priest; he refuses to explain his parables to the crowd, and much of his other teaching in public and private, even to the disciples. Why, for example, does he tell them that they will continue to "follow" him after his death, apparently at great cost, without explaining what he means (13:9–11)? From the calling of Simon and Andrew by the Sea of Galilee (1:16–18) until his arrest in Gethsemane, Jesus does not pressure the disciples, and they faithfully accept his resistance to their attempts to pressure him. Though not quite equal, the mutual freedom of his relations with them and theirs with him is sustained until, in terror, they abandon him. And this is precisely the relation Mark achieves with his readers throughout the Gospel but especially in his account of what happened on the morning of the first day of the week after the death and burial of Jesus. We may "follow" his narrative if we can and if we wish. We are in the same kind of relationship with Mark's words as the disciples were with Jesus himself. It might even be said that in ending the Gospel as he does, Mark abandons us.

The young man in the tomb is dressed in white. The only other occasion on which white clothing is mentioned in the Gospel is when, in the presence of Peter, James, and John, Jesus's "garments became glistening, intensely white" on the high mountain (9:3). It is up to us whether this is significant.

The young man's words to the women need careful scrutiny. He says:

> Do not be amazed; you seek Jesus of Nazareth. He is risen, he is not here; see the place where they laid him. But go, tell his disciples … "he is going before you to Galilee; there you will see him, as he told you."[23]

Two serious issues arise. First, Peter's being mentioned after the other disciples instead of before them is unexplained. Up to now he has invariably been mentioned first. It is almost as if he were no longer a disciple Second, the young man was not present when Jesus made the prophecy about going ahead of the disciples to Galilee, so he must have been told that Jesus said to the disciples on the Mount of Olives, "after I am raised up, I will go before you to Galilee" (14:28). But Jesus said nothing about the disciples *seeing* him in Galilee.

On the assumption that the young man is saying what he has been instructed to say, his utterance registers a series of utterances and utterances within utterances. In order these are:

1. Jesus to the disciples: "But after I am raised up, I will go before you to Galilee."
2. Words addressed to the young man: "Say to whoever comes to the tomb, 'He has risen … But go, tell his disciples and Peter, "He is going before you to Galilee; there you will see him, as he told you."'"
3. The young man to the women: "He has risen … But go, tell his disciples and Peter, 'He is going before you to Galilee; there you will see him, as he told you.'"
4. The women to the disciples: "The young man said to tell you, 'He has risen … But go, tell his disciples and Peter, "He is going before you to Galilee; there you will see him, as he told you ."'"

23. In the Vulgate, the Authorized Version, RSV, and the New Revised Standard Version of the Gospel According to Mark, "that" precedes "he is going before you." However, the young man does not shift awkwardly into indirect speech as these translations suggest. Mark frequently introduces direct speech with "that," so the young man is simply telling the women the specific words they are to use to the disciples.

5. Peter or the disciples to the narrator or his source: "The women said, 'A young man told us to tell you, "He has risen . . . But go, tell his disciples and Peter [*or* me], 'He is going before you to Galilee; there you will see me there, as he told you.'"'"
6. The Gospel account.

No other utterance in the Ancient World has so exactly and convincingly preserved a series of communications on the same subject. The ultimate proclamation is crystal clear, yet gossamer-frail,[24] characteristically muddled, and innocently authentic.

The reaction of the women is confused: "trembling and astonishment" come upon them, and they run away saying nothing to anyone because they are afraid. There are all sorts of fear—fear of their nightmarish experience, fear of being caught up in some covert activity that might put them in danger with the authorities, fear of the burden that has been put upon them—who would believe such a story from three highly stressed women? Fear of this sort would be comparable with that felt by the disciples at the second Passion prediction (9:32) and as they approached Jerusalem (10:32). But there is the fear also of Manoah and his wife. On the two occasions when Jesus displays supernatural mastery of the sea (4:41, 6:51), and at the Transfiguration (9:6), the disciples experience what may well be *religious* fear of this kind, the fear that in the Jewish Scriptures falls also on Jacob (Gn 28:17) and Moses (Ex 3:6) in the presence of the Divine.

It is entirely up to Mark's readers to engage with the women's speechless terror as best they can. Nevertheless, the fact that somehow their story burst upon the world, and that Mark recorded it, is a matter of incalculable importance and (for some) great joy. Not the least moving aspect of that joy is that our freedom as Mark's readers can operate as a kind of counterpoint to the freedom of Jesus bound,

24. Kermode, *Genesis of Secrecy*, 56–57, 68; Myers, *Binding the Strong Man*, 358.

beaten, crucified (and risen?). A small minority of scholars suggest an early date for the Gospel According to Mark.[25] It has even been argued that it is the earliest of the New Testament writings. Early or late, it comes across to me as foundational, so that the rest of the New Testament can fruitfully be read as explaining, modifying, amplifying, and complementing it.

It is the most open piece of writing in the history of the world; it is inexhaustible, forever, and essentially needing overinterpretation. And it is so because it makes no attempt to reveal the center that it so confidently proclaims at its beginning. Mark's readers must find that for themselves, with whatever resources of mind and heart are given to them.

The one who truly possesses the word of Jesus is able to hear his silence as well.[26]

25. Hengel, *Four Gospels and the One Gospel of Christ* 16; *Jewish Annotated New Testament*, 55.
26. St. Ignatius of Antioch, *Letters*, 235.

Bibliography

Scripture

The Holy Bible. Revised Standard Version (RSV). 2nd Catholic ed. San Francisco: Ignatius Press, 2006. [Scriptural quotations are from this source unless otherwise indicated.]

The Jewish Annotated New Testament. New Revised Standard Version. Oxford: Oxford University Press, 2011.

The New Jerusalem Bible (NJB). London: Darton, Longman & Todd, 1985.

The New Testament. Translated by Nicholas King. Buxhall, UK: Kevin Mayhew, 2006.

Other Texts

Aquinas, St. Thomas. *Summa Theologiae*, in *St Thomas Aquinas' Works in English*. dhapriory.org/Thomas, n.d.

Austen, Jane. *The Novels of Jane Austen*. Vol. 5, edited by R. W. Chapman. 3rd ed. London: Oxford University Press, 1959.

Baggini, Julian. *Freedom Regained: The Possibility of Free Will*. London: Granta, 2015.

Baker, Robin. *Sperm Wars: Infidelity, Sexual Conflict and Other Bedroom Battles*. Darby, PA: Diane Publishing, 1996.

Barthes, Roland. *Image Music Text*. Translated by Stephen Heath. Glasgow: Fontan/Collins, 1977.

Baukham, Richard. *Jesus and the Eyewitnesses: The Gospels as Eyewitness Testimony*. Grand Rapids, MI: William B. Eerdmans, 2006.

Blake, William. *Complete Writings*. Edited by Geoffrey Keynes. London: Oxford University Press, 1966.

Brown, Raymond E. *The Gospel According to John*. Translated by Raymond E. Brown, SS. Vol. 2 of *The Anchor Bible*. London: Geoffrey Chapman, 1982.

———. *The Death of the Messiah: From Gethsemane to the Grave. A Commentary on the Passion Narratives in the Four Gospels*. 2 vols. New York: Doubleday, 1994.

Bruno, Saint. "Letter to His Sons the Carthusians." In *The Divine Office: The Liturgy of the Hours According to the Roman Rite*. Vol. 3. London: HarperCollins, 2006.

Chalybäus, H. M. *Historical Development of Speculative Philosophy from Kant to Hegel*. Edinburgh: T & T Clark, 1854.

Chesterton, G. K. *The Everlasting Man*. London: Hodder and Stoughton, 1925.

Clark, T. J. "Frank Auerbach's London." *London Review of Books* 37, no. 17 (2015): 8–10.

Coleridge, Samuel Taylor. *Biographia Literaria with His Aesthetical Essays*. Edited by J. Shawcross. London: Oxford University Press, 1962.

Dames, Nicholas. *Amnesiac Selves: Nostalgia, Forgetting, and British Fiction*. Oxford: Oxford University Press, 2003.

———. *The Physiology of the Novel: Reading, Neural Science, and the Form of Victorian Fiction*. Oxford: Oxford University Press, 2007.

Darwin, Charles. *On the Origin of Species by Means of Natural Selection, or the Preservation of Favoured Races in the Struggle for Life*. London: John Murray, 1872.

———. *The Formation of Vegetable Mould through the Actions of Worms with Observations of Their Habits*. London: John Murray, 1904.

Dennett, Daniel C. *Brainstorms: Philosophical Essays on Mind and Psychology*. Brighton: Harvester Press, 1981. [Reprinted in 1986.]

———. *Elbow Room: The Varieties of Free Will Worth Wanting*. Oxford: Clarendon Press, 1984.

———. *Consciousness Explained*. London: Allen Lane / Penguin, 1992.

———. *Freedom Evolves*. London: Allen Lane / Penguin, 2003.

———. *From Bacteria to Bach and Back: The Evolution of Minds*. London: Allen Lane / Penguin, 2017.

Derrida, Jacques. *Writing and Difference*. Translated by Alan Bass. London: Routledge & Kegan Paul, 1981.

Descartes, René. *Key Philosophical Writings*. Translated by Elizabeth S. Haldane and G. R. T. Ross. Edited by Enrique Chávez-Arvizo. Ware, UK: Wordsworth, 1997.

Despland, Michael. *Kant on History and Religion with a Translation of Kant's "On the Failure of All Attempted Theodicies."* Montreal: McGill-Queen's University Press, 1973.

Dickinson, Emily. *Selected Poems and Letters, Together with Thomas Wentworth Higgins's Account of His Correspondence with the Poet and His Visit to Her in Amherst.* Edited by Robert N. Linscott. Garden City, NY: Doubleday, 1959.

Diski, Jenny. "Schrödinger's Tumour." *London Review of Books* 36, no. 21 (2014): 23–24.

Einstein, Albert. *The Principle of Relativity: A Collection of Original Memoirs on the Special and General Theory of Relativity*. Edited by A. Einstein, H. A. Lorentz, and H. Monkowski. Translated by W. Perrett and G. B. Jeffery. London: Methuen, 1923.

Eliot, George. *The Letters of George Eliot.* Edited by G. S. Haight. New Haven, CT: Yale University Press, 1954–78.

———. *Essays of George Eliot.* Edited by Thomas Pinney. London: Routledge and Kegan Paul, 1963.

———. *Middlemarch: A Study of Provincial Life.* Edited by W. J. Harvey. London: Penguin, 1981.

———. *The Mill on the Floss.* Edited by A. S. Byatt. Harmondsworth: Penguin, 1985.

———. *Daniel Deronda.* Edited by Terence Cave. London: Penguin, 1995.

Fenton, J. C. *St Matthew*. Harmondsworth: Penguin, 1963.

Frankel, Hermann. *Early Greek Poetry and Philosophy: A History of Greek Epic, Lyric, and Prose to the Middle of the Fifth Century.* Translated by Moses Hadas and James Willis. New York: Harcourt Brace Jovanovich, 1973.

Freud, Anna. *The Ego and the Mechanism of Defence.* London: Hogarth Press, 1937.

Freud, Sigmund. *Civilization and Its Discontents.* Edited by J. Strachey. New York: W. W. Norton, 1962.

———. *Dora: An Analysis of a Case of Hysteria.* Edited by Philip Reiff. New York: Collier Books, 1963.

Greenson, Ralph R. *The Techniques and Practice of Psychoanalysis.* Vol. 1. New York: International Universities Press, 1967.

Hagiiouannu, A. *The Man Who Would Be Kipling.* London: Palgrave Macmillan, 2003.

Hamilton, Sir William. "Philosophy of Perception." In *The Edinburgh Review*. Edinburgh: Ballantyne, 1830.

Hardy, Thomas. *The Collected Poems of Thomas Hardy*. London: Macmillan, 1930. [Reprint, 1962.]

———. *Jude the Obscure*. Edited by Patricia Ingham. Oxford: Oxford University Press, 2002.

Hengel, Martin. *The Four Gospels and the One Gospel of Christ: An Investigation of the Collection and Origin of the Canonical Gospels*. London: SCM Press, 2000.

———. *Studies in the Gospel of Mark*. Eugene, OR: Wipf and Stock, 2003.

Hext, Kate. *Walter Pater: Individualism and Aesthetic Philosophy*. Edinburgh: Edinburgh University Press, 2013.

Hofstadter, Douglas R., and Daniel C. Dennett, eds. *The Mind's I: Fantasies and Reflections on Self and Soul*. Brighton: Harvester Press, 1981.

Homer. *The Odyssey*. Translated by T. E. Shaw (Colonel T. E. Lawrence). New York: Oxford University Press, 1956.

Hooker, Morna D. *The Gospel According to Saint Mark*. London: Hendrickson, 1991.

Hopkins, Gerard Manley. *Poems and Prose of Gerard Manley Hopkins*. Introduction and notes by W. H. Gardner. Harmondsworth: Penguin, 1966.

Hume, David. *A Treatise of Human Nature*. 2nd ed., edited by L. A. Selby-Bigge. With revised and variant readings by P. H. Nidditch. Oxford: Clarendon Press, 1978.

Ignatius of Antioch. *Letters*. In *The Apostolic Fathers*. Vol. 1, edited and translated by Bart D. Ehrman. Cambridge, MA: Harvard University Press, 2003.

Jones, Ernest. *The Life and Work of Sigmund Freud*. Edited and abridged by L. Trilling and S. Marcus. Harmondsworth: Pelican, 1964.

Kant, Immanuel. *Prolegomena to Any Future Metaphysics*. Edited by Paul Carus. 3rd ed. Chicago: Open Court, 1912.

———. *Critique of Judgement. Part I, Critique if Aesthetic Judgement. Part II, Critique of Teleological Judgement*. Translated by James Creed Meredith. Oxford: Clarendon Press, 1952.

———. *The Doctrine of Virtue: Part II of the Metaphysics of Morals with the Introduction to the Metaphysics of Morals and the Preface to the Doctrine of Law*. Translated by Mary J. Gregor. New York: Harper & Row, 1964.

———. *Critique of Pure Reason*. Translated by J. M. D. Meiklejohn. London: Dutton, 1969. [This edition contains relevant references to the work of Sir William Hamilton.]

Kenny, Anthony. *Will, Freedom and Power*. Oxford: Basil Blackwell, 1975.

Ker, Ian. *John Henry Newman: A Biography*. Oxford: Oxford University Press, 1990.

Kermode, Frank. *The Genesis of Secrecy: On the Interpretation of Narrative*. Cambridge, MA: Harvard University Press, 1979.

Kipling, Rudyard. *The Seven Seas*. 2nd ed. London: Methuen, 1896.

———. *The Day's Work*. London: Macmillan, 1964.

———. *The Works of Rudyard Kipling*. Ware: Wordsworth, 1994.

Knox, Ronald. *God and the Atom*. London: Sheed and Ward, 1945.

Kümmel, Werner Georg. *Theology of the New Testament According to Its Major Witnesses Jesus—Paul—John* (1972). Translated by John E Steely (1974). London: SCM Press, 1980.

Lacan, Jacques. *Écrits: A Selection*. Translated by Alan Sheridan. London: Routledge, 1993.

———. *The Four Fundamental Concepts of Psycho-analysis*. Edited by Jacques-Alain Miller. Translated by Alan Sheridan. London: Penguin, 1994.

Levenson, David B. "Messianic Movements." In *The Jewish Annotated New Testament (New Revised Standard Version)*. Oxford: Oxford University Press, 2011.

Locke, John. *An Essay Concerning Human Understanding*. Edited by Peter H. Nidditch. Oxford: Clarendon Press, 1975.

MacIntyre, Alasdair. *Dependent Rational Animals: Why Human Beings Need the Virtues*. London: Gerard Duckworth, 1999.

Magee, Bryan. *Ultimate Questions*. Princeton, NJ: Princeton University Press, 2016.

Maleuvre, Didier. *The Religion of Reality: Inquiry into the Self, Art and Transcendence*. Washington, DC: Catholic University of America Press, 2006.

Markovits, Stefanie. *The Crisis of Action in Nineteenth-Century English Literature*. Columbus: Ohio State University Press, 2006.

Mill, John Stuart. *On Liberty*. In *Essays on Politics and Society*. Edited by J. M. Robson. *The Collected Works*. Vol. 18. Toronto: University of Toronto Press, 1977.

———. *An Examination of Sir William Hamilton's Philosophy and of the Principal Philosophical Questions Discussed in His Writings*. Edited by J. M. Robson. *The Collected Works*. Vol. 4. Toronto: University of Toronto Press, 1979.

Miller, J. Hillis. "But Are Things What We Really Think They Are?" *Times Literary Supplement*, October 9–15, 1987.

Milton, John. *Complete Prose Works*. Vols. 6 and 7, edited by John Carey and Alistair Fowler. New Haven, CT: Yale University Press, 1980.

———. *John Milton: A Critical Edition of the Major Works*. Edited by Stephen Orgel and Jonathan Goldberg. Oxford: Oxford University Press, 1990.

Mitchell, Juliet. "Love and Hate, Girl and Boy." *London Review of Books*, November 6, 2014, 11–12, 14.

Monod, Jacques. *Chance and Necessity: An Essay on the Natural Philosophy of Modern Biology*. Translated by Austryn Wainhouse. London: Collins, 1972.

Myers, Ched. *Binding the Strong Man: A Political Reading of Mark's Story of Jesus*. New York: Maryknoll, 1988.

Myers, F. W. H. "George Eliot." *Century Magazine* 33 (1881): 62.

Myers, William F. *Milton and Free Will: An Essay in Criticism and Philosophy*. London: Croom Helm, 1987.

———. *The Thoughtful Heart: The Metaphysics of John Henry Newman with a Fully Annotated Reader's Text of Newman's Discursive Enquiries on Metaphysical Subjects*. Milwaukee, WI: Marquette University Press, 2013.

Nagel, Thomas. "What Is It Like to Be a Bat?" In *The Mind's I: Fantasies and Reflections on Self and Soul*, edited by Douglas R. Hofstadter and Daniel C. Dennett. Brighton: Harvester Press, 1981.

———. *The View from Nowhere*. Oxford: Oxford University Press, 1989.

Newman, John Henry. *Parochial and Plain Sermons*. 8 vols. London: Rivingtons, 1869.

———. *The Arians of the Fourth Century*. 5th ed. London: Pickering, 1883.

———. *Loss and Gain*. London: Burns & Oates, 1891.

———. *Callista: A Tale of the Third Century*. London: Longmans, Green, 1893.

———. *Who's to Blame? (Addressed to the Editor of The Catholic Standard, by Catholicus)*. In *Discussions and Arguments on Various Subjects*. London: Longmans, Green, 1899.

———. *Newman's University Sermons: Fifteen Sermons Preached before the University of Oxford 1826–43*. London: SPCK, 1970. [Reprinted from the third edition, 1871.]

———. *An Essay in Aid of A Grammar of Assent*. Notre Dame, IN: University of Notre Dame Press, 1979.

———. *Apologia pro Vita Sua*. Edited by William Oddie. London: J. M. Dent, 1993.

Nietzsche, Friedrich. *The Portable Nietzsche*. Translated by Walter Kaufmann. New York: Viking, 1954.

———. *The Birth of Tragedy* and *The Genealogy of Morals*. Translated by F. Goffing. New York: Doubleday, 1956.

Nineham, D. E. *The Gospel of Mark*. Harmondsworth: Penguin, 1963.

Nodet, Étienne, and Justin Taylor. *The Origins of Christianity: An Exploration*. Collegeville, MN: Liturgical Press, 1998.

Noth, Martin. *Exodus: A Commentary*. London: SCM Press, 1962.

O'Connor, D. J. *Aquinas and Natural Law*. London: Macmillan, 1967.

O'Hanlon, Joseph. *Mark My Words*. Slough: St. Paul's, 1994.

Parks, Tim. "Bitten by an Adder." *London Review of Books*. July 17, 2014.

Pater, Walter. *Marius the Epicurean: His Sensations and Ideas*. London: Jonathan Cape, 1927.

———. *Essays on Literature and Art*. Edited by Jennifer Uglow. London: Dent, 1973.

Pears, David. *Wittgenstein*. Edited by Frank Kermode. London: William Collins Sons, 1971.

Phillips, Adam. "Against Self-Criticism." *London Review of Books*, March 5, 2015, 13–16.

Polanyi, Michael. *Personal Knowledge: Towards a Post-Critical Philosophy*. 2nd ed. London: Routledge & Kegan Paul, 1962.

Quine, Willard Van Orman. *The Roots of Reference*. Chicago: Open Court, 1974.

Rendtdorff, Rolf. *Canon and Theology: Overtures to an Old Testament Theology*. Edinburgh: T & T Clark, 1993.

Ricoeur, Paul. *Freud and Philosophy: An Essay on Interpretation*. Translated by Denis Savage. New Haven, CT: Yale University Press, 1970.

———. *The Rule of Metaphor: Multidisciplinary Studies in the Creation of Meaning in Language*. London: Routledge & Kegan Paul, 1978.

———. *Oneself as Another*. Translated by Kathleen Blamey. Chicago: University of Chicago Press, 1992.

———. *Freedom and Nature: The Voluntary and the Involuntary*. Northwestern University Studies in Phenomenology and Existential Philosophy, translated by Erazim V. Kohák. Evanston, IL: Northwestern University Press, 2007.

Rosmini, Antonio. *The Philosophy of Right*. Vol. 1, *Introduction—Moral System: The Essence of Right*. Durham: Rosmini House, 1993.

———. *A New Essay on the Origin of Ideas*. Vol. 2, translated by Terry Watson and Denis Cleary. Durham: Rosmini House, 2001.

Rossetti, Christina. *The Works*. Ware: Wordsworth, 1995.

Russell, Bertrand. *A Critical Exposition of the Philosophy of Leibniz with an Appendix of Leading Passages*. London: George Allen & Unwin, 1937.

———. *The Autobiography of Bertrand Russell, 1872–1914*. London: George Allen & Unwin, 1967.

Sanders, E. P. *Jesus and Judaism*. London: SCM Press, 1985.

Schillebeeckx, Edward. *Jesus: An Experiment in Christology*. London: Collins, 1983.

Sillem, Edward. *The Philosophical Notebook of John Henry Newman*. Vol. 1. Louvain: Nauwelaerts, 1970.

Smith, Martyn John. *Divine Violence and the Christus Victor Model: God's Reluctant Use of Violence for Soteriological Ends*. Eugene, OR: Pickwick, 2016.

Spencer, Herbert. *The Principles of Psychology*. London: Longman, Brown, Green and Longmans, 1855.

———. *Autobiography*. 2 vols. New York: D. Appleton, 1904.

Spinoza, Baruch. *Spinoza's Ethics and De Intellectus Emendatione*. Edited by Andrew Boyle. London: J. M. Dent & Sons, 1959.

Strawson, Galen. *Selves: An Essay in Revisionary Metaphysics*. Oxford: Clarendon Press, 2011.

Strawson, P. F. *Freedom and Resentment and Other Essays*. London: Macmillan, 1974.

Tennyson, Alfred Lord. *Poetical Works*. London: Macmillan, 1926.

Vermes, Geza. *The Authentic Gospel of Jesus*. London: Penguin, 2004.

———. *The Passion*. London: Penguin, 2005.

Volosinov, Valentin Nikolaevich. *Marxism and the Philosophy of Language*. Translated by Ladislaw Matejka and I. R. Titunuk. New York: Seminar Paper, 1973.

Wilde, Oscar. *The Letters of Oscar Wilde*. Edited by Rupert Hart-Davis. London: Rupert Hart-Davis, 1962.

———. *The Works of Oscar Wilde*. Edited by G. F. Maine. London: 1963.

Williams, Rowan. *On Christian Theology*. Oxford: Blackwell, 2000.

Witherington, Ben, III. *The Many Faces of Christ: The Christologies of the New Testament and Beyond*. New York: Crossroad, 1998.

Wittgenstein, Ludwig. "Lecture on Ethics." Presented to the Heretics Society, Cambridge University, November 1929. Text prepared by Robert Charleston, October 10, 2002, sackett.net.

———. *Tractatus Logico-Philosophicus*. 3rd ed., translated by G. E. M. Anscombe. Oxford: Basil Blackwell, 1968.

———. *Philosophical Investigations*. 3rd ed., translated by G. E. M. Anscombe. Oxford: Basil Blackwell, 1968.

Wojtyła, Karol, Cardinal/Pope St. John Paul II. *The Acting Person*. Translated by Andrzej Potocki. Dordrecht: D. Reidel, 1979.

Wordsworth, William. *Selected Works*. Edited by Stephen Gill. Oxford: Oxford University Press, 1984.

Wright, N. T. *The New Testament and the People of God*. London: SPCK, 1992.

———. *Jesus and the Victory of God*. London: SPCK, 1996.

Žižek, Slavoj. *The Metastases of Enjoyment: Six Essays on Woman and Causality*. London: Verso, 1994.

———. *The Indivisible Remainder: An Essay on Schelling and Related Matters*. London: Verso, 1996.

———. *The Plague of Fantasies*. London: Verso, 1997.

Žižek, Slavoj, and Friedrich Wilhelm Schelling. *The Abyss of Freedom/Ages of the Word: An Essay by Slavoj Žižek with the Text of Schelling's Die Weltalter (Second Draft, 1813)*. Translated by Judith Norman. Ann Arbor: University of Michigan Press, 1997.

General Index

Biblical Index